CU00730725

Jim Spark's The Keepers is vetted by comp
Mack and Linda Moulton Howe, and reads .
notes of a great discoverer. The Keepers documents Spark's unique recall of an Extraterrestrial civilization's human genetic-farming and educational outreach (aka "Abduction") programs, as well as Sparks first hand witnessing of time travel teleportation technology (originally meant to solve humanity's urgent environmental problems) apparently transferred by the same ETs to the U.S. Government, which has misused it for military-political purposes. Speaking through The Keepers, the ETs give us an important public policy message: Public disclosure and sharing in this vital ET technology can come about through a South Africa-style Truth Amnesty process covering the criminal acts accompanying the 60 year public embargo of this ET technology. The Keepers is a work of importance to Exopolitics and to our human future.

—Alfred Lambremont Webre, J.D., M.Ed.

Author, Exopolitics: Politics, Government And Law In The Universe.

Host: Exopolitics Radio.

We have had hundreds of guests on our UFO Files radio program, however, Jim stands out as one of the best. His story is dynamic and vivid and the book is a great read, something that Hollywood would be proud to do and have great success, only Jim lived this in real life.

The Keepers is a keeper.

— Jerry Pippin, www.jerrypippin.com

Sparks has a message for humanity courtesy of the ETs: that we are on a spiritual path, but we have to act to ensure the survival of Earth. Sparks is not the first to carry such a message from aliens, but surely we should wake up to our responsibilities regardless.

—Nexus, March - April 2007

Sparks' writing is lively, conversational and interesting...

— MUFON UFO Journal

"This is one of the best books I have ever read. Page 233 alone is worth what you pay for the whole book!"
— Robert Hieronymous, 21st Century Radio, Baltimore


A few quotes from readers at Amazon.com:


Very convincing revelation. Mr. Sparks has presented a riveting report of his experiences that rings true. His interaction also makes sense if these other cultures are trying to learn how to interact with we primitives. All & all a very interesting book, well worth the money to add more perspective to your own lines of personal analysis.
By J. Morrison (NC) - April 4, 2007


After hearing the author on Coast-to-Coast AM; I was so intrigued I just had to buy the book. …well-written, entertaining, and thought provoking first person account of the authors experiences with strange phenomenon and visitations from cosmic travelers over the past 16 years. I highly recommend this book to anyone who is interested in learning about the possibilities and opportunities when we explore both inner and outer space.
By Cheryl L. Semerjian "Sheri" (Ogden, Utah) March 29, 2007


Mr. Sparks can write a story. It is very interesting, entertaining and moves along at a good pace. I believe that Mr. Sparks was/is an abductee. This book is definitely worth a read. Mr. Sparks is bright, vocal, verbal and presents well over the air-waves, where I have heard him speak.
By N. A. Wisznia, March 25, 2007


I think Jim has done a very good job here. He has been able to relate his experiences in an everyday manner and so giving the reader the feel of his encounters. It is a sad reality that many people will laugh at Jim and have no idea that what he tells is the truth. It's time society woke up to what is really happening. Well done Jim.
By Mr. Robert Freeman March 17, 2007

# The Keepers

# The Keepers

An Alien Message for the Human Race

Jim Sparks

Wild Flower Press
An Imprint of Granite Publishing
P.O. Box 1429
Columbus, NC 28722

Library of Congress Cataloging-in-Publication Data

Sparks, Jim, 1954-
The keepers: an alien message for the human race / Jim Sparks.
p. cm6.
Includes bibliographical references and index.
ISBN 0-926524-68-2 (alk. paper)
1. Sparks, Jim, 1954- 2.
2. Alien abduction--United States
3. Human-alien encounters--United States.
I. Title.
BF2050.S63 2008
001.94--dc22
2008015004

All artwork has been produced by: Galante
Initial Manuscript Editor: Joe Filippone
Final Manuscript Editor: Brian L. Crissey
Book Design: Pamela Meyer
Cover Design: Phillip Dizick

The Publishers thank the following people for their comments about the author,
Daved E. Rubien, Lyle J. Michel, Nancy Smoot, Anita L. Albright,
and Donald E. Ware

Printed in the United States of America

Address all inquiries to:
Wild Flower Press
P.O. Box 1429
Columbus, NC 28722

# Dedication

This book is dedicated to Harvard Psychiatrist
Dr. John Mack, a man of integrity who disregarded his
colleagues' ridicule to pursue the investigation of alien
abductions because he was a true scientist who
believed in pursuing the unknown.

-----

When colleagues asked John Mack why he was so
interested in the UFO/ET phenomenon,
he responded by asking,
"Why aren't you?"

# Table of Contents

# List of Figures

# Prologue

by Linda Moulton Howe

In 1995, I first met Vincent Sparacino, also known as Jim Sparks. Jim was born to Italian parents on November 15, 1954. He grew up in southern Florida, graduated from high school and spent a couple of years in a local college studying real estate. He moved on to Houston, Texas, in 1979, and then to North Carolina where he purchased raw land, divided lots for housing construction, and always felt a strong need to preserve the trees at his developments. Happy, married and thriving, by 1988 at age 34, Sparks says he suddenly came face-to-face with beings from other worlds.

Jim insists he has had completely conscious encounters with "small, grey, drone worker types; taller true aliens, or supervisors; and tall reptoids with big human-shaped bodies covered with scaly, reptile skin." Jim Sparks sees himself as an interpreter or translator — or at least an elementary grade student in an alien "school." Jim says he was forced by the grey beings to learn English letter and number equivalents to alien symbols. After eight years "of being close enough to breathe their rotten-egg smelling skin," Sparks thinks he has some insights into the alien agenda, but admits he has "a thousand more questions than answers." He is frustrated that he cannot prove his repeated and conscious contacts with alien beings since 1988.

Jim permitted me to tape record several hours of our discussions about his experiences, which I first published as Chapter 3 of my 1998 book, Glimpses of Other Realities, Vol. II: High Strangeness. I was always impressed by Jim's no nonsense, "call a spade a spade" attitude. He has always been straightforward in his descriptions, even if he did not always understand what he was seeing or experiencing. I would like to share one of Jim's insights now, before you begin his important first-person account:

"I understood better their nature and agenda. They are neither benevolent nor evil. They have been among us in secret for thousands of years, maybe longer. But the length of time isn't as much the issue as why they have been among us. I believe they have been farming us for raw materials…. But now there's a problem, and their investment is in trouble. The aliens have spent a lot of time, travel and effort to farm us. But we are on an almost irreversible path of self-destruction…. But if we environmentally destroy ourselves, the aliens still have an excellent insurance policy. They've been collecting seeds from plants, animals and humans. Through semen and ova extraction, the aliens can start us, or other Earth life, all over again here, or somewhere else."

Linda Moulton Howe
Emmy Award-winning TV Producer and
Reporter and Editor Earthfiles.com
Albuquerque, New Mexico
February 19, 2005

# Foreword

by Dr. John E. Mack, 10/4/29 to 9/27/04

Many Americans are having experiences which have come to be known as "alien abductions." Despite the readiness of people who are not familiar with the details of the phenomenon to offer psychiatric or other conventional explanations, none of these has even begun to account for the strange nature, richness and awesome power of these experiences. Those who are willing to pay attention to what is going on here are confronted with an intriguing mystery of expanding scope.

Jim Sparks's case has many of the features that have been reported now in hundreds of instances, but it is also unusual in several respects. His account provides one of our richest and most detailed documentations of an abduction history. In addition, he shows clearly how the experiences evolved, together with shifts in his own consciousness. But above all, Sparks's recall is altogether conscious, i.e., without the benefit of hypnosis, relaxation exercises or any other use of a non-ordinary state of consciousness for the exploration of buried memories. This should help to settle what may still remain of the suspicion that these experiences are somehow the product of a narrator trying to please a hypnotist. As for myself, I met Jim Sparks for the first time in March, 1996, and although we have had two interviews and several other conversations, I cannot be regarded as complicit in bringing forth his knowledge, as his book was far along before we met.

Sensing that he has something important to teach us, Sparks has avoided reading about "alien" abductions, lest his prior knowledge contaminate his account. Nevertheless, his story is in many ways consistent with the narratives and lives of other abductees I have seen or whose cases have been published. He has the passion, curiosity, and self-doubt of an authentic, truthful voice. There would be little reason to question the reality of what he has written except for the fact that from the standpoint of the materialist worldview that still dominates our culture, what Sparks has to tell us is simply not possible. We are then faced with the choice of rejecting his story prima facie or allowing ourselves to expand our notions of the possible by attending to what he has to say.

Jim Sparks is an Italian American who was in the residential real estate business when his experiences began. Those that he remembers began a decade ago. He has been informed by the alien beings that they are concentrating their contact now upon ordinary people (he regards himself as an "average person") because agreements with Earth's leaders to "correct the environmental condition of your planet" were violated. Furthermore, Sparks is so convinced that information about alien cultures and activity of great importance for human health and the future of the Earth has been illegally suppressed by government officials that he initiated a National Security Information Amnesty bill that would allow records to be opened and these individuals to come forward with what they know, without fear of reprisal.

Initially Jim's experiences, which occurred as often as several times a month, were primarily intrusive and terrifying, including the oft-reported forced extraction of sperm. Furthermore, he had been brought into a "mind-boggling" world where known physical laws were broken — passage through solid objects, shape-shifting, and instant, apparently thought-activated, transport. Something, he tells us, had "invaded my being right down to the core." A process, totally outside of his control, had befallen him which utterly broke down his will, "probing through to the deepest fiber of my mind." Sparks tried desperately to relate what was happening to him to familiar notions, thinking at first that he was being taken over by evil spirits.

Little by little Sparks was able to put aside his rage, overcome fear and accept that he was encountering some sort of technologically advanced non-human intelligence from which he could not escape, beings with the "ability to scan the deepest fiber of your soul," before which he was quite powerless. As he was able to surrender, the experiences transformed. Sparks found that he had been inducted into a kind of "alien boot camp," a school of training and testing that made heavy use of riddles, ambiguity, paradox and symbolization, where much of the communication occurred telepathically or via connection with the aliens' dark, mysterious eyes.

The purpose of his schooling seems to be two-fold: to create a hybrid race as an "insurance policy" for the future, and to awaken us to our mindless destructiveness, so that we may halt the devastation we are bringing to Earth. Sparks's articulate and moving expression of his awakening of consciousness in relation to this danger (a "different point of view" in "sharp contrast to earlier feelings"), which appears to be the core significance of the abduction experience for him and so many others, gives his book power and importance. The human race is "isolated" in the cosmos "by ignorance," he has learned, not "ready to join the intelligent life" that exists in other realms and "too dangerous" to "be set free in the universe to do as we please." As Sparks has moved beyond his resentment, he has come to feel quite fortunate to have somehow been chosen to "participate" in such a great "adventure." He is unwavering in his conviction that we must heed the beings' warnings in order to stop the destruction of the environment and the death of the planet.

This central message is stressed repeatedly and relentlessly in Sparks's book, and is the reason for its power. Through Sparks the beings, or whatever may be the intelligence behind this extraordinary phenomenon, tells of our failed stewardship of this magnificent planet. In several of his abductions Sparks was shown on TV-like screens scenes of such breathtaking natural beauty that they left him "completely mesmerized." But they would inevitably be followed by visions of "mankind's destructive ways," as the images showed once-beautiful forests "now brown gray and dead looking instead of healthy and green," or dead, bloated fish floating on top of the water. Sparks writes, "This made me feel very sad and depressed." Suddenly after one of these experiences a telepathic voice said, "YOU ARE KILLING YOUR PLANET. YOUR PLANET IS

DYING." In some of his experiences Sparks was confronted with the dangers of overpopulation, breaks in the food chain and the dangers of nuclear and biological contamination. "There are better ways," he was told, of "deriving your energy and food needs, without causing your planet any damage." Our mindlessness seems, in Sparks's experiences, to have cosmic proportions. "In the galactic neighborhood," he was taught, "there seems to be an order" which our species is violating.

In a certain sense, the reality or truth of all this is well-known, so why should we pay attention to Jim Sparks, who has been informed by strange beings we do not even acknowledge exist? And if the aliens are so concerned with the Earth's ecology, why don't they just stop us? These are difficult questions to answer. First there is the emotional and transforming power of the environmental "education" for Sparks and many other abductees, which leads to a more total kind of commitment to changing direction. Also there is the sense in these experiences that the message is coming from a higher, or divine, source of great potency, should we be able to acknowledge its authority. Finally, as Sparks and other experiencers have been told, the changes that may result from "training" like his must occur through shifts in consciousness of the human race, especially on the part of ordinary people, rather than by direct intervention. With the failure of leaders to take responsibility for the planet's plight, Sparks was told, "we are now concentrating our energy on the average person."

Sparks writes of changes in his own consciousness and psychic powers, an "ability to see in other dimensions," a "sixth and seventh sense." "These extra senses seem to lie dormant like an atrophied muscle," he says. "One just needs the tools, or technology, to tap into these realms. In my case exposure to alien technology heightens the senses."

Sparks is to be commended for having the courage to "come out" and tell his remarkable story. Many experiencers are ridiculed privately and publicly for truths that run so counter to the official reality of our culture. He hopes that if he can provide an example of leadership in this regard, he may contribute to overcoming the denial that characterizes the prevailing reaction to the great dangers facing the Earth. To the end Sparks, like all abductees, remains mystified as to the source of his expe-

riences but feels that what he has learned is of immense power, importance and credibility. "What is wrong with us then," he asks at the end of
the book. "Are we blind? Maybe so, because it is taking cultures from
God knows where to warn us."

I asked Sparks to tell me how his experiences had changed him. In a
letter sent to me by FAX he wrote the following:

Prior to 1988 [when he began to recall his experiences] about 95%
of my energy was focused on business, marriage, recreation and living as
carefree as possible. I had some concern for the environment. I tried to
save as many trees as possible when I bought land and sold lots for home
sites.

My experience with advanced cultures in the last nine years has
changed my life and expanded my awareness. Clearly the Earth is alive,
and we have cut off her arms and legs. Truly we have damaged her
severely. She is a living body fighting for her life because we are attacking
her vital organs. The heart and lungs of this plant lie in the rain forests of
Central and South America. The attack on these vital organs is beginning
to show signs that the Earth is having a difficult time trying to cleanse herself. As land is destroyed, diseases are released, along with [the loss of]
potential cures. The list goes on and on.

My life has changed to the point that I am forming a foundation that
will purchase and preserve valuable forest land.

(Publisher's Note: see chapter 'Your Earth' for more information
on this foundation.)

Jim Sparks

# Introduction

I can remember a time when I looked up in the sky and didn't see much. I can remember a life where I was just a normal guy, living a normal life. I worked hard, I took what life offered as best I could, and I loved and appreciated my family, without a whole lot of questions. Then things changed. I found out that things in my life, in your life, aren't, as they seem to be.

My name is Jim Sparks, and I have been contacted by extraterrestrial beings.

Today I refer to them as advanced cultures. It should be made clear there are many different species of intelligent life that have been interacting with humans since the dawn of time. In this story we will be focusing primarily on a race commonly referred to by researchers as Greys.

My contact with these creatures has been one on one, face to face. I have been abducted so many times since 1988 I have lost count. Most abductees have fragmented memories. I have better than 95% total conscious recall.

Listen to what they have said to me and what they have to say to us all. It's right here in this book.

Whether they are extra-terrestrial or extra-dimensional or just plain extra-curricular, I can't say. I'm no expert. And why they've chosen me I don't know.

However, I can make an educated guess. They track family lines for many thousands of years, in my case since day one. They came to me totally out of the blue in 1988, and the first several years were a trauma-filled hell. I felt as if I had been drafted into a war that no one knew existed. I refer to this as an alien boot camp in which the M.O. is isolation, fear and confusion. This completely disrupted my life those first few years, but now I have come full circle. I wouldn't trade these experiences for anything in the world. My eyes have been opened.

They are like us in some ways, but for the most part not like us at all. Technically speaking they are light years ahead. However in some cases we are catching up. Here are a few examples:

- They radiate an energy either naturally or technically enhanced that paralyzes you when they are just a few feet away.
- They can transmit and receive hundreds of thoughts at the same time.
- They are completely telepathic and can create any reality they wish you to believe.
- Their technology is thought activated.
- They can pass through solid matter, travel dimensions and distort time using their understanding of science.
- Their technology is so advanced it almost seems like magic.

This is a small part of it; I'm just getting started. All I can do is to tell you about them and relate my story to the best of my ability.

The literature of alien contact has been around for over half a century. Everyone has heard of UFOs. I'd heard of UFOs before 1988 when this began, but I'd never seen one that I remembered.

I'd never heard of the famous UFO abductees such as Betty and Barney Hill or Whitley Strieber. And, I didn't read any other books that were causing people to take alien abductions seriously. Know what? I had other things to do. I guess I just didn't care.

Why should I care? Why should you? After all, the conventional point-of-view in this world says that it's best for everybody if you just toe the line, believe what you're told to believe. As an enthusiastic Capitalist American, you'd better believe that's just what I did. That's the way I was until 1988, though, when things changed and the alien abductions began.

So I hear you thinking, "Hey, there are plenty of alien abduction stories. What's so special about this one?" That's easy. You can check the reports of researchers like Budd Hopkins or the late Dr. John Mack and the many other serious scientists who are working with people who have had these kinds of experiences. Mostly they're troubled, and the therapist has to get to the memories through hypnotherapy and such. With me, I remember most of what happens to me when I get taken. And I'm putting that down here, in my words, right now.

Moreover, these creatures, these "Visitors" if you want to call them that as Whitley Strieber does, have allowed me to keep my memories for a very particular purpose.

It's the 21st century, and we're in a crisis. Whether you're talking nuclear meltdowns, political emergencies, global warming, environmental catastrophe, religious awakenings, consciousness risings or paradigm shifts — we're in the midst of vast changes. Like I say, I'm just a regular guy, but for some reason I've got something that these "Visitors" could use to teach me a lot of amazing things that just might help humanity get through these changes.

Here, then, is what these aliens are telling me.

Here, now, is my story.

# CHAPTER ONE

# Abducted by the Mafia

Fort Myers Beach, a beautiful town on the Gulf coast of Florida, is where I grew up. It's also the place I fled to when my life seemed to be unraveling in Texas and North Carolina.

I have family here. There's nothing like family to steady a soul. At first my family wasn't sure how to take all of this. They seemed quite certain I'd lost it. Over time they came to support me.

The Gulf of Mexico is a gorgeous sea. Its waters are warm and mostly calm. Every large body of water has its own scent and I love the smell of home. The nights are mostly clear and filled with stars.

When I see a sunset of gold and orange, I relax. Even when these strange creatures come and take me elsewhere I know they will bring me back here to this community, where I only have to walk a short way to run into an acquaintance, or even better, a friend.

Fort Myers Beach will always be small because it's an island, just fifteen miles off the mainland from metropolitan Fort Myers. It is close enough to enjoy Fort Myers's historic areas, yet far enough to be a great vacation spot. If you want sand, beaches, sun, and surf — we've got it here.

When I was a boy, Fort Myers Beach was just a fishing village filled with natural charm. Today it's a tourist mecca, although it still has a fishing fleet that gives it a lingering charm. There's nothing like sitting near this beach eating fresh gulf shrimp, stone claws and oysters along with a tangy ice tea with lemons that were just hanging from trees earlier in the morning.

Even as I sit here now writing of aliens and the future, I can smell the marvelous aromas of smoking fish from the Smoke House on San Carlos Boulevard. It has been around a long time, since Fort Myers has always been a fishing port. The fishing boats bring in a bountiful haul of grouper, snapper, tuna and bonita every day, and some of it goes to the smokehouse where wood and fire do their magic. I never get tired of this place, even though lots of tourists have found it —especially, alas, college students on spring break. It makes me feel good.

The Gulf radiates peaceful energy for me. There are playful dolphins here and brightly plumed tropical birds. The sunset is spectacularly beautiful every day. Afterward the stars are bright. It's pretty astonishing to think that one of the scariest and most unusual contacts started right here on a beautiful, moon-swept Fort Myers Beach night.

March 7, 1994, is probably the most significant date in my story. The aliens had taken me away many times before, but I want to tell you about this day first because of what happened that night.

In that fateful winter of 1993-1994, I'd just gotten back together with my wife Teresa after tumultuous times. The calming effect of Fort Myers Beach worked on me, and I was getting my act together after a lot of insanity.

We had a beach house — a nice one with ample rooms. Although my marriage had improved, I still slept alone. I'm a restless sleeper, and I guess Teresa didn't really mind being relieved of that part of me.

On that evening, March 7, instead of sleeping on the living room sofa as I usually did when I slept alone, I decided to use one of the extra bedrooms in the back of the house. We were about a100 yards or so from the Gulf with a few outer houses between the surf and us.

With the help of a pleasant night with Teresa, I went to bed around midnight and fell into a deep sleep without dreams.

At 3:47 A.M. a hand gently shook my foot, and I woke up.

I could hear the waves lapping on the beach, and a breeze played through the trees outside. The room smelled like a troubled memory.

"Teresa?," I said

2

Enough moonlight crept through the window for me to discern a dark shape at the end of the bed.

I was afraid. Just because this wasn't the first time something like this happened, it wasn't exactly old hat either.

Fear is fear, and fear is what I feel whenever this thing happens. Yank my chain, push my buttons — what's in me comes out. What comes out when I know I'm about to get on the Abduction Special is stone-cold fear.

A pale light rose up in the room.

At first I thought it was just a man. He wore a jacket with wide shoulders and baggy pants, a black dress shirt, and a black silk tie — up tight against this neck. His suit was an Armani or some other fancy designer cut. A wide-brimmed fedora hat slouched low across his features.

Those features, I came to see, were not human, but rather they were the strangely shaped head and almond eyes I'd come to know too well. I guess the cat's out of the bag as far as what these creatures look like. X-Files did an okay job in depicting them. In the flesh, the aliens have a definite look, a presence, an other-worldliness about them, and the human instinct in their presence is to be very afraid.

This time was different. Where the eyes of my abductors before had been indifferent, this guy's eyes seemed cruel.

Here before me was an alien dressed like some 1930s style Chicago mobster. Those words rattled in my baffled brain, and I repeated them out loud in confusion.

He said, "The boss wants to see ya."

I wish I could say I wasn't still afraid. It's not often that an alien abduction starts out with a comedic slant, though, and the idea of being in some intergalactic farce was not as nuts as it might sound and is a hell of a lot easier to swallow than most of what I've been through.

Why did the alien that night come dressed like Humphrey Bogart in Angels With Dirty Faces?

3

Do these "Visitors" actually have some warped sense of humor?

Putting aside the Men In Black, one doesn't find a lot of slapstick comedy in the alien stories we hear. I was not familiar with UFO movies or literature then — I was mostly just stunned, and only a little less freaked. Now I wonder whether the aliens sometimes use our own cultural icons to communicate with us. As you'll see, they may well have time-travel capacities, and this joker's last touchdown may have been the late '30s in America. Then again, perhaps these things are just so alien, just so off the map of what a human can grasp that my mind sometimes short-circuits and substitutes impressions as ludicrous as a gangster masquerade to allow these experiences to be assimilated.

It's hard to believe that there's a sense of alien humor in these guys, but then maybe they're slapping their knees behind our backs right now.

"Despite the outfit," I said, "You're scaring me."

Those alien lips weren't moving, but it hit me then that the movie-mobster's voice was sounding in the middle of my brain.

I don't read science-fiction or psychic-powers books, and I never knew anything about telepathy until I started actually experiencing it.

The being's face changed, morphing from a ruddy scowl to a more human, softer look. Then I realized what was happening. This was what I have come to know as "screen imaging," kind of like "virtual reality," only without visible computers.

The visitor was playing with my perception of visual reality. Maybe that's where it had found the dusty costume trunk to play Halloween with — from all the old movies in my head.

"Everything will be all right. You'll be fine," he said in a friendly manner.

"Why are you wearing that old style suit? Why a suit at all?" I managed to say.

The transition was instantaneous. One moment I was in my warm bed. Next, I stood in the backyard, with the Gulf breeze on my bare back. I felt the being's hand on my arm. At this point, you might think that I would have panicked. There was nothing at all dreamy about it — it was exhilarating, exciting — and so real!

Before in these situations, I had always been paralyzed. This time, I wasn't, though I noticed I had very little peripheral vision and my reaction time was slowed, but I could walk, and move around. I turned to him and said, "Where are we going?"

He said, "You'll be just fine. Just come with me." As he held my right arm, we started walking in the direction of the beach.

We walked slowly through my neighbor's back yard, his hand guiding me, not forcing me. We walked across the street, and I remember feeling upset because he didn't even look to see whether there were cars coming, he just charged ahead. We headed down to the footpath that leads to the beach. I remember sea oats along the path.

This seemed odd, since I hadn't noticed sea oats along that path before. Sea oats are common scruffy plants that grow here and there in patches along the beach. In this heightened state, however, I finally noticed what I'd ignored all along.

I could feel the breeze, but I wasn't cold. The smell of the beach — that fresh, fishy scent — was vibrant and alive, and the night seemed incredibly awake. The sand was cool beneath my feet as we walked toward the breakers. We just kept on walking.

"We're not stopping!" I said. You're going to walk us right into the water. We'll drown!"

Again he said, "You'll be just fine."

Just at the water's edge, the cold foam touched my bare feet, and we stopped.

The night was clear. The stars hung in the sky with an incredible splendor. I had a sense of expectancy, as though we were waiting for something.

Then about fifteen feet straight in front of us, from out of nowhere, a small circle of dim white light appeared, floating about ten feet above the water. There wasn't really anything impressive about the white light, believe it or not. Somehow it looked perfectly ordinary, as ordinary as a sailboat leaving a light hanging from its side so other boats can see it at night.

The visitor's grip on my arm was not strong, and I could have run away.

But, as in previous abductions where I had no chance to escape, I was going along voluntarily. Was I curious? I don't know. I just know I wasn't frightened any more.

I was enjoying this new experience, just standing there with him on the beach. In a sense I had come a long way. Perhaps this time I could have escaped, almost as if the choice were mine. How out of character this was, because at that particular moment we were on human terms — two intelligent life-forms standing on the shoreline.

As we stood I couldn't help but think how many trillions of miles these beings may travel to get here, and how many dimensions they span. Yet, here we were on the beach.

All of a sudden, there was a blinding flash of white light. The small circle of light turned into a huge rectangle of white light about 25 feet wide and fifteen feet high. It appeared to be a doorway made of light.

At first I thought this opening appeared from nowhere, or that they had ripped a hole into another dimension. I know they have the technology to do this. However, in this case the ship was cloaked or invisible. The small white light was a marker. The larger rectangle opening was emanating light from inside the ship. At this point, this light was much brighter than the light that normally illuminates the inside of the ship.

With my lack of peripheral vision, I hadn't noticed anyone else with us, but now another alien of the kind I'd seen before — I call them "workers" — stepped in front of me. He was smaller than the guy beside me — short, skinny, with a big head and eyes. Then he jumped into the light and disappeared.

"Go ahead," said the alien in the suit. "Step into it."

I hesitated.

"You'll be all right," he said reassuringly. "Just step into it." I did. Pain flashed up my leg.

•FIG. 1: A MAN IN BLACK LEADS ME TO HIS SPACE CRAFT

I'd stubbed my right foot's big toe. That was all. So banal, and yet it reinforced the reality of all this.

"You have to step up," he said.

I thought sarcastically, why didn't you mention that before?

I stepped up, and I walked into that huge, overwhelming light.

I blacked out and awoke in a dimly lit room. Standing in front of me were three aliens. Two were small "worker" types, and one was taller — a true alien, as I call them — kind of like a supervisor. Beside them was something akin to a hospital gurney or examination table.

After six and a half years of abductions, this was the first time I was in complete control of my motor functions. Again, I could have run, but I didn't. They seemed to understand me. They seemed to know that I wasn't going to give them any trouble this time — that somehow, for some reason I now knew they wouldn't hurt me!

I heard the supervisor's voice in my head. "Would you please lie on this table?"

After years of forced procedures, this guy was actually asking me? "Sure," I thought. "Why not?" I crawled up on the table and once more lost consciousness.

When I opened my eyes, I had no sense of how much time had passed, and no memory of what had happened on the table. I pushed myself up and scooted to the edge of the table. Ten feet before me, two aliens at another table asked me to come to it.

I was floored. Asking me? Again? Had these guys suddenly gotten social skills?

You have to understand the intense feelings of terror and helplessness I'd had before. Now I felt as though they considered me almost a significant person. They had some sense of respect.

Still, that overwhelming sense of strangeness kicked in, and I felt those familiar old feelings again.

Have you ever wakened from a deep sleep, or after sleep walking and found yourself in a strange place — and not known who you are? Contemplate this, and then add alien beings, and you might get an idea of the feelings I'm talking about.

"I'm sorry. I'm afraid this time," I said.

•FIG. 2: DOORWAY OF LIGHT OPENS

I suppose it was too much to ask that they be warm and friendly with great big smiles. Instead, with that "screen reality" talent of theirs, they reached into my head — and suddenly that cold and gleaming metal examination table became green and felt. It looked like a Las Vegas dicing table. Were we going to play craps?

9

Abruptly, my fear drained. Of course, they knew that I enjoyed a little gambling in Vegas from time to time. They had mucked around in my head enough!

I wasn't exactly laughing, but I hopped off and went up to them. Well, they'd designed the table wrong — bad odds on this felt. Abruptly, this realization twisted something in my head. Blink. The Vegas exam table was just a normal alien examination table again, if such a thing can ever really be considered normal. Still, they seemed to be trying to be considerate. They weren't forcing me.

I got up on the table, lay down...and blacked out again. When I came to, I was alone.

It seemed quite strange to be alone like this. Always before there had been aliens in these rooms. Not only that, but I also had complete physical and mental control of myself. I sat up and looked around the plain, gray room and wondered what I was going to do next.

The doorway was open, and it led into a hall. The lighting was dim and ambient, not from any fixtures, but seeming to leak from the walls, ceiling and floors. Should I just sit and wait?

I stewed about that for a few moments, but boredom and curiosity got the best of me. "The hell with it," I said out loud, "I'm going to walk around!" This felt wonderfully daring, as though I were challenging their authority.

I got off the table and held onto it, as though it were some life buoy in a strange sea. I peered out and down the hall — not able to see much.

Okay. Take a deep breath, I thought. Here goes nothing.

I pushed off and ventured into the narrow hallway. It went about 25 feet down, then made a sharp left.

I took the turn and walked a few more feet, coming to an open doorway. I stopped for a moment, debating with myself.

Should I just go back and park myself on that examination table and be a good little abductee?

10

No. I had to find out more. I had to find out the truth. Why had they abducted humans all these years? Why was I selected? I had the power now, and I was going to use it.

I walked into that room in that alien ship, and the moment I saw what was there, something deeper than fear gripped me.

It was a kind of overwhelming panic.

There, before me, was The Future.

# CHAPTER TWO

# Dream, It's Just a Dream

Prior to 1988, you could never have convinced me that alien abductions were anything other than strange psychological fantasies.

Prior to 1988, I considered myself an average American in pursuit of the American dream. I wanted success, a happy family, and whatever fulfillment an average life had to offer.

Let me tell you a little more about who I was before 1988, then I'll talk about the year that everything changed.

I was raised in south Florida, born to a couple named Sam and Rose, an old-fashioned hard-working Italian-American couple. I worked odd-end jobs throughout all of my schooling.

After graduating from high school, I took two years of college, mostly taking courses related to real estate and investing. I then went to work for a major condominium firm. In 1978, the firm transferred me to Houston, Texas.

In 1984 I met Teresa, a slender, blonde woman. She was pretty and down to earth — my kind of person.

Teresa is the youngest of eleven siblings in a poverty-stricken family. She was raised in North Carolina and was forced to pick tobacco instead of going to school. She left home at fifteen and began to work full-time. At the same time, she got her high school diploma and took a five-year college Bible course. She literally taught herself how to read and write. She's strong-willed and vital — qualities very attractive to me. In 1985 we married and purchased our first home.

For years I have always been a hard worker, putting in ten or twelve hours a day, six to seven days a week. After twelve years of working for someone else, I took all my savings and started my own natural land development company, J & J Properties. I would buy land and divide it into home site lots. My main development was called Ashley Estates.

When buyers bought home sites, the deed allowed them to clear enough space to build a home, but forbade the cutting of more trees than necessary.

Although I lived in Texas, I did most of my business in North Carolina. This work kept me away from home seven to ten days a month.

I would go to a town and live in a hotel that had a restaurant and bar. I would eat at the hotel restaurant and have a cocktail in the evenings. After several weeks, the natives considered me a local. All this time I would keep my ears open and do research. I would find out where the building growth was heading. Afterwards, I would buy raw land a few miles ahead of the growth. Then I would harvest pine straw while waiting for the growth to come to me. When it did, I would divide and sell.

At the time, Teresa managed a large apartment complex in Houston, and was quite content with her work. We had everything we needed, it seemed. We were young, happy, healthy, and successful.

In mid-1988, though, my abductions began, and everything changed. It started with a dream.

I would have the same dream over and over again for a period of weeks. When I woke up in the morning after each dream, I was paralyzed. I was completely conscious but unable to move. After a few moments, I gradually gained mobility. Sometimes I didn't have the dream and I'd wake up and be able to hop out of bed, feeling fine, no problems. But whenever I had that terrible dream, I couldn't move when I awakened.

This was the dream:

I feel something beside my bed. I am pulled up by strange entities and guided out of my bedroom, down the hallway, and into the guest room of our house on the ground floor. It had a large double-paned window with blue drapes and white mini-blinds. I walk to this window, then walk right through it, without stopping. My escort and I go across the front lawn, over the street and into the woods adjacent to the house.

In our front lawn we had honeysuckle bushes. I don't think there's anything sweeter than the smell of honeysuckle. In my dream, I could smell that honeysuckle quite vividly. When in bloom, the tiny flowers that had fallen to the grass would stick to my feet. I remember looking down and seeing the blossoms on my feet just as I entered the woods.

I have no memory of what happened in those woods during those dreams. However, I always emerge out of that blankness and cross the street again, walking through that solid window into my home. Down the hallways I march and end up back in bed. Upon waking, I would have vague, incomplete memories of my "dreams" and would be unable to move for a while.

These dreams occurred from May until early December of 1988, maybe two or three times a week. For whole stretches of time they didn't happen. Even when I had them, I just shrugged them off and went about my daily schedule. Dreams fade quickly under the light of the sun. The one aspect that did bother me was the temporary paralysis. That was so odd, I would think about it from time to time. Still I never mentioned it to anyone.

Then, in early December, things shifted.

I had my dream and woke up unable to move, but this time the paralysis lasted longer than usual. When I was finally able to move, I walked down the hallway and looked into the guest room.

•FIG. 3: FOOTPRINTS THROUGH THE WALL.

Honeysuckle flowers were strewn across the carpet. They clung to imprints in the pile carpeting. The heel of one imprint was in the yard and the toes were on the carpet. I thought, "How could this be?"

I remembered what I thought had been my dream, but this was cold, hard reality staring me in the face.

I panicked and phoned the police. When two officers arrived, I regretted the call, but I showed them the evidence that someone had come into the house — and walked right through a window and wall. There was a right footprint on the lawn outside, and a left footprint on the pile car-

15

peting. Also, there was that footprint, half on the grass and half on the carpet.

"Was a crime committed?" one of the policemen asked.

"No. I guess not."

They went away and probably had a good laugh back in the squad car.

If I had a history of strangeness in my life, I might have taken this all in stride. But the truth was that I'd never had a paranormal experience before in my entire life. Surely this kind of thing just didn't happen to a businessman! As I got out the vacuum cleaner from the laundry room and vacuumed the carpet, making sure to remove every flower, twig or blade of grass, I thought how relieved I was that Teresa was out of the house. I wouldn't tell her, not yet.

I couldn't hide this from myself. I was consumed with questions about what had happened. I wanted to talk to Teresa. I was pretty rattled, and I started flubbing up on my job. But I also didn't want to scare my wife, and I certainly didn't want to give her cause to think I was crazy. No, it was best to just wait and make sure myself. I would wait for it to happen again.

Also, I decided that the next time I had one of those weird dreams, I would make an effort to remember more detail.

About a week later, the same dream came to me again, and I sensed a presence at my bedside.

Teresa lay beside me, sleeping soundly, and I can remember thinking in my semi-conscious state: "Dream! It's just a dream!" My resolution to remember kicked in.

I was going to try to see who was doing this.

Focus, I thought. Pay attention. Who — or what — was this presence? In the dimness, I was able to make out that these beings were shorter than the average human.

Then the familiar dream unrolled. Being pulled from the bed, walking down the hall, the shock of passing through the window and wall into the lawn, crossing the street and going into the woods beyond. Then the aroma of honeysuckle.

Next morning, as soon as I experienced the familiar paralysis, I headed straight for the guest room. Sure enough, there were the footprints in the carpet, and the honeysuckle flowers.

While I had gained a valuable piece of information about these events, why was I being carried from my house by short creatures?

Strange and upsetting as all this was, though, it was nothing compared to the events that came next. With all my strength and will, I thought, if this bizarre experience happens to me again, I will be present and conscious. I will remember!

I showed Teresa the honeysuckle, told her about the incident and my feelings. She insisted I was playing some kind of strange joke. People in the bedroom? "I would have heard them," she said. "Don't be silly."

So the next few times it happened, I just vacuumed up the honeysuckle, leaves and grass, and kept mum. So far, I wasn't getting anywhere in remembering what went on in the woods. I felt frustrated, and my work suffered.

Still, I was determined to stay conscious during these strange occurrences. Finally, after many more "dreams," I was successful.

In late December of 1988, I was having a difficult time sleeping. Finally, after much tossing and turning, I nodded off. I woke up to see the digital clock read: 3:30 A.M. I drifted back to sleep, but then, quite suddenly, I woke up.

I couldn't open my eyes or move my body. I heard a low-pitched whirling sound, which slowly got louder.

A strange sensation grew from the pit of my stomach, creeping up my torso towards my heart. When this sensation filled my chest, my heart began to race, and louder and faster came that whirling sound.

Deep instinctual fear overwhelmed me, but I couldn't even open my mouth to scream. Cold sweat covered me as I screamed silently. My heart was thumping so fast I thought it was going to jump out of my chest. My head filled with that sound...whirling, whirling...until the whole universe was that sound, and it wanted to burst open my head.

Then I felt a tremendous rushing feeling. I was accelerating as if I were going down the steepest grade of a roller coaster, without any kind of safety harness.

"I don't want to die!" I screamed inside. "I don't want to die!"

Then it all stopped — the sensation of acceleration, the sound in my head, and the feeling of imminent death. My heart had calmed, and I was breathing normally. There was one big difference here, though — I was sitting now on some sort of hard bench. "Where the hell am I?"

Oddly enough, the panic had vanished. I was alive, and I guess that was enough.

Concentrating hard, I tried to move my eyelids. Slowly I was able to open my eyes. The first thing I saw was that I was leaning against a table. It wasn't any normal table — it was a flat TV or maybe a big, blank computer screen. I seemed to be in some sort of dimly lit room. I could only look ahead, though. I had no peripheral vision. The room smelled sulphurous, like rotting eggs. It was warm and humid.

I was still unable to move, and my thoughts seemed to be in slow motion. When I realized I could raise my head, I saw that there was a wall about eight feet in front of me — a wall holding another, smaller video screen. I strained to get up, but I couldn't. I could only move my head up and down, so I could only see that strange table, that wall screen, and the light from nowhere yet everywhere, which was a dim white.

I sensed I wasn't alone in that room — some kind of tingling awareness made me cognizant of activity to either side, but when I tried to look, I couldn't turn my head to the right or left. When I gazed down again, I noticed I could slightly move the wrist and forefinger of my right hand. When I moved my forefinger, it left a gray line or trail on that glass screen table, almost as if my finger were a pencil and the surface were some kind of electronic paper.

I smelled something ancient and foul. There was the hum of some kind of energy subtly surrounding everything. It felt as though I were deep in the guts of some very old computer.

"Why am I here? What the hell is this all about?" I thought.

The fear was coming back, in a different, dreadful flavor. I didn't know if I could speak aloud or not because I was too frightened to try. Then my head went up, moved by some force other than myself. My eyes involuntarily fixed on that gray wall screen.

In the middle of my head, I heard a voice say, "YOU WILL LEARN THIS."

This Voice did not vibrate my eardrums. God! I can't possibly describe my alarm as each separate word rang through my head. The sensation was so very odd — I know the concept now — telepathy — direct mind-to-mind contact.

Not only that, but as each word was enunciated, I saw a word appear on that wall screen. A word not in English, but in some strange language.

I heard the Voice again, "YOU WILL LEARN THIS."

I didn't know where I was or why I was there. And here was some booming Voice in my head telling me what to do. I guess my Italian emotions took over here, because instead of becoming more frightened, I felt anger and rage.

"No, I won't!" I screamed.

The sentence burst from my mouth and surprised me. Definite sounds, yes — much different than that neutral, antiseptic voice booming in my brain.

The letter "A" appeared on the wall screen.

Next to it was some strange hieroglyph. Somehow I sensed that it was supposed to be another language's equivalent.

The alien letter faded, and then traced itself out again, as though to instruct me on its formation. I grasped immediately that I was supposed to write the alien letter out on the table screen before me with a forefinger.

"No!" I said.

•FIG. 4: MY TEACHERS WATCH ME LEARN ALIEN LETTERS.

It was worse than any school. It was worse than being told by a teacher what to do. It was a strange omnipresent intimidation by a force with no compassion or understanding of my feelings.

I would not cooperate with this kind of bizarre coercion!

"No!" I repeated.

Again, the letter "A" appeared and this time the air pressure changed in the room. It pushed against my head and my ears, becoming quite painful. My heart pounded again. I could taste fear again — body fear, fear of more pain that might come. Everything tightened and I was quite uncomfortable. I sensed that this discomfort would continue unless I cooperated, unless I drew that alien "A" on the screen.

Still, I can be a stubborn man.

"No!" I said. "What kind of stupid school is this? I don't know who you are, or why I'm here, and I'm not going to write your damn letter!"

The alien "A" reappeared.

FOOOMP!

The air pressure increased, upping my discomfort and anxiety.

I knew that unless I obeyed, it would go up again. I was still angry though — and maybe something about wanting to remember these experiences made me hang onto that pain.

"No!" I said, "I won't do it."

I could bear only so much, though. After the next level of agony, it felt as though I were about to die.

I cried out, "I don't want to die!"

I looked down at the table screen. With my right forefinger I traced the first stroke for their version of the letter A.

Instantly the air pressure dropped. Quickly, my heart rate dropped down toward normal. The anxiety and the fear faded.

Moreover, I felt euphoric. The contrast was remarkable. A very pleasant sensation flooded me.

The message was plain — "cooperate and feel good; refuse and receive pain."

But they didn't seem to think I'd learned that lesson yet.

"A!" said the Voice. The alien "A" appeared on the screen. Simultaneously, the air pressure went "Foomp!" and a low level of discomfort ran through my body.

I was still stubborn, though, and still determined to take this to the maximum. After a half a dozen levels of increased pressure and discomfort, I couldn't take it anymore. I copied the second stroke to this odd interpretation of the letter A.

Euphoria.

As I sat there in this artificially relaxed state I attempted to move, but my body was still completely paralyzed, my vision was a complete blur.

Anger stabbed through the pleasant feeling again. "Who are you bastards?" I demanded. "You don't have the right to do this to me!"

The telepathic response came back: "WE HAVE THE RIGHT! WE ALWAYS HAVE! WE ALWAYS WILL!"

That declaration had a touch of finality to it.

I sensed it was time to go, that this lesson was done.

Sure enough, my eyes closed even though I willed them to remain open. That whirling sound came again, and I felt the pressing of G-forces — of acceleration. All the terrifying cycles of this process unfurled, and I found myself lying flat on my face.

The softness of my own bed, the smell of my clean sheets, and the hushed bedroom air surrounded me like a gentle balm.

It was still night, but dawn light was beginning to filter through the curtains. I was back in my own bed. Beside me was Teresa's still, comforting form, her smell and hair spilled upon the pillow. Teresa didn't wear make-up. She didn't need to. She smelled sweet and clean, and she had on her worn, long cotton nightgown, the one she always wore, the one I always liked.

Gratified that I was able to move, I got out of bed and turned on the light. Yes, definitely, there was Teresa, sleeping.... This was home.... This was safety.... What, though, had happened?

I slapped myself. Again, harder. I was awake. This was no dream.

The funny thing was that despite the sound of my slapping and all the ruckus I was making, Teresa had not roused, despite being a light sleeper. I knew quite well that even the slightest sound, light or movement wakes her up.

Concerned, I leaned over and touched her. No response. Then I shook her slightly. She didn't wake. I shook her harder and it was then that I noticed something on my hands.

On the back of my hands were several small cuts that had not been there the day before. These cuts, however, were closed over and pink, not red with blood. They were almost healed, but they had not been there the day before.

I was worried about Teresa. I shook her some more, maybe getting a little frenzied — a little panicky.

Anyway, I knew she was alive when she moaned. She was stone asleep, though, and short of maybe throwing some cold water on her, I couldn't get her out of her stupor.

The digital numbers on the clock claimed I'd been gone about two hours. I went back to bed, but I couldn't go back to sleep. When Teresa woke up, she did so just as she always did, groggily but without any other trouble.

Lying awake, I'd considered unburdening myself about my bizarre experience, but, staring at her over the eggs, bacon and coffee, I just couldn't. I hid myself in the paper. It was just too much to believe in the cold, jittery, painful morning.

The rest of the day I was a basket case. I thought the light of day, some lunch, a few real estate calls, and some number-crunching would straighten me out, but by the time dinner, which I barely touched, was over, I started feeling even worse. Looking out at the dark made me feel cold, alone, and upset. I felt aftershocks of the fear, from the aches and discomfort I'd felt the previous night. I got through some TV and banal monotone chatter with Teresa, and she conked out at midnight. The whole idea of going to sleep again was just horrific. I just sat on the sofa, thinking, "I'm a logical guy. I'm a rational fellow. What took place last night doesn't make sense. How can I tell Teresa? How can I tell anybody? First of all, they won't believe me. Second, it just sounds like...nonsense!"

Unfortunately, I had a business trip to North Carolina planned for the next morning. Should I take Teresa along to hold my hand? Just say,

23

"Hey, could you come and keep me company? North Carolina is getting creepy!" More than that I was wondering if this house was safe. If I left her alone...maybe those things, whatever they were, would come and play intergalactic alphabet with her. She wouldn't be safe!

Rationally, some part of me was assured that she'd be in no danger. I had the feeling that these creatures were after me, not her. The idea of getting away seemed vital. Besides then I could talk to Jim Johnson, who was a close business friend of mine. I found I'd been able to discuss things with him that I couldn't talk about with other people. Why not strange presences forcing me to learn alien letters?

I met Jim Johnson over 20 years ago in Jacksonville, Florida. He was my first sales manager. He didn't like me at first because I was new at selling and my hair was a bit long. Jim tried to get rid of me by assigning me impossible sales territories. To his surprise, I closed every deal he sent me on. As he got to know me, he got to like me, and since then we've been friends.

Jim speaks with a deep Southern drawl and reminds me of a Southern plantation owner or General Robert E. Lee. His wife Peggy is a lovely woman with a sweet Southern voice. Like Lee, Jim has white and gray hair and a beard. Peggy is petite with long, reddish hair.

They had their own real estate brokerage company, but our partnership was Pine Straw. When he or Peg sold my lots, they got a percentage. If I was going to make that trip to see my partners, though, I sure was going to need some rest.

Somehow, with the help of a glass of beer, I went to sleep on the sofa. When I awoke, the luminous hands of the clock on the wall said it was 3:30 A.M. Why always 3:30? I thought.

I felt a wave of paralyzing fear.

It was deja vu with a different view. Not again! I thought. I was frozen solid, I simply couldn't move. My whole body was so tight, I could hardly breathe or swallow.

Then came a different sensation — a feeling that's difficult to describe. It felt as though I were being bathed in a field of intense static

24

electricity. Only one other time had this powerful unnatural sensation occurred — on that strange bench-and-screen room the night before. Only now I was in my own living room.

I tried to scream, but I couldn't open my mouth.

I thought, "Oh God, I can tell they are close!"

"Who was close? And how would I know?" echoed another part of me. Then, all of a sudden, on the living room wall a green glow appeared — it was almost like a cloud roiling there between a couple of picture frames. It expanded and contracted, expanded and contracted. Then it began to take form.

For an instant, that green cloud looked like a hairless two-dimensional stick man with large, unforgettable eyes.

Then it shifted into what seemed like a hologram of an owl — a green and ghostly owl.

# CHAPTER THREE

# The Fringe of Sanity

As I mentioned before, I had never read any books or magazines about the kinds of experiences I was having. I avoided anything associated with UFOs. Before my experiences, I simply wasn't interested. Afterwards I purposefully did not read any literature or see any movies or TV shows on the subject, because I didn't want to confuse or cloud any of my experiences with suggestions or anything else. Despite my terror, despite my confusion, inside of me burned a stubborn urge to know, to understand what was happening to me on my own terms. Now, I wonder if that was the right choice. I might have found a lot of comfort by going for help to the right people immediately. However, I did not. Perhaps this was why I had the kind of experience that I had, and why the Visitors were so interested in me. They were working with someone unprejudiced by immediate cultural or scientific interpretations of what was happening to him.

Mind you, just because I wasn't into UFOs then didn't mean that I didn't think there could be other intelligent life in the universe. Before being abducted, in fact, I took a logical common sense approach to the whole business. It didn't take much thought to realize that there are billions and billions of stars out there, and that there was a damned good probability of planets around many of those stars. So more life in the universe? Why not? And there was no reason that other life-forms wouldn't visit our planet, if they knew about it. I guess in the '80s, I was too busy finding and selling real estate to think too much about it.

Later, however, because of specialists who helped me understand that I was not alone in these experiences, I learned that while every abductee has his own unique encounters with aliens, there are some elements of the abduction phenomenon that keep recurring, for instance, this translucent owl, which gave me the feeling of the presence of a great wisdom. Now, whether or not that was because I'd always thought about owls as symbols of wisdom, I don't know.

My friend, Tim, from my Alien Abductee Support Group (which I didn't join, alas, until years after my first experiences) told me owls figured prominently in Whitley Strieber's Communion. Strieber saw lots of owls in the woods by his cabin where he had many of his abduction encounters.

The Visitors like symbols, I guess.

To me, it soon became apparent what this spectral owl signified — it meant school. It meant time for class. I got to know it as a symbol meaning, "Get ready to learn, Jim Sparks." Almost every time the Visitors take me, they show me a symbol. Perhaps it keys off some kind of subliminal response in my psyche.

I gather from my abductee brothers and sisters that Whitley Strieber's thoughts on owls have gone very deep in the abductee mindset. For me, though, it was simple — a representation or symbol of an owl meant to adjust my mind-set to learn.

It's become obvious to me that there are subtle shadings of meaning introduced with the alteration of these holographic forms.

That night, though, sitting on my couch staring at that perched owl with large, strange, round eyes, horns, feathers, beak and talons staring down at me, you can bet I wasn't paging through Freud's book about dream meanings.

My body finally relaxed. Though I could move, I felt completely drained of energy, exhausted. Enough of this, I thought. I have to get some sleep.

Somehow, strangely enough, despite the adrenalin pumping through me, I slept.

How long I slept I cannot say. Abruptly, I was snatched from slumber. I felt like I was strapped into that invisible rocket again and hurtled toward the moon. Anyone who's been on a roller coaster, or even a rapidly accelerating car has felt G-forces, and this was rough, heavy-duty acceleration. Maybe worse than before. I honestly thought it would kill me this time.

Again, there was the room, the bench, those screens, and the faintly acrid, neutral smell of the place. Again, I felt the warm and humid air, then the slight chill....

Mercifully, the G-forces stopped, and I caught my breath. I breathed raggedly, angry and confused. Once more, I had tunnel vision — I had to look directly at something to see it.

Even as I was recovering, maybe even thinking of just getting up and hurtling away from this madness if I could, something walked across that line of vision. One of my captors, one of those short people.

The first time I saw one of the Visitors I noted how slender its body was, and how large its head was. It kind of moved strangely, too — like Gumby, as though it had a different kind of bone structure, maybe more cartilage than bone. It wasn't wearing clothing, but somehow it didn't look particularly naked either. That head though. If I weren't scared silly, I think I might have laughed. It looked ludicrous, like some elf's head. It had these great big eyes like slanted rounded jewels. I didn't need a Ph.D. in biology to see that it wasn't human.

But then it was gone.

I held onto my anger. I pitted it against my fear and I cried out, "You bastards aren't human! Who are you? What are you?"

The non-human being had gone back into the shadows, and my head was jerked back to stiffly face my assignment.

Dead center in the screen, strange lines of symbols formed. Before each one appeared, a telepathic alien voice sounded in my head.

"I AM," that Voice said.

Then, a symbol for what I guessed represented each individual involved would fade in for a moment, and then disappear, like some spirit roll call.

The funny thing was that the Voice in my head always sounded the same, even though each individual symbol was unique.

I don't know if I'll ever get used to it, but in all the years these guys have been talking to me, never once have I heard them use any kind of vocal chords for communication. They always communicate directly with my brain. The Voice sounds deep inside of me, all knowing, unbearably intimate. Each time I saw one, I'd get a quick jolt of adrenalized fear, as I waited for the voice to resonate inside of me. It felt like a jealous God of yore pronouncing law.

These name symbols continued, each preceded by a deep "I AM" that had all the authority that the burning bush had to Moses.

Then the Voice said, "YOU ARE…"

My name, in English script, appeared. Beside it was my name in alien symbols. The flow and form of the alien symbols were quite beautiful. Amidst the fear, I felt a kind of awe that I didn't feel was artificially induced at all.

The alien version of my name disappeared and that Voice pronounced in my head:

"YOU WILL LEARN THIS."

Then the letter "A" appeared. Next to it was the alien equivalent. At the time I thought it was a conversion from our alphabet to theirs. I'm no linguist, but I figure that just because the English alphabet has 26 letters doesn't mean that alien creatures from wherever have an alphabet or language of their own that directly corresponds to our alphabet. However, for some reason, this was the way they taught. There must have been some other kind of process going on inside my mind, and this was the way I interpreted it in a literal kind of way. Whatever, these guys sure were working on my wiring.

The thing that struck me about the process was that they never, ever said, "We'd really like you to learn this," or "Would you learn this,

29

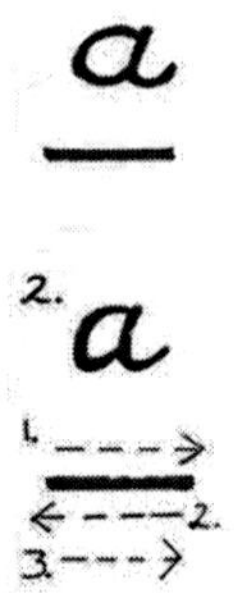

*a*

———

2.

*a*

ı _ _ _ →
← _ _ _ 2.
3 - - - →

•FIG. 5: ALIEN A

please?" It was always "YOU WILL LEARN THIS."

This coercion fired me up. I think it countered the fear and helped me keep my sanity. I must say, though, I didn't feel like going through that pressurization business again, so I started tracing out that alien symbol on the electronic etch-a-sketch.

I did a few of these symbols as best I could, and it got less scary, because they were hitting me with the euphoric stuff again, I guess. I mustered up some courage, and I squeaked out: "Who are you people?"

The Voice responded:
"WE ARE STAR PEOPLE."

I realize now they were teaching the fundamentals of telepathy, something all of us are capable of learning.

"Star People," I thought to myself. What's that supposed to mean? It sounded kind of cheesy, like something out of a bad Sci-Fi movie from the 1950s. Even the name upset me. It was like they were treating me like some monkey moron!

Then I felt the whirling, swirling and pain, and I was whisked away from Star People School and plopped back into my bed, with an Earth-human flavor of reality in a place called Houston, Texas.

# CHAPTER FOUR

# Falling Fast

The next morning I was to leave for North Carolina, and I was furious when I awoke. I managed to get through a hot shower and sausage and eggs, but not even a cup of strong Columbian coffee made me feel better.

In the past months, the concept of being abused by aliens had entered my mind, but I was in denial about it. After my previous night's experience, I was not only convinced of their otherworldly identity — I was also totally unnerved and offended at a core level about their methods, intentions and their lack of compassion for humans, including their treatment of me.

The morning of my Carolina trip, I managed to get off with a kiss for Teresa and not much else. I mean, what was I supposed to say? "See you next week, dear — oh, and by the way, I was hustled off again by 'Star People' who are teaching me an Alien Primer."

North Carolina is a lovely place, quite a contrast to Houston. The gorgeous foliage of the trees greeted me, and the sweet smell of the cold, bracing air seemed to snap some of the fear out of me as I arrived. This was Central East North Carolina, hilly with winding roads through lots of woods, which caused me to get lost more than once. I stayed at my friend Jim Johnson's house that trip, and it was good to be around him. My nights were untroubled, and my boiling mind calmed somewhat as I immersed it in work.

31

A couple of days later, sitting around with Jim and listening to some music after a hard day's work, I felt comfortable enough to broach the subject with him. I gave him a brief overview of what I'd been through.

Needless to say, he was very concerned. "Sounds like some sort of Devil Cult. That, or you're losing your mind!" He took a drink from his tinkling glass of iced tea as though he wished it were something stronger.

I assured him there was nothing devilish about it. It just didn't feel that way. It was scary, sure, but not in a spiritual or demonic kind of way. "You've known me for years," I said. "I'm a pretty level-headed guy, right? I haven't been in and out of a shrink's office, and I don't make things up!"

Jim's the salt of the Earth — a big, burly guy, middle-aged with that North Carolina drawl distinguished with an occasional stutter. He moves gracefully, and boy, does he love his music! He's a great jitterbug dancer, too. He grew up with a slew of famous '50s rock and blues musicians amidst poverty and obscurity, but he never became a musician himself.

"Yes, guy! But... aliens? I don't know what to say," Jim said.

I could understand his reaction. On one hand it was great to talk about it, and let it out. Unfortunately, even as I spoke I realized how totally absurd it all sounded. I didn't want Jim to think I was crazy.

At first, I allowed that maybe I'd been working too hard and was having delusions, but even as I spoke, I knew I was lying.

I got angry at the situation and myself.

"Bullshit," I said as I spilled my drink. "I'm not crazy! And these weren't delusions. These things happened... Period!"

Jim was taken aback, but he recognized the real me all right. "Whether it happened or not, you seem to believe it happened. That's going to have to be good enough for me."

He kind of cocked an eyebrow and said, "I hope whatever the hell is going on with you doesn't happen here!"

I chuckled and felt a little better. "Believe me, if it does, you'll be the first to know!"

I could tell he simply couldn't accept the reality of it all, but I will say he tried to understand, and he did listen. He just really couldn't wrap his mind around the concept. I really can't blame him, or anyone else. There's not a whole lot of proof around for visits from extraterrestrial life. There is, however, plenty of evidence for lapses in human sanity.

Still, of all people, I was really hoping against hope that Jim would be the one who would believe me, no matter what, but of all my friends, Jim Johnson tried the hardest.

That trip to North Carolina lasted ten days, and I didn't get dragged off to Star People School, which was fortunate indeed. I didn't get near the subject again with Jim, as I could tell it made him feel uncomfortable. I just savored my sanity, wrapped myself in work and North Carolina, and got some vital rest. I tried to eat right and exercise. The house was a large and comfortable ranch home with a big kitchen, where Jim loves to cook.

By the time I left, Jim wasn't giving me strange glances. Hell, I wasn't giving myself strange glances. I felt better — ready to face Texas again.

I wish I could say that it worked out okay. The smell, the taste, the presence of my own bedroom back at home got to me. I simply couldn't sleep there. The first night back I tossed and turned, and this time Teresa was not in a stupor. I ended up on the living room sofa again.

During the third sofa night, after days and nights of apprehension, the Visitors came again — whirling, acceleration....

My butt thumped on that bench. I saw the screens. I tasted the peculiar, ancient taste in my mouth, and I felt the warm mustiness of that room around me....

And then the "A."

By now, I knew what I was going to do.

Letting my anger override my fear, I concentrated. Carefully, with my finger I sketched out that alien symbol for A, just as they seemed to want me to do.

"GOOD."

The word appeared on the alien screen.

Simultaneously, that's just the way I felt — good. The fear left, the pain left, and a blessed relief poured through my veins — refreshing and pure. I think, there in that Somewhere Else place I actually smiled grimly to myself.

"I've got you figured out! You bastards are trying to brainwash me!"

I was feeling pretty smug, and I didn't really think they'd respond. But they did respond and quickly.

"NO."

The word appeared on the screen. Simultaneously, it reverberated in my head, and wiped the smile off my face.

It didn't keep my mouth closed though. "Sure, that's why you're doing this. Admit it! When you make me feel good, it's just like some scientist rewarding a laboratory mouse."

Now, I was still almost completely paralyzed, but my hand was free enough to do the drills they wanted. I rapidly tapped my right forefinger on the table screen, hard as I could. "No!" I shouted. "No! No! No! No!" For the first time I felt I had some sense of control. Suddenly my mouth became paralyzed. That didn't stop my brain though. If I could hear them telepathically, maybe they could hear me as well. "No! No! No! No!"

I continued to tap my finger emphatically on the table screen.

Suddenly, in my field of vision two of the creatures I'd seen before scurried in. I got a fuzzy, blurry impression of them at first, and I knew they didn't like what I was doing. They were about to use screen imaging, which is something like shape shifting, but I just kept at it. Then those blurry images changed and sharpened, and abruptly started looking like two policemen....

Then another blurry change and they became two military soldiers. I could see what was up, and it didn't get to me.

"Sorry!" I yelled inside my head. "You're not frightening me. That's not going to stop me!" I was just whistling in the dark. I was dead frightened. Still I knew instinctively that I would hang onto this consciously by putting up a great big stink with my will.

They changed back into their previous big-head, skinny elfish bodies again.

"Hey," I thought to myself, "these guys can be distracted."

I continued my finger banging. I almost felt triumphant — for about a second or two.

Then a wrenching sensation passed through my whole body. It particularly throbbed through the right side of my gut with deeply reverberating pain and anxiety.

I felt a distinct tingling in the right side of my head, and I felt a presence just out of sight — a powerful, significant presence. It was very strong. I'm not sure why, but I had the feeling that it was a male presence. For some reason, I think of most of the Visitors as being male.

I stopped my ruckus.

The energy radiating from this being was so strong that I can't really find the words to describe it. Overpowering? Overbearing? All this and more. I guess the nearest comparison I could make would be if I were strapped in a chair while some Tyrannosaurus Rex was sniffing me, thinking about whether it was hungry or not.

I could sense this being leaning down. I could feel its head no more than three inches from mine. I couldn't quite make him out directly, but I got the suggestion of an outline of a face and a taller body.

In retrospect, I realized that this thing was some sort of manager or supervisor, while the others were underlings. This was organized like a beehive, with drones and workers. As I think back on my experiences now, I realize that I noticed something about those first two aliens I encountered. They seemed a little robotic, with rather unnatural movements. Their mannerisms were more programmed and methodical, whereas the larger supervisors had a fluid, more definitively biological movement.

Even then I thought, the "workers" were the creation of the other, taller Visitors! The workers are shorter, with large eyes and featureless, blank faces — leather-like in appearance. Some have wrinkled foreheads.

•FIG. 6: MY LEARNING OF LETTERS IS SUPERVISED

The supervisors, as I was beginning to make out now, were tall, with that same leathery texture to their faces. Their eyes and heads are a little bigger than ours, but not nearly as large as the workers, and their eyes are much more focused. Both the supervisor beings and workers have bodies that are very skinny, almost atrophied.

These observations came to me in the middle of what seemed like some sort of three-dimensional monster movie! Even though I was still frightened, I knew that my plan was working. I was keeping my mind going, I was taking all this in, I would remember it!

The Voice inside my head said, "LOOK," and the letter "B" appeared on the screen.

I cried. I couldn't deal with the idea of having to go through this process 26 times, or God knows how many times. Maybe there were more letters in the alien alphabet that I had to learn to trace. I was already emotionally drained, and now this.

"The whole damned alphabet?" I sobbed.

"YES," appeared on the screen, followed again by "B," and then what must have been the alien equivalent. And, as though they anticipated me giving them more trouble, along with the "B" I got a zap of increased air pressure against my ears and head, along with stepped-up anxiety.

I put up no fight. As well as I could, I learned to trace out that next alien symbol. The sooner I got it to their satisfaction, I figured, the sooner I could go home.

Something was becoming apparent to me that may have already occurred to the reader, who is not under so much stress. The screens I was working with were part of a larger machine that could read my thoughts, anticipate my reactions, punish and reward. It had the ability to record my emotions, invading every private thought mercilessly. I felt I was being used just as callously.

When this "learning machine" perceived that I was proficient at tracing the symbols for the letters "A" and "B," the word GOOD appeared on the wall screen. Just like a lab rat, I knew it was time for my reward.

Then, on the wall screen the word LUST appeared, with the alien symbol for the letter "A" beside it. Just to the right of LUST appeared POWER and the symbol for the letter "B."

Okay, I thought.

•FIG. 7:
ALIEN B

If I write down the letter "A," I get some kind of reward that has to do with lust? I write down the "B" I get a reward associated with power?

Again, I just wanted to get all this over with, but the notion of pleasurable rewards was a sight better than the pain part.

I sketched out the alien symbol for "A." Instantly, floating before me, appeared a full-sized hologram of a beautiful, dark-haired woman. "Bizarre," I thought. On the wall screen the word FASTER appeared. I drew the symbol again, faster. The hologram moved and the woman began to teasingly disrobe. This was the reward session, and I sensed that I could fulfill any fantasy. The woman was beautiful, and my manhood wanted more. I couldn't give in to this. I couldn't let them have anything on me.

"No," I said. "I don't want anything to do with this anymore."

The hologram disappeared. I thought it odd that they should honor my demand on the pleasure part.

Then, I heard that low-pitched whirling sound again, spinning faster and faster. The pitch slowly got higher, and the whirling sound began spinning. My heart began to race.

Thus, was I taken home.

I had the desolate feeling that I would return to that dreadful place again soon. There were so many letters yet to learn.

# CHAPTER FIVE

# Life Falls Apart

The lesson continued there in that twilight world, in that screen room of strange beings. It could have been on some ship, some distant planet dimension... or in an abandoned warehouse in Brooklyn, for all I knew. I learned, I suffered, and I was rewarded. Time after time in that strange and foreign place, my mind was mauled by pure alienness. It seemed a continuum, a permanent time/space platform.

It seemed as though time stood still in that place. Perhaps it did. Generally it was warm and humid there, although at times weird, cool air would filter in from somewhere.

The aliens experimented with emotions, and it seemed there were other things about humans that particularly interested them, things like individualism, war and uniforms.

I always gave them their money's worth in those early years when it came to emotions.

In real life, though, things started falling apart. I was an emotional mess. All the things that keep a normal life functioning — friends, family, business, and personal life — began to disintegrate. People began to suggest to me that I seemed to be having some sort of psychological difficulty. I knew that already. They just didn't know why.

In mid-March 1989, the strain was too much. I was on the verge of losing my mind, and I felt like a pressure relief valve about to blow. Should I confess to Teresa? I was still concerned that it would frighten her and maybe wedge something between us. I knew nothing about people like Budd Hopkins, or alien abduction support groups at that time.

You would think I'd go to a library and research. All I can say was that I just didn't realize that other people could be like me. I just wasn't media-connected, and besides, I guess I just wasn't thinking straight.

Several years before 1988, I volunteered for a local church. Though I'm not much of church person, I had enjoyed helping the sick, poor and old people in my spare time. I respected the pastor of that church, whom I'll call Reverend Ed. He seemed to be an intelligent, wise person, with advanced college degrees. I'd never asked him for anything before, except to have him marry us, but I called him.

I told him I needed help with a strange problem.

"What do you mean by strange?" he asked.

"I'm having experiences... with strange beings.... They're forcing me to learn some kind of alien language." I gave a few more details and he listened patiently.

"Well, Jim," Reverend Ed said, "judging from what you're telling me, if it's okay with you, I would like to bring someone else along who perhaps would be more qualified to consult with on this matter."

I'm not sure if I felt better after my call to the pastor, but I felt I was doing something positive. I almost wished I was crazy at the time, so I could get treatment from a doctor. Maybe that's where the pastor and his friend would direct me. I probably should have headed straight to a shrink, but as I said, I wasn't the most rational of individuals at that time.

Besides, the core of me knew the truth. The core of me was quite sane, and it was that part that was clinging to the memories of my experiences. They were reality. They were happening. I wasn't crazy.

"Pulled" was the word I started to use with myself to describe the transition between here and there. The previous night I'd been "pulled" into the alien school experience.

I'd just called Reverend Ed, and I was feeling slightly relieved, but I was still exhausted. Doing the real estate work I needed to do seemed impossible.

I was just sitting in my easy chair in the living room just trying to grab a spot of safety amidst this whole mess. All at once I felt as if I were surrounded by a field of static electricity. I looked around, stunned. Dust balls and lint were sticking to my skin! I started to wipe them off, when I caught a whiff of a foul smell, sort of like rotting eggs or sulfur.

Then, out of nowhere, three marble-sized balls of green phosphorus light materialized. They hovered five feet in front of me, right over my coffee table. They formed into a triangle, and in the midst of this triangle a projection flashed into existence —an owl, a perched owl, stared at me with hooded eyes.

"Leave me alone!" I cried. I was never excited about the prospect of school, especially so soon after the last episode. But in the afternoon?

The owl disappeared. From the corner of my eye I caught a glimpse of two figures. When I turned my head to face them, nothing was there. Then I heard what sounded like footsteps coming from my attic. "Why can't you leave me alone?" I cried.

I still felt electrically charged. I jumped up with anger, and some knickknacks flew from the coffee table. I seemed to be charged with some kind of an electromagnetic force.

"Okay," I thought, amidst my alarm, "comic book times." Yes, I was still thinking sarcastically from time to time.

But truly, from the very earliest stages of my abductions, there were side effects involved. I now call the electromagnetic stuff and its ilk all part of "the residual effect." There always seemed to be something clanking about in the house after one of my abductions, which I tried to ignore, and oddly enough so did Teresa. Now, though, my theory is that it's all involved with the kind of technology they use.

Previously, I had thought that what I had been experiencing — dancing knick-knacks, etc. — was odd poltergeist activity, but now before me — here in my own house, away from that twilight zone computer screen room — was physical evidence that something real was happening.

I'm no rocket scientist, but I have enough education to deduce that all that was going on wasn't supernatural. It was science-fiction writer Arthur C. Clarke who said, "Any sufficiently advanced technology will appear indistinguishable from magic." So if what we had here was

•FIG. 8: I SEE A LARGE OWL IN MY LIVING ROOM

advanced technology that involved magnetism, electricity and light, then perhaps I was feeling the after-effects of whatever field they used. I've learned over time that they use this field for all sorts of purposes — invisibility for instance. They can render any form of matter invisible. They can transport themselves or others (including, alas, me) quickly and efficiently, just like the transporter on Star Trek, only without dematerialization.

This was also about the time that, despite my ragged state, I was beginning to perceive other strangeness, and I began formulating a theory — namely that these things, or creatures, may not be from another planet so much as from another dimension.

I'd noticed that when I saw them in this world, they only seemed to be partly here. Also, I would see these Visitors walking through walls. My dimension theory would explain this, since it would afford them the ability to work in our dimension, and yet be in theirs at the same time — a kind of phasing effect, if you will.

42

Anyway, that's what I was starting to think, and future experience bore me out. This business with the dancing knickknacks in the house was the result of my interaction with the field. The more I got abducted, the stronger this residual effect got. The paranormal activity, I discovered later when I got involved with researchers and groups, happens to most abductees, as do precognitive activities, which I'll discuss later.

So, on a Monday, I got a trip to School again, this time in midday. Another session with my schoolmasters certainly didn't help my mental state much, and I had to wait until Friday until I could meet with the pastor and the qualified guy he wanted me to meet. The emotional trauma affected my eating and my sleeping. I was losing weight and maybe getting one or two hours of sleep a night. I avoided my wife as much as possible. Teresa could tell I wasn't myself, and she asked me what was wrong. I told her I was just worried about business. We were both independent sorts, single-minded people. She had her projects, and I had mine. We required our own spaces, so it was natural for us to avoid each other from time to time. Therefore, Teresa seemed to accept my excuse.

Thursday night before my meeting with my pastor, I fell into a deep sleep. At 3:30 A.M., that phosphorous ball showed up again. I was so exhausted. I looked at it, knew it was "Time for School," and then I fell back to sleep.

Acceleration.

I guess they had to pry open my eyes this time.

"Hello, assholes," I said.

The Voice said, "THIS IS NOT PLEASING TO GOD."

"To God?" I was incensed. "To God, you say? How dare you say that? Do you think for one minute you're going to trick me into thinking you have anything to do with God? I'll tell you what, turn me loose and I'll squeeze your big heads off your skinny little necks. So do it! Turn me loose! Because I can't hurt God, can I?"

From the corner of my eye, I could see two of the workers. They were staring at each other. They had no expression, of course, but I could tell they were stumped.

That was the last time the Voice presented itself as God, and I wondered if other prophets had heard the same thing.

It seemed as though they'd try almost anything to weaken my will, in order to get my cooperation. What happened next didn't get my full cooperation, but it sure got my attention.

We were moving along in that alien alphabet by now. I'd passed "D" with flying colors, so I figured that "E" was next. So we spent the first part of the session with me proving my skill with those first letters. I was tired and I needed that positive feeling of euphoria, and they gave it to me, whatever it was. I performed admirably. Instead of "E," though, the number 1 appeared, then 2 and so on upward to the number 6. I cooperated, and traced out the symbols for each. Slowly I was becoming acquainted with their writing style, which made it faster and easier to learn. They stopped at the number 6, and then I said, "Okay. What about 7?"

"NO," said the Voice.

"What do you mean, no?"

"OUR NUMBER SYSTEM IS BASED ON THE SIX."

That upset me for some reason. Maybe it was the resentment I'd stored, going through those numbers for them like a good little slave. "The hell with your base six number system! I like mine better."

I drew out the number 7, my style. It disappeared from the screen. I traced it out again. It disappeared again, like a shaken Etch-a-Sketch. This happened over and over again, and I got a perverse sense of enjoyment. This was probably aggravating them! After a while I stopped writing the number 7, I shrugged and went back over the alien symbols for 1 through 6. I did well.

"GOOD," came on the screen, and the Voice sounded it in my head as well. I got that pleasant rush of euphoric reward.

"TIME TO COMPETE."

Mild euphoria turned to anxiety. "Compete with whom?"

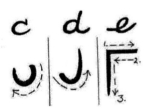

•FIG. 9: ALIEN C, D, E

"LOOK!"

I was able to turn my head, so I looked around. To my right was a corridor, through which I could look into another room. I was so shocked by what I saw that I almost fainted.

The room was a duplicate of mine — tool, screens, everything, but, instead of me sitting on the stool, it was my wife!

"Teresa!"

She turned her head slowly and then stared straight through me, as though I weren't even there.

"TIME TO COMPETE. GO!"

Quickly, Teresa turned her attention back to the screen. She started writing the complete alphabet on the screen — symbols I hadn't seen yet. She was fluid and fast, as though she'd been doing this for years.

"COMPETE! COMPETE!"

"I can't keep up with this!" It was such a heart-rending sight, seeing Teresa there. "Stop! Stop! Please stop!"

"SHE'S GOOD, ISN'T SHE?"

"That's my wife! You bastards have my wife!"

"SHE'S NOT YOURS. SHE'S OURS. ALWAYS HAS BEEN, ALWAYS WILL BE."

"She doesn't belong to you or anyone. Teresa is my wife."

"NO. SHE HAS ALWAYS BEEN OURS."

I cried out, "She's mine! That's my wife!"

"LOOK."

Straight ahead of me, three or four feet in the air, a scene appeared like a projected holographic movie. It was a hospital room. A child was being born. The scene faded into another scene, this one showing a four or five-year-old child sleeping in a bed. To my disbelief, I realized it was Teresa as a child. Then the next scene was Teresa as a teenager, making out with her first boyfriend. This was some sort of chronological representation of different periods of Teresa's life, right up to our marriage.

"Enough. That's enough. Now I understand. I don't like it, but I understand. You've been keeping track of her all her life. Me as well?"

"YES."

"Why?" I asked. No response. When I asked again and still got no response, I said, "I hate you more than anything I've ever hated in my life. You have invaded me to my core being. From all I can tell, nothing is

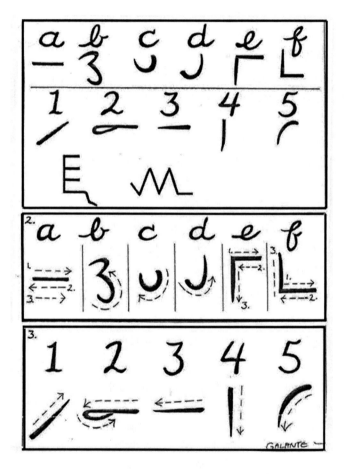

•FIG. 10: PARTIAL ALIEN ALPHABET[1]

_____

1. The complete alien alphabet can be seen on page 239.

sacred to you. What a pathetic existence you endure! Sure you have the technology, but you're like robots — empty and hollow. I'd like to kill you all."

No response.

"You don't have emotions. Do you? Answer me! Do you!"

Nothing.

Suddenly I just felt empty. I almost felt sorry for them, and I almost apologized for my desire to kill them. In any case, they certainly were getting full value from this particular abductee!

"Teresa!" I said. "Teresa... is she okay?"

They said nothing. They were as silent as the spaces between the stars.

The terrible whirling of acceleration drew me back to an Earth life that was growing stranger than my alien school room.

# CHAPTER SIX

# The Devil or Drugs

Home. I can see it now, the pretty Italian tile in the entry way, the oak railings, the high ceilings in the living room with sun windows, the fireplace, the large color TV and Teresa's excellent housekeeping. Even at the worst of times, she always made sure that our house was clean.

I could tell by the softness of the couch below me, the aroma of last night's dinner in the air, and the familiar smell of the heating system that I was back on my couch.

Nonetheless, I couldn't move. More than that, I was in some kind of haze. A timelessness hung over me, and I felt a drowsiness that I couldn't shake. All I could think of was seeing Teresa in that alien school. Was she all right? What did this mean? I was tortured by worry and doubt, all wrapped up in one great big ball of helplessness.

I had awakened in the dark, and it seemed to take a very long time for light to come. In between I fell into some kind of glazed half-consciousness, filled with sluggish nightmares.

When I finally was able to move, it was fully light. The clock claimed it was ten in the morning. I couldn't believe that so much time had passed. I didn't waste my ability to move. I rolled off that couch and rushed through the hall to our bedroom, half expecting to find Teresa gone — either gone to work or still controlled by those beings somewhere in the Twilight Zone, maybe reading alien Dick and Jane books already.

But there she was, my wife, still sleeping snugly in our bed, looking pretty and untroubled.

48

And safe! Thank God she was safe!

However, as soon as I got past my relief, I realized that what was before me was something rather odd. Usually Teresa is up every morning by 6:30 A.M.

Calling her name didn't wake her. I shook her.

"What time is it?" she mumbled.

"Past ten, dear. Are you okay?"

She nodded and blinked. "I feel weak. I must be getting a cold or something."

"I'll call your work for you and tell them you're sick."

I made us some coffee. It was time to talk.

When I gave her the coffee the way she liked it, she seemed a little more awake. I told her I'd make her breakfast as well, if she wanted it, but we needed to talk first.

"Teresa. Who are those strange creatures that have been taking us away?"

Her brow furrowed as she sipped at her hot drink.

"What creatures, Jim?"

I looked away and thought for a moment. How should I deal with this? She had an evasiveness about her. I decided that I needed to be stern.

"You know what I'm talking about. Who are they, Teresa? You seem to have been around them awhile."

She still seemed a little addled, a little confused, and she said, "What, you mean my Helpers from Heaven?"

Helpers from Heaven?

A whirlwind of thoughts flashed through my head. The creatures had tried to convince me they were from God, but it didn't work. However, they'd conned Teresa into thinking they were Helpers from Heaven. Then I thought back to days of old, to ancient man, thousands of years ago. The minds of that day, seeing everything religiously, would think the Visitors were either from heaven or hell.

Helpers from Heaven was an odd name for them, but that phrase still rings in my ears, and I was so grateful. It meant that I wasn't alone. Moreover, I wasn't losing my sanity.

"I don't think they were Helpers from Heaven, Teresa. I'd say they were aliens! Don't you remember seeing me last night?"

"No." She was suddenly alarmed, as though fully realizing who was talking to her. Her eyes flashed darkly as she stared up at me. "We're not supposed to talk about it."

Yet more relief.

Here was someone that was acknowledging that yes, Jim — this hasn't been a warped dream. Everything that has been tearing your mind apart has really and truly been happening.

On the other hand, this was a vital matter. We were not only husband and wife, we also shared this experience. Why shouldn't we talk about it? I desperately needed to discuss it!

"What do you mean?" I urged.

"We're not allowed to discuss it."

I shook my head. "Even between us?"

"Yes."

Well, they sure never told me that, but then maybe they figured pretty quickly that it would be worthless. Maybe they even instructed me to discuss it with anyone and everyone.

"Come on. You just admitted we were both there in that... that... place. You've seen them," I said, straining to get the words out. "Please. I need to know what the hell is going on!"

She turned away from me. Her words turned cold.

"Don't ask me any more, because I won't talk about it!"

I implored her, to no avail.

Finally, I just threw up my hands and went off and tried to take care of myself. That one time was the only time that Teresa ever acknowledged our mutual experiences, but the fact that she refused to discuss it was almost a confirmation.

The aliens had her intimidated, and I really can't blame her that much. We've all felt fear, some more than most, but can you imagine yourself experiencing these "things" with their slender unearthly fingers on your deepest instinctual triggers?

No, I didn't blame Teresa, but I guess I wish we'd been a bit less independent and had the kind of bond that not even unfeeling creatures from beyond understanding could break.

Despite Teresa's declared intention to follow party lines, I was determined not to.

I was going to get to the bottom of this, no matter what the cost. Oh yes, and there was a cost — a cost most dear.

After getting some breakfast for us, I sighed.

"Look," I said. "I'm sorry you don't want to talk about it, but I asked the pastor to come over to counsel me about this. He's bringing someone he says might be qualified to help. I respect how you feel... but could you at least say something helpful... I mean, so that they won't cart me off to some institution?"

She nodded. "I'll try." She had the kind of stony expression I recognized in her from five years of marriage, a look I'd see many times again.

It was almost 11:00 A.M., the time when the pastor said he'd arrive. I didn't have time to shower or shave. So I just went into the bathroom to splash some water over my face and run a comb through my hair.

I looked at myself in the bathroom mirror after doing what I could to fix my appearance. Staring back at me were puffy, red eyes peering out of a tired, pale face. My pants kept sliding down because of the weight I'd lost.

The doorbell rang. It was the pastor.

Reverend Ed is a short, stocky, strong, middle-aged man of German descent with blond hair. He's gentle but strong. Beside him was a short middle-aged man with glasses whom the pastor just introduced as "Tom." They both gave me firm, concerned handshakes.

I did my best to get them refreshments, and then I sat down with them, feeling a little relieved to be able to get help, but also suddenly wondering if I'd called the right people. Tom looked stiff and uncomfortable, and he had the attitude of a man who had already made up his mind about what was in this universe and how things were supposed to run.

"Now, Tom, before we jump to any conclusions, let's let Jim share some details," said the pastor.

I took a deep breath and jumped into my story. I gave them a 45-minute summary. I included the fact that I'd seen my wife on board the craft, or whatever it was. I mentioned my recent conclusion that she'd been influenced by these aliens for years, if not her entire life.

Well, I held their interest. That was for sure. They seemed entranced, but when I finished my story, Tom said, "Without a doubt there is demonic activity taking place here."

"I completely agree," said the pastor, nodding gravely. "The ways of the Devil are confusing."

"The Devil!" I shook my head. "I'm not talking pitchforks and barbed tails or horns! I'm not even talking evil... I'm discussing a possible starcraft. I'm talking about amazingly advanced technology. We are not in the middle ages! These are aliens!"

The pastor sighed. "I'm sorry, Jim. If this isn't satanic work... well, then I'm afraid you must be taking some kind of drugs."

Tom nodded smugly. "In my experience, drugs and evil spirits are always linked."

"I almost wish this were so, fellows! But please believe me... these aren't devils. Look. I'll get Teresa. She's more religious than I am. Maybe she'll convince you."

When Teresa came out, she looked at me in a funny way. She'd brushed her hair and put on her dressing gown. She gripped a Kleenex and still claimed she had a cold.

"I was telling the pastor about what happened last night, about the creatures who kidnapped me, and about you being there too," I said.

She gave me a look of sorrow, then turned to the man who had married us. "I have no idea what Jim is talking about."

I felt devastated. I snatched at straws. "Okay, Teresa. What about the people you call your Helpers from Heaven?"

She shook her head. "I've never said anything like that, and I have no idea what you're talking about, Jim."

"Is Jim taking some kind of prescription drug or illegal substances?" the pastor asked.

"Not here," Teresa answered, "not that I know of, anyway. I'm not sure if that's the case when he goes up to North Carolina on business."

I had to fight for control. Inside, I was raging with frustration. I was asking for help and understanding here, and getting patronizing preconceptions. They weren't dealing with me as a person. They were doing just what I've seen so many people do — come at things with prejudiced world views.

So I had a choice, according to them, this could be either the Devil or drugs! Quite peeved, my Italian anger lashed out. "Drugs! That's it. You figured it out. Thank you for your expert opinion on the matter!"

They told me I should go into rehab and get professional help. I promised to consider that, thanked them for coming and suggested that they leave.

"I'll get the phone numbers you can use," promised the pastor. "I'll call you back."

When Teresa and I were finally alone, I confronted her. "Why didn't you tell them the truth?"

Aloof and defensive, she said, "I couldn't. I didn't want them to think I was crazy." Crazy, or in my satanic cult, or shooting drugs with her hubby.

Well, whatever. From then on, I never pressed my wife for answers or even support. In fact, from then on she would get hostile if I were even to mention or hint about the subject. Her way of coping was denial.

I can't tell you how isolated I felt, how alone, how abandoned. I'd reached out, and I'd been handed presuppositions and platitudes.

I had to regroup or I'd be totally lost. After that dreadful meeting with the pastor, I went for a walk.

I sat down on a bench in a park. I knew they could probably "pull" me back from anywhere, but daytime abductions were rare so far. I didn't feel safe necessarily, but I felt I had some space. Again, my indignation and anger was what kept me going. I would make a plan, I thought, managing to steel myself.

I outlined the pattern of the abductions in my head. Okay. 3:30 A.M. Awaken. Strange lights. Holograms. Symbols. Terrible fear. Static electricity. Despite all this hoopla, though, immediately after the dramatic prologue, there was always an overwhelming urge to go back to sleep.

Next time, Jim — 3:30 A.M. Lights... camera... action. No back to sleep, guy. Jump out, get in your car and drive as fast and as far away as possible.

This was a pretty simple plan, but it kept me together over the next two weeks. True, I wasn't totally myself. The nights were still hard, but I had a plan. I knew what I was going to do.

In April, 1989, my tormentors came for me again.

# CHAPTER SEVEN

# Nowhere to Hide

Sleep is important. Some people resent it because they can't go out and earn money or play or whatever, and scientists still don't understand it totally. What they do know is that while you're sleeping, things get fixed inside your head and body, and maybe most important of all, the chemicals that make life bearable — like dopamine — get manufactured and released.

I don't have to be a scientist to know that getting too little sleep in that period of my life was doing me no favors. I felt wretched. I would try to sleep, yes, but it would be a fitful sleep. I had a plan, and I knew that even if I got abducted I'd come back. That didn't help the incredible instinct-level fear and pain that the experiences caused in my head. You can tell your core self that everything is going to be okay — but you are still going to have terrible emotions if something terrifying is happening.

And if someone knows those pain-and-fear circuits and where exactly to hit your buttons to get the responses they want... some people would call that torture.

I'd call it my life in 1989.

It was 3:20 A.M., two weeks after the last encounter, to the day. Somehow I'd managed to fall asleep after the requisite tossing and turning, and when I saw those numbers on the digital clock, I pretty much knew what was up.

A glowing, green ball of light suddenly emerged from the living room wall. It shimmered and spun, like something from Industrial Light and Magic Cinema effects, only immensely creepier. The ball of light changed, wiggled and elongated. Slowly it described what looked at first like a figure 8, or maybe the sign for infinity. Wobbly. Phosphorescent.

Unaccountably, I muttered to myself: "Time for an experiment."

Even as the words escaped my lips, I had no idea how I knew this. It felt like a fact, but I don't remember ever being told this before.

The familiar fear struck, and with it came adrenalin, which sparked memory.

My plan!

The urge to fall asleep again rolled over me, but this time I fought it off. "No way," I snarled.

I managed to force myself off the sofa and lumber back to the bedroom where I threw on some clothes. Teresa was in bed, sleeping. The way I felt about her betrayal had made me think I could just drive off without her. Now, though, I realized I simply couldn't abandon her to these whatever-they-weres.

I woke her up. I threw her robe on her. She was groggy but compliant. I led her out to the garage and our car.

At the time we lived about 35 miles southwest of Houston in a subdivision called Pecan Grove Plantation. I sped the car away as quickly as I dared, just putting as much distance as possible between me and that glowing twist of light. I'm not sure why, but I took the first turn I could.

Unfortunately, there were no lights about, no houses, and no other autos on this road.

Smart, I thought. A dark and lonely road, but I pressed on, still trying to gain that distance.

Teresa said, "You need to pull over."

She said it quietly. But her voice and what she said unnerved me. She didn't ask me what we were doing or where we were going. She didn't request that we go back.

I ignored her and if anything sped up.

Louder, she said it again.

When I didn't respond, she did something I never thought she might do; it was so out of character. Teresa's generally a prudent and cautious person, the type that looks all ways before she crosses the street.

"Pull over!" she screamed at the top of her lungs. She grabbed the steering wheel and tried to wrench it from my grasp. The car swerved wildly, the lights from our headlights bouncing all over the place. I was so alarmed, it seemed like I had no other choice. I veered to the shoulder, right by a large cow pasture. The odor of manure wafted through my open window. It was pitch black beyond our lights. There was no one about for miles.

"Why did you do that?" I demanded.

Instead of responding, she just fell back on the seat. Whether she passed out or fell asleep it was hard to say, but she was out and wouldn't wake up even though I shook her.

As though that sleep was contagious, a tremendous wave of weariness passed over me. I felt so drowsy, the prospect of driving along a back road seemed ludicrously dangerous. As my exhaustion increased, I realized I had no choice. I turned off the engine and lights, and leaned my head back. Just for a moment... I promised myself. I'm going to close my eyes for just a bit and then I'll feel better. Then came....

The sensation of something near....

The crunch of gravel as though through cotton....

The feeling of being moved....

My eyes fluttered open. Just beside me was my car — the outside of my car.

"How did I get here?" I thought and then I realized that something was holding on to my right arm. I was standing up, walking like some kind of zombie. I was guided through the field that stretched out beyond my parked car. I don't know how long I walked, because everything was disjointed and wavering. But then I saw something like a dome rising up high from the ground outlined by trees.

Some sort of craft?

The fog just drifted over my brain, heavier, until it enveloped me. The next thing I knew I was exactly where I'd been trying to avoid — the alien schoolroom, with its hard bench, screens and grim schoolmaster included.

I had the presence of mind to conclude that the dome I'd seen, the vessel-like thing, was where I had been taken. Even as I sat there, feeling the familiar feelings and getting ready to take my instruction, I realized that without the awful acceleration that seemed to tear my cell structure apart at its seams, I wasn't quite as angry as usual, nor in exactly the same terrorized state I usually suffered.

If the other way of getting to the room was the hard way, then this was the easy way.

This was the way I started to view my arrivals here.

Needless to say, over the years I experienced both ways many times. And although it might be concluded that I prefer the easy way of abduction, it's no treat. It's disorienting, and confusing. You get wrapped up in that interdimensional field and sometimes you think you've left vital parts of your soul behind.

So here we were again, having come in via a different portal to what I came to think of as alien boot camp.

And I had company now, other than your friendly neighborhood gumby workers and supervisor.

There was this ant. It was a big red ant, and I recognized its type immediately. It was a bull ant, or perhaps a farm ant. It was crawling around in a circle maybe eighteen inches in circumference, right there on the table. And it was a perfect circle! I couldn't see what was keeping the bull ant right on the border of the circle.

The Voice inside my head said, "EXPERIMENT."

As soon as the word registered with me (and fitted into my interpretation of that twisted coil that looked like a figure 8) another word bloomed in my head.

"KILL," said the voice.

Simultaneously, a symbol I knew must be the alien term for "Kill" flashed on the screen, noting that it would be easy to duplicate. I had an uneasy feeling about all this....

The Voice said, "DRAW THE SYMBOL TO KILL THE ANT."

"No!" I said loudly. "I won't kill."

They didn't like that.

I got the increased air pressure treatment.

"KILL!"

"No!" Again, the air pressure upped again. My beating heart shifted into overdrive. It felt like there was some kind of heart attack coming on, but I managed to snarl out through gritted teeth: "You will never force me to kill."

All I had to do was to draw the symbol and my pain would cease. I tried to rationalize the fact that I wouldn't actually physically kill the ant, but I realized that there was cause and effect here — so it would be the same damned thing.

"Killing is wrong," I said.

This was the most tormenting moment so far. The agony just got way up there. Desperately, I tried one last tactic. "You bastards will have to kill me first because I won't do it! Go ahead. I'm not afraid to die!" The last bit was a total lie. Somehow, despite all I'd been through, I still had the will to survive.

I watched the supervisor approach. Well, were they sick of this? Were they just going to put me out of my misery? But then I could feel some kind of probing, mental fingers pushing through the fibers of my mind, searching for a weakness.

Suddenly, a three-dimensional image sprang before me. I saw, in this video-like image, my brother in a hospital room, clutching his heart, his face red, clearly at death's door.

The implication was clear. I had to draw that symbol, or my brother would die.

The pain I was experiencing was one thing, but the thought of harm coming to my brother was more than I could bear. I broke down and copied that symbol.

Coincidentally, my brother did have heart trouble ten months later, but he recovered fully. Nonetheless, right there, right then, the big red ant curled into a ball and was still. It died. At the same time, the discomfort ceased.

The supervisor alien backed off, turned and left. I just sat there. Tears came to my eyes. Weeping, I said, "Why did you do this to me?"

"WE HAD TO BE SURE."

"Be sure of what...?"

"THAT YOU'RE NOT A KILLER. YOU'RE NOT."

I completely blacked out. I was put back in my car — a door handle. A wheel and gear shift. A glove box. Pine fresh deodorizer.

Slowly, things phased back in for me, resolving into a familiar scene. My car. I was sitting in the driver's seat of my car. There was a kink in my neck. My head was twisted back onto the seat in an uncomfortable position. I gasped but couldn't move. I was able to make out a dim form next to me — Teresa, slumped on the seat beside me.

Slowly the power of movement flowed back into me. I just wanted to get out of that place, so I turned on the ignition. The sound of the engine rolling over woke Teresa. "Why did you turn off the road?" she asked.

She didn't know? "I was tired. I pulled over." It seemed pointless to explain.

"Emergency?"

"Teresa, how long do you think it's been since we left the house?"

She blinked. "Just a few minutes."

Well, just a glance at the clock told me that we'd been gone a couple of hours.

"What did we leave for in the first place, Jim?"

I was far too gummed up in my head, too upset and confused to try to explain everything. "I needed to take a ride, and I wanted you with me," I answered, lamely.

"Jim, I think you need help."

Yes, I needed help.

But I knew that I wouldn't be getting help from my wife.

The whole of the next day I was numb inside both mind and body. "Damn!" I was thinking. "Those things can get you anywhere!"

However, over the next few weeks they left me alone.

I tried to open up, talk to friends, but they just looked at me oddly and patronized me. No help there!

I tried to get my life and my business back together. In May of 1989, I devised a strategy. All my problems were centered around the whole abduction experience. If I could get somewhere where I couldn't be whisked away, surely then I could concentrate on getting the rest of my life — and my work — back together.

I found a hotel — the tallest building in downtown Houston. Surely here I would be safe!

I asked Teresa to come along with me, and she agreed to give it a try.

Even as I checked in, I felt better. It was a nice room, and although home is always nicer, home lately had been a place of terror. I managed to eat a decent dinner, and I took a long bath. I promised myself that tomorrow would be a full work day.

I woke up in the middle of the night. The room seemed cold and strange. The clock read 3:00 A.M. exactly.

Something fluttered on the other side of the bed.

My heart in my mouth, I turned and looked over Teresa's form, asleep beside me.

Hovering overhead, like some ghost, was a translucent owl.

Time for School.

This time, I didn't bother to wake Teresa. I hopped out of bed and grabbed the suitcase I'd left packed for just this possibility. I rode the elevator down to the garage, got my car and headed for another part of downtown Houston.

As I pulled into the parking lot of another hotel, I thought, sardonically, "At least they can't get me while I'm driving."

Rousing the clerk, I requested a room smack in the middle of the hotel. No windows, please. How long would I be staying?

"The whole night," I said. "I hope."

When I got to the room, I threw down my suitcase and flopped into bed.

Surely I was safe here! Surely they can't get me here!

I fell asleep immediately.

I don't know how long I slept, but it seemed like no time at all. The next thing I knew, I was being swept away again with that low-pitched whirling sound to the place where I did not want to go.

Acceleration.

"Oh, God!" I whispered. "Is there nowhere to hide?"

# CHAPTER EIGHT

# Abandoned Home

I was falling into a deep depression. My hair had grown quite long, and I wasn't showering. My fingernails were long and dirty. I was drinking a great deal of alcohol. One evening I sat in my easy chair with a fifth of Smirnoff Vodka, drinking straight out of the bottle. My right hand gripped the neck of the bottle and my left hand held a.357 Magnum cocked and ready to shoot, as my right forefinger massaged the trigger. I was going to shoot anything and everything resembling aliens — even holograms.

Part way into the bottle a loud thump sounded on the roof. I was certain a small scout ship had landed on my roof. I waited, feeling my hackles rise and perspiration growing on my forehead and underarms. Then I heard shuffling footsteps in the attic and then another noise. It sounded as though those things were moving my boxes around up there. I tried to pinpoint the exact origin of those sounds and tracked them with the muzzle of the gun. My finger tightened on the trigger. My heart was pounding and I was sweating like a racehorse. I closed my eyes — but didn't shoot. "No, not yet," I thought. "Wait until they come into the living room."

Moments later, the waiting seemed unbearable. "Why don't you freaks walk through the walls like you usually do?"

A few seconds later two of the aliens walked from the hallway into my living room, their big eyes shining. They looked so odd as they entered my living room, like curious children. They examined my belongings, played with the lamps, walked into knick-knacks like clods, and knocked things over. One of them was moving the ashes around in the fireplace. The other kept staring at the TV.

Trigger cocked and barrel pointed at the back of his bulbous head, I took a large gulp of vodka, began to squeeze the trigger, and yelled, "Pretty pathetic! You walk through walls and travel the universe, but you can't figure out how to turn on the TV! I'm going to kill you!" But even through the alcoholic haze, I heard what they had recently told me, "WE KNOW YOU ARE NOT A KILLER."

The sentence sounded through my head, and I knew they had been right. I lowered the gun. The creatures stayed in the house until daybreak. When daylight came they were gone.

If the Visitors, or whatever you want to call them, want to get you — there is nowhere to hide. In 1989, I thought there was no hope, no help at all. As those things whisked me away from that hotel room, I didn't know if I was going to be able to survive, at least as my full self. However, I did survive. Whether as my full self, I don't know. Maybe I lost something in these experiences, maybe I've gained something. I just knew the whole while that I had to understand what was going on!

In the years that followed, even stranger things happened, and I became more and more convinced of the absolute reality of what was happening to me, that I was being instructed by the aliens for a reason. It took me a long time to understand that, but I learned. I also learned that I wasn't alone.

In 1994, I took a step that would change my life and put my contact with these other beings in a totally different perspective. In that year, I found real help.

Believe me, Houston, was not a good source of compassion for someone who claimed the things I did. Neither, for that matter, was North Carolina. Both are pretty much set in their ways, and those ways are generally either secular or religious. So, professionals wanted me to take prescription drugs and talk about my mother, while religious therapists wanted to throw holy water on me and pray that my demons would be cast out.

I'll get to what happened between '90 and '94 soon, I promise, because those years contain much of what I learned from the aliens, about what I was supposed to do and say as I went out and spoke to people about them.

One of the best things I did was move back to the Ft. Myers Beach area. My family probably did think I was more than one card short of a full deck, but they were caring and supportive, and I'd decided that South Florida was where I should be.

I guess that South Florida is a lot more free-thinking about things, since it's a mixture of people from around the world. In any case, two significant things happened as soon as I moved back.

Number one, I started to hear more about the whole UFO abductee phenomenon. Call me unattached to media, if you like, but I didn't get much of that in Houston! In South Florida, however, there's a lot more talk of such things. Maybe the Visitors work there more, or more likely, people are willing to talk more about it.

In any case, soon enough I learned that there were others who had had abduction experiences. I was still pretty mentally disturbed about the whole situation, and so it took me a while to get up the nerve — being at my wits' end was an incentive.

In any case, the news filtered down to me: In Florida there was something called the Southwest Florida Abductee Support Group.

The founder and leader was a man named Tim Wilson. I called Tim, nervously. I was used to dealing with people who regarded me as an escapee from the loony bin. This seemed to be my last hope for understanding, and I do confess I was perspiring somewhat, and my hand shook a little as I rang him on the telephone February 24, 1994.

Tim was wonderful. He listened patiently and asked just the right questions.

"Look," he said. "I know this has been rough on you. You need to talk about it. I want to assure you, you're not the only one who's had these kinds of mind-breaking experiences, and believe it or not it really helps to share and compare notes and support others as you are supported. Most of all, it's great to listen — and to be listened to — without judgment. We have a meeting the last Saturday of every month, which means there's one this Saturday evening. Why don't you come? I, for one, would love to hear your fascinating story."

At first I was elated. Yes, I would be there! Tim Wilson's family owned a motel, which was the site of the monthly meeting.

After my agreement, however, I was worried.

I began to think of some of the things that had been happening in recent years. Most prominent were the experiences I had had with men who would come to my home in Houston, after my talk of aliens and abduction, and explicitly tell me to be quiet. Then I would see them following me. Suffice it to say, it had a two-edged effect. For one thing, it made me realize that others took me seriously, even if only "Men in Black." But it also made me quite paranoid about others who considered abductions serious business. Perhaps this was one of the reasons I hadn't worked as hard as I might to seek out this kind of people.

I got into the car and made the trip to the meeting. Oddly enough, I lived only a mile from the address that Tim had given me, so it wasn't hard to get there physically that Saturday night. Still, I was upset and hesitant as I drove, and I tried to let the beauty of the scenery absorb some of my anxiety.

Southwest Florida has a unique mixture of foliage and wildlife, particularly the birds and trees. It's one of the few places where you'll find coconut trees, pine trees and orange trees growing together in a clump. Still, the closer I got to the motel, the more uncomfortable I became.

I'd been used to ridicule, but I didn't think I could take any more. Was that what was in store? Or worse, was this some sort of plot — reel in the UFO experiencers, track them, get their stories, and then control them through these groups? These and far wilder thoughts crossed my head, like, "Were these aliens themselves in disguise... testing me?"

The motel was nice — one of those cottage-style motels, tucked into a relaxed, wooded setting. When I pulled into the macadam parking lot, I noticed the sign immediately:

## THE MEETING

———————————▶

I followed the arrow below the words to an open door past which I could see people. I half-expected wild-eyed lunatics, but they looked absolutely normal — the sort of folks you'd see in a middle-class mall somewhere.

A guy stood up.

"Hi. I'm Tim Wilson."

Just a guy. No antennas. No ray gun.

"Hi. I'm Jim," I said.

Tim introduced me around. Tonight we had present a nurse, a warehouse manager, a geriatric care-giver, and a wide range of individuals in different vocations — and all just people — normal people.

"We usually have about twenty people at these meetings," said Tim. "It's a smaller group tonight."

"There is just one rule here," Tim explained. "To attend these meetings, you have to have had alien-abductee experiences."

It didn't take long to realize that Tim was intelligent and friendly. He was a person who went out of his way to make others feel comfortable, and the way he dealt with everyone in that room showed me that he was firmly committed to helping people involved in this phenomenon. He too was a victim, and he made no secret of that fact. Tim had a calming effect on me, and I was glad that I had come.

A few people spoke. They had anxiety, a sense of some kind of abuse, psychological disturbances, and maybe a few vague notions and images, sounds and smells, but no one recalled their abductions as vividly as I did. I almost envied them.

When it was my turn to speak, my relaxation crumbled. My chest began to tighten and my heart raced. This wasn't just an ordinary fear of speaking in front of a group. I'd felt that before, and I knew the difference. No, this was a feeling that was much more familiar. I knew then that as I shared my story, I would relive the trauma.

But these were good people, and I knew that they would do their best to understand. I told them a short version of my experiences, and although it wasn't easy, neither was it as difficult as I feared.

Later, it became much easier, and I became a regular attendee at the meetings. Tim Wilson, bless him, also met with me regularly. We hashed out my experiences, and he helped me interpret them.

Through Tim and the others, I got to know about people like Budd Hopkins, John Mack, and others who worked with people who had experienced alien abductions. I still felt that I shouldn't read about this subject for fear that it would mar my personal understanding and detailed recall of the events in which I had participated. Now, though, through the group I could actually learn more, and I did not feel as though my interpretations would be tainted.

I discovered I had similarities with the group of people, but there were also big differences. I remembered.

I remembered just about everything.

I remembered, for instance, being pulled from that hotel room in downtown Houston and set back into that awful room to face an experience I never would — never could — forget.

"H."

That was the problem letter.

That was the letter that hung me up, — the alien version of the letter "H." I just couldn't get the stroke down right.

I paused and looked up. The two workers were standing there, placidly staring at me as usual.

"Can't do it. Sorry. Maybe I could use some help."

Suddenly my arm and hand felt like a long glove that someone had slipped their fingers into. My right forefinger began to move on its own, drawing out each stroke of their symbol perfectly. Amidst my fright at being controlled, I also felt astonishment.

"Thanks," I said.

After going through the paces before, I had gotten tired, and I appreciated this new kind of attitude toward me.

"What are you creatures that you can do something like that?"

The energy they radiated was not a bluff. I knew they were going to give me a truthful answer.

"WE ARE STAR PEOPLE."

"Okay. So you say, but what exactly is that supposed to mean? Star people. Like, you're from another star. Okay. But people? Look, humans are people. And you're not human, certainly."

They had no response to that.

But I'd been thinking about something else, and as long as they seemed to be listening to me, I figured I might as well let go with it.

"Okay. So you're from another star. Which means you get back and forth in some sort of starship. So, if I wanted to go with you — you know, travel the universe — would you take me?"

"YES."

Much time passed in thought because I knew they meant what they said.

"If I didn't like it — would you bring me back home?"

"NO."

Clearly, they could do what they wanted with me at any time. They'd proven that. Nonetheless, I sensed that they were telling the truth. They would take me away if I requested it, for whatever reason. They were actually responding and listening to me, and I found their offer intriguing. Then I began thinking, "No more hot dogs, hamburgers, steaks and, Oh my God, no beer!" Plus the smell of cut grass that gave me a warm feeling.

I contemplated this for a moment, then said, "I love the Earth, and as much as I'd like to go, I'd better pass for now, but just for now."

As I ponder the first years of my interaction with the aliens, I can't help but consider that, somewhere between the fear and the pain and the disoriented feelings, there were good moments. This was one. I felt a real sense of two-way communication here, and although I turned down that trip, I might just take them up on it some day.

After this interchange, there was no time lost on getting me back to letters.

As before the words LUST and POWER appeared, and next to each word was a symbol for new letters I had just learned. There was no fight left in me. I decided to go along with their agenda. However, instead of picking LUST as before, I chose POWER. I briefly lost consciousness. When I awoke, I found three items before me — a ball, a cube, and a pyramid. Each was the size of a large marble.

Then on the table screen a letter appeared. With my right forefinger I drew one of the new symbols that I had learned. Instantly the ball began to roll slowly across the table. I noticed right away that it would move to the rhythm and direction of my forefinger. When I moved my finger to the left, right, up or down, the ball would roll accordingly. In order to keep the ball's momentum going, and to control its direction, letters and symbols would intermittently appear on the table screen. These were there for me to duplicate. If I copied them wrongly, the ball would stop. On the other hand, if I duplicated the symbols correctly, I then had more power or control.

I don't think this was an experiment. They were teaching me something.

After I felt I had mastered the ball's movement, I telepathically heard the word THINK and at the same time it appeared on the table screen. "Think?" I thought to myself. Then I said aloud, "What do you want me to do, use psychokinesis to control the ball's movement by thought?"

"YES."

I stared at the ball. I concentrated. To my surprise the ball slowly began rolling back and forth. When it became what I'd have to call a mental struggle to move the ball, a previously learned symbol would appear, so that when I drew it or duplicated it, I would have more control or power over the ball's movement — mental control.

70

After mastering this assisted mental ability, I began to concentrate my efforts on the cube. This was a much more difficult task because the only way it would move was end over end or by sliding. This took much more effort than just rolling a ball. As before, the more efficiently I traced out those previously learned symbols, the easier it was to mentally turn the cube end over end. In fact, from time to time it would slide across rather quickly, completely out of my control.

I then worked with the pyramid, which was extremely difficult. I got the hang of it, though.

"This review isn't about power, is it? You're teaching me how to use an elementary form of your thought-activated technology! That's what you're doing, isn't it?"

No response.

"Isn't it?" I demanded.

I got no response, but I kept asking the question because, for the most part, the aliens don't like to answer direct questions. They answer in riddles. But I can somehow tease the truth out, and I can feel whether they're telling me the truth or not.

I never did get a response. Then or ever.

What I got was unconsciousness. When I came to, I found myself nose to bedspread on that downtown Houston hotel bed.

It took me a few moments to reorient myself. But as soon as normal reality kicked in, my previous urge and inclination returned. I wanted to get away from those things.

Maybe getting away from Houston, totally, would do the trick. They hadn't found me in North Carolina. Maybe if I were away from this vicinity, I'd be safe.

At that point, I no longer cared about my marriage, business or my personal well being. All I wanted was for them to go away and leave me alone.

There was another thought in my head, though, that upset me even more. In some odd way, despite the fear, and the crazed feelings — all this

71

was getting interesting. Mental powers to move things. Telepathy! Aliens! An offer to tour across the universe....

That was too much. I don't know why I was feeling this way. I just had to point my car in a direction and drive, drive, drive.

Weariness eventually took over on my highway journey. I found a small town off an exit, and I turned into the first available motel.

It was well past dawn, and I knew I looked rather rough. The hotel owner looked quite leery of me, but I had plenty of money and flashed some credit cards as well.

The motel room was small and dingy. I was drained.

I did have the smarts to get some breakfast. I hadn't been able to keep much down, but I needed something. I went to the vending machines, got a candy bar and soda and brought them back to my room. I sat on the bed, flipped on the TV and managed to get the candy and soda down.

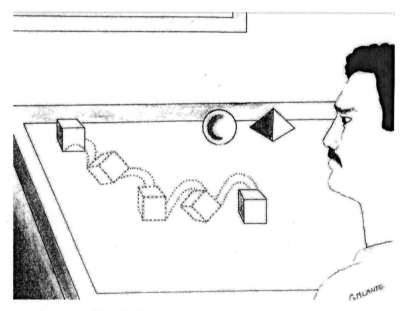

•FIG. 11: I LEARN TO MIND CONTROL A BALL

A little revived, I shook my head and began to think a little more clearly.

How had they been able to find me in those hotel rooms?

Well, they had advanced technology. More advanced than ours, certainly. What was comparable?

The only science courses I took were in high school, but I watched enough TV to know that homing devices can be attached to animals, to track them in the wild. Was something like that happening to me?

I started to mull this over, energized by the sugar I'd consumed. One thing I had noticed about the aftermath of each abduction was that I'd always return with a variety of cuts and marks on my hands.

Implants?

For all my squawking about remembering so much, I sure don't remember watching them put anything in like this, but later, when I got to know more about the phenomenon from experts, I learned that this is indeed what happens.

Musing on this, I watched a movie on the television. It put me to sleep, fortunately, because sleep was just what I needed.

When I awoke it was dark again. I felt queasy and lost, and I struggled to turn over and look at my digital clock. No digital clock. Not at home.... The shred of memories pieced themselves back together again, and I realized I was in that seedy, nameless motel room, and the TV and lights were off.

But I had left them on!

I felt a presence. With a gasp I flopped over. There on the other side of the bed was a transparent image of a stick man with large round eyes. Immediately, this faded away, replaced by a symbol I did not recognize.

A mumble passed through my lips: "Time for medical procedures."

"Okay," I thought. "Where did that come from?"

I felt frightened, but simultaneously that urge to sleep passed over me. I slumped back down into the motel bed and was gone.

I had the sensation of travel....

Acceleration....

I woke up, expecting to be in my usual situation — bench, screens, letters, and symbols. Instead, I was flat on my back.

I lay on a hard, cold surface that I could feel through my paralyzed body. The only thing I could move were my eyelids, and that wasn't easy. When I pried my lids open, I could see a white glowing ceiling. The light in this room was a soft white, which seemed to be emanating from everywhere.

Something was missing here....

Then I got it. What the hell? This was the most upsetting position to be in yet, and I wasn't scared.

Metal clanged. It sounded sort of like silverware rattling around in a tray. I knew I was on board the same craft I'd been on before, but somewhere altogether different.

Something murmured in my head. I could hear talk — telepathic talk, only it wasn't that one Voice. There were, rather, Voices.

It was a struggle to make out what was going on, but I managed to make out three or four aliens standing near my head. They seemed to be conversing telepathically with another group of aliens who were standing by my feet. I couldn't tell if they were workers or supervisors, because I could only make out skinny torsos and arms. It must have been a mix of both. At that point I did not sense the strong energies I'd felt before from the supervisors.

How come I could understand their communications? Had I started learning their language? Or was this telepathy not in language as such, but in concepts which translated in my head to English because of what they'd drilled into me?

In any case, I could understand what they were talking about, and I didn't care for it.

They were talking about extracting semen from my body.

# CHAPTER NINE

# Trying to Lose Myself

Later, of course, when I met other alien abductees, and heard researchers, and other counselors speak — I allowed myself to hear what others had experienced. I heard about alien surgical procedures, anal probes, and alien reproductive experimentation, or "abuse" as the case may be. However, I have no memory of anything like that before this experience of mine. At that point, as far as I knew, the aliens only wanted to kidnap me, terrorize me, and make me learn their language.

You can understand how this talk of semen extraction was a shock and an upset. It was bad enough that these strange-looking gnomes wanted to fiddle with my gray matter, but my privates? As they buzzed telepathically in that group around me, they were discussing whether my semen should be extracted artificially or naturally. By inference, I got the gist — should I be milked, or aroused and manipulated. This is definitely something you don't normally talk about in public — according to my upbringing, anyway. But I want to get everything down here. I feel I owe it to myself and to the world of my fellow human beings.

After my shock, I started wondering how they expected to extract anything from me naturally. How could I be aroused under these circumstances? As I lay there, I tried to speak vocally with no success, so I tried to move my mental muscles and speak telepathically. I pretty much told them that I thought what they had planned seemed unlikely. "Look, for one thing I couldn't do it with you standing there and staring!" They stopped speaking and turned to me.

"THAT'S NOT A PROBLEM," they said in my head. Immediately, I was blinded, and I got angry.

"Do you bastards think that just because I can't see you, that will make a difference?" I got no response. All I could do was lie there. Again, the telepathic buzz:

"WE WILL DO IT NATURALLY AND ARTIFICIALLY."

What could they mean by that? Again, that clanging.... Several pairs of hands grasped my right shoulder and waist. They turned me onto my left side — and gently at that. I'll never forget as long as I live what that felt like — those hands grasping me. The fingers were strong and bony, and although they were not rough, they were certainly not human.

I lay on my side for awhile, when suddenly my sight was restored. In front of me was a metal table, like a gurney, with some sort of gadget on its surface. One of the aliens was pushing it towards me, so I strained to see what this machine could possibly be. A supervisor arrived, complete with powerful, emanating energy, which impacted me tremendously, blurring my vision.

Things were cloudy for a moment, but when they cleared I realized there was something beside me, or rather, someone — a woman. She was lying on her side and she wore no clothing. Her back faced me, and she was curved as gracefully as a cello. She was on a table beside me. I could still add two and two, so I knew what she was there for. She turned over. She was blonde with blue eyes and she was quite beautiful. It all seemed academic, though, as I couldn't move any limbs, and certainly not the one they wanted to work. I told them I knew what they wanted, but I couldn't perform — sorry, no way.

Then one of the supervisors came forward with some sort of dark metallic or plastic rod. He touched my testicles with it. I felt a tingly electric warmth pass through my groin. Almost instantly, to my astonishment, my penis became erect.

Two workers pushed her on me. I felt no womanly warmth or comfort. Everything was mechanical, as I was forced to mate with her. Within five seconds, they got what they wanted.

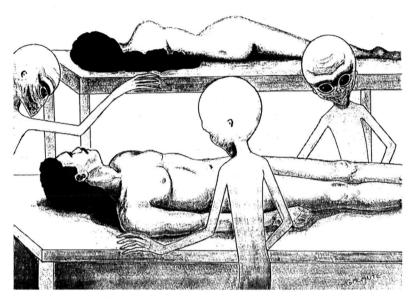

•FIG. 12: I SEE THE SCREEN-IMAGE WOMAN

As they pulled me away, I couldn't help but notice that some of the smooth lines of this woman seemed squarish now. She was decidedly less organic. I sensed that "she" wasn't really a woman at all, but rather a machine — some kind of apparatus that the aliens used to extract semen. Using their skill of illusion, of masking and "screen imaging" they'd been able to trick my senses enough for their purposes. There's more to this process, I found out quickly enough, than their simply taking semen.

I'm sorry to say that this experience was only the first of many times that I "donated" sperm in this manner, and there was never much joy or pleasure in the process, believe me. This first time, I lost my sight again and I just lay there, enraged, feeling used and manipulated.

Then acceleration.

I was back in the hotel room. I could see, but it took a few moments for the paralysis to wear off. Dawn was breaking and the TV and lights were still off. As I lay there, troubled and exhausted, I thought about all of this.

77

Pardon me if I'm getting a bit ahead of myself here, but I think this topic is important enough to elucidate now. During many reward sessions, the workers and supervisors from time to time would bathe me in sexual energy. I believe that this energy also rewarded the workers in some way. It's hard enough making clear how unusual these cultures are. However, it seems pleasure is still important in these advanced races.

On many reward sessions I had the choice between what I term "Power" and 'Lust." Sometimes "power" would be the privilege of playing with the aliens' thought-activated technology. At times I could obtain any sexual fantasy I wanted, which would then appear in hologram form, just hanging in the air as the aliens looked on. Around this hologram, different (previously learned) symbols would appear.

As I traced each symbol with my right forefinger, stressing direction, motion, feeling or sounding it out in my mind, the sexual hologram slowly became more vivid. As each symbol was traced to perfection, the hologram took on depth and color. As I proceeded, it would take on motion. At this point, the workers and often the supervisors would mentally aid me in the process. When this occurred, I experienced ecstasy beyond compare.

I must say it was rather odd. There was never any physical contact. My whole body, though, at these points was in euphoria. The aliens would then somehow capture this sexual energy and pass it around. They would add to it and take from it. They would create symbol patterns. Each time it came back to me, the whole experience was amplified. At times I would pass it to the hologram, which seemed to take on its very own life.This was a truly amazing experience, and I suspect that I don't have the necessary vocabulary and command of words to express what happened to me, but I wonder if anyone truly does.

Peripheral phenomena also occurred — disturbance of electronic items like the TV, lights, even my dining room light. One time, a few weeks before, I had left the dining room light on. I could see the switch from the couch in the living room. It wasn't an on-off switch, but rather one of those dial-operated rheostats that adjusts the level of illumination.

After waking up from a deep sleep in the middle of the night, just before one of my abduction experiences, I sat up. The light in the dining room was fading. I looked at the switch and noted that it was turning on its own. The switch was being twisted to the off position by some invisible force.

As I mentioned, there's some sort of electromagnetic field associated with what the aliens do, and it affects electronics in the vicinity. I'm convinced also that there's a residue on me that interacts with electronics, and I was wondering how much that affected the TV and lights there in that motel room. Later, of course, I found that other abductees reported the same kind of thing going on in their waking lives.

When I regained my motor functions, I felt defeated. I sat up, slumped and just ran my hands through my hair despairingly. I might as well just go home, I thought. It was no good trying to hide — at least here in Texas. Texas — that was where they'd been taking me, so I'd go to North Carolina, of course. I had not been abducted even once from there! Yes, I'd spend some time in North Carolina. I was just together enough to be able to figure this out, and I knew I needed some kind of relief. Everything was still emotionally turbulent, and I needed space. The notion of escaping to North Carolina gave me fresh hope.

I needed to go home first, to talk with Teresa, despite my urge to just hop a plane immediately. When I got home, she wasn't there, and I felt relieved. I guess I really didn't want to face her. I dashed off a quick letter: "I know you don't understand," I wrote, "and perhaps you think I'm crazy, but I have to do what I have to do. So I'm going to North Carolina for a while. Try not to worry, and I'll call you tonight. I love you." I gathered up some extra clothes and left for the airport.

When I arrived in North Carolina, I notified my friends Jim and Peggy. After renting a car, I checked into the hotel where I usually stayed. I was still pretty rattled. I left my suitcase in my room and headed for the small restaurant-lounge area. The whiskey was a pleasant amber color — a good Kentucky whiskey — and I listened to the ice tinkle as the bartender poured the jiggers into the clean, clear glass.

It smelled and tasted strong, and I finished half of it in a gulp. My hand was shaking. Slowly, it stopped shaking. I finished the drink, and ordered another one. Two whiskeys blended into three. Three slid into four. After some nice mellow music from the jukebox, and five or six drinks, I was thinking I had no friends. I had nothing but the booze. Things became kind of jumbled, and I remember thinking "I'm falling fast," before I actually managed to pick my butt off that bar stool and haul it to my room. I fell onto the bed and passed out.

In the morning, my head spun and ached, and my mouth was sour and grim. The hungover face that stared at me from the mirror didn't look like Jim Sparks at all, but two aspirins, a hot shower and a leisurely shave made me feel physically better and happy. Yes, happy. I had not been abducted during the night!

I went down and ordered breakfast — sunny side-up eggs, Carolina bacon and Virginia ham, along with hotcakes and juice, toast and hashbrowns, with some green peppers in them, and sweet milky coffee. This was the first solid meal I'd eaten in months. I felt groggy afterwards, despite the coffee, and I had nothing planned, so I thought I'd just relax a little more. I ended up napping most of the day, and it was a good nap, because I don't remember waking up in fear once.

Later I woke up and watched some TV. As evening rolled along, though, anxiety teased its way up my spine. "Well, so far I'm okay," I thought. But I remembered that I'd felt absolutely no anxiety after that first drink, so I figured I'd try that again.

As I'd left a nice tip the night before, the bartender was very friendly and quite generous with the whiskey. Most of the way into my first one, some of the fog lifted, and I felt as though I had a space in which to try and sort this all out. Alien creatures? Come on, Jim! But I couldn't deny it. It was all just as real as the rest of my life. I went over it all from the dream-state of the first encounter to the stark reality of the most recent event. I drank more. As the booze swam through my head and numbed my concerns, it seemed to be my only true friend.

Finally, when I felt up to it, after I had enough drinks under my belt, I got around to calling Teresa. Pleased was not the word of the day. Nonetheless, she did not give me a hard time and told me to take care of myself.

"What were these things doing?" I asked myself. "Why me? This was the strangest form of contact.... Why not go to the President or someone else and make them learn? Why not come out and show yourselves?"

There are speculations and possible answers to all of these out there in the respected community of scientists and psychiatrists who think about these things. In that motel, with the help of Dr. Jack Daniels, I was coming up with a few of my own.

I was thinking, "It can't be just me! This must be happening somewhere else, and there has to be a logical reason for it."

I sure wasn't handling all this well. To tell you the truth, I'm glad I was drinking while I was reflecting on all this, because although I knew that behavior was wrong and it went against my grain, it kind of kept my mind from breaking. I was certainly no drunk, and it was the only comfort I had.

Aliens! It's one thing for an average guy like me to go see "Star Wars" or "E.T." or play "Space Invaders." It's quite another to meet the otherworldly and bizarre, to confront something from far beyond the confines of our safe reality, face to face. No — mind to mind.

You know, since I've gotten to know some of the people who are brave enough to not only confront this concept, but to also seek it out — those brave souls who work hard to bring out the truth from the past, from now — for tomorrow — folks in MUFON, writers like Whitley Strieber, Jacque Vallée, Stanton Friedman, and many more who actually accept that we are being visited — the more I agree with what they say about why authorities who know about this, who have evidence of alien contact aren't coming out with it.

Here's the truth, the bald reality that I was facing there in that hotel, floating in a cushion of booze: It's too much!

The concept is hard enough to deal with, but the actual experience itself is simply mind bending. The average person can't deal with it. How well do you think you'd deal with something like this happening to you? Do you think that the people in your community, church, synagogue, or whatever, would believe you if you claimed that little people were shuttling you off to learn their alphabet, to test and play with you? I don't think so.

And I think that anyone who's in charge knows this. In retrospect I realize why all this is shadowy and secret with the military, the government, and the people who actually could prove all this is happening. I don't think average folks could take this.

They'd do about as well as I was doing then in that hotel room, quaking and quivering. I don't think regular people are ready for the kind of dissociation all this brings, and the reality that we are not in charge. Societal boundaries could crumble; people might not function; things could fall apart.

Mind you, as the years have progressed since the advent of the atomic age, and ideas such as star travel and alien life have started to get out, general society has been adjusting. But look at what happened to me! A modern businessman in the late 20th Century, successful, well adjusted — look at what happened to me. What would happen to you? Believe me, our minds and our lives are more fragile than you think.

So this is why it's taking a while to disseminate this knowledge, this truth. In my heart of hearts, maybe even then, scared out of my mind and drinking a lot, I realized that I was part of something huge.

Now I think that there's a strong possibility that everything's about to change on a worldwide basis. I believe that fairly soon, things will be so different that we can't totally comprehend now how different.

I believe from my experience that the world is being geared up for direct contact — contact that no one in high places is going to be able to deny. Contact that will be just so definitive that nothing will ever be the same again.

How well you pay heed to my story, how well you let this assimilate in you, could well be an important factor in your survival, in your coping... in your understanding. That's one of the messages I have here for everyone, so listen closely.

Believe me, you don't want to grab a bottle of Jack Daniels and head for a North Carolina hotel!

I discovered it did no good to hide my head in the sands of whiskey in another state, because it turned out I wasn't safe in North Carolina either.

The Visitors knew exactly where I was, and eventually, they came and got me.

# CHAPTER TEN

# "The Boss Wants to See You"

You know the part in Alfred Hitchcock's "Vertigo" where James Stewart is falling? Twirling, whirling, grabbing for a hold, terrified?

That's kind of what it feels like to be "pulled" during the acceleration process. It's this carnival ride you want to shun; it's a kind of falling up into insanity.

One moment, I was woozy and boozy in North Carolina, numb and feeling safe, the next I was transported from my room onto that ship again.

Right down onto that same seat. Right in front of that same screen. This time, there was not even the hoot of an owl to get me prepared.

There, of course, to either side of the screen were Mutt and Jeff — the two alien drones, skinny and almond-eyed. I don't know what they did, but the alcohol got kicked out of me. I was stone-cold sober, there in that grim room.

I immediately launched into my lesson, as though nothing had changed, and started to learn more as though my mind were some kind of machine that they'd just turned on.

During this drinking period, there were times when they would wait hours for me to sober up, all night long if need be, and get me just before dawn. However, this was also when the time dilation effect truly reared its head.

Sometimes they would take me and let me sober up in the cell before beginning my lesson. Ten hours would pass in the learning chamber, but only two would have passed when I was returned to bed. These creatures are not only able to traverse dimensions, but distort time as well.

After the lesson, I guess I was sort of expecting — maybe even looking forward to — the reward part. They had me pretty well trained by that time.

Instead, on the screen before me flashed pages upon pages of text. Not alien text, mind you. Paragraphs upon paragraphs in quite legible and understandable American English. Maybe twenty pages worth, I'd estimate.

I began to read. It didn't take long to realize that I was reading a story about the life of a close friend of mine. I was enthralled. The text described intimate details of his life I'd not known. It began with his name, where he was born, where he went to school, his childhood likes and dislikes, his teenage years and so on. I read page after page right through to the present.

The story didn't stop there, though. It continued into my friend's future, as though it had already happened — nothing Earth-shattering, mind you, just trivial minutiae of his daily life.

I was pretty amazed, but I was even more stunned with what happened next.

After I had read all the pages, two more pages appeared on the wall screen to the right of the pages I'd just read. These were not in English, but in the alien language I was learning. The stunning fact was that I could comprehend what the alien symbols said.

"Wow!" I couldn't help but shout. "WOW!"

Moreover, this alien text described the exact same information I'd just read about my friend in English. Instead of twenty pages, though, it took only half a page of alien script. Then another page appeared.

This page had the alien alphabet in what seemed like a shorthand version. For example, it showed the letter "A," then next to it the alien's version of "A," then next to that a short hand version of the letter "A."

Then another page appeared with one single symbol on it about the size of a fifty-cent piece. After looking at this symbol, I almost fainted with amazement. This one single small symbol that I could read in a matter of a few seconds, housed twenty pages of detailed information in English. [See Fig. 13, page 87.]

Incredible!

Thinking back on it, it seems impossible. I don't know quite how it works, but it does. Were there other aspects of this language that I had not picked up on yet? Dimensional quirks and symbologies? Depths and intonations only telepathic mental processing could properly decode? I honestly don't know. All I knew was what it must feel like to a kid when he not only learns to read, but when the words fall away and a magical story appears in his head.

A Voice sounded in my head, "YOU WILL LEARN THIS."

"You mean you want me to learn the short version of your alphabet?"

"YES."

"Why?" I got no response.

"WHY!" I demanded.

I guess by then, the conditioning kind of let loose. Up until then, I was just absorbed in the experience. However, I'd had enough freedom in North Carolina to regain some of my mental independence. The true me, a rebel at heart, got into the game. "Why? Why me! I demand an answer, you bastards!"

My mouth froze. They'd paralyzed it.

For all the good it would do!

"Why me? Why me? Why me!" I screamed the outrage again, blasting with my mind. Yeah, sure, they could lock up my mouth, but hell if they could shut down my mind. They'd have to kill me first! I was furious!

And I knew they could hear me, because they read my mind — and I think I was learning telepathy as well.

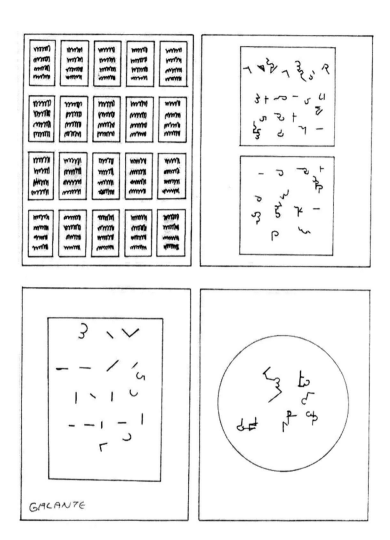

•FIG. 13: ALIENS CONDENSE 20 PAGES OF TEXT INTO ONE SYMBOL

"Why me? Why me?" I tapped my right forefinger hard and loud on the table screen and continued my mental scream. Suddenly, the two alien drones morphed into large American-style cops. No riot gear, just your garden-variety blue uniforms, polished shoes, cap and scowl, all-American police officers. I don't know what they're thinking when they do this. Tapping into my sense of authority? Are they trying to manipulate and control me with my cultural conditioning? It was almost laughable, about as subtle as a sledgehammer in an egg house.

So these alien cops were glaring at me, and I could hear one of them bore into my brain with a telepathic command, a constant repetition of "NO." I've always tried to be a law-abiding citizen, and I do respect officers of the law. Clearly, though, these were nothing of the sort, not really. I honestly wished they were! I'd ask them to arrest the damned supervisor for kidnapping!

"You don't scare me!" I glared right back. Again a morphing, this time into a couple of military policemen of the nasty, ham-shouldered Marine persuasion, complete with generic crewcuts. I shook my head. "That doesn't scare me." I think I even managed a chuckle. Again the images wavered, then transformed, this time into two fully dressed Army generals laden with medals.

"Bullshit!" I blasted at them with my mind. I just kept on tapping that finger, and thinking, "Why me? Why me?" Every few seconds, I thought, "Hey, you bozos! I'm just going to keep on tapping and asking 'Why me?' until you answer!"

Nothing. Mexican standoff. This didn't last too long, though, because very soon indeed I felt an overbearing mental presence swarm into the room. The thing almost smelled of power, of swelling symphonic music, of a mighty and dominant presence. You get that feeling sometimes with strong, charismatic individuals, and I certainly recognized the telltale signs of this thing.

It was the supervisor. I didn't see him right away, but I sure could feel him. I could sense him staring down at my head and I thought, "Damn! You are powerful!" I could feel him probing through my mind. I stopped the tapping.

"WRITE YOUR QUESTION OUT THE WAY WE TAUGHT YOU. ONLY THEN WILL WE ANSWER."

I wanted that answer. I wanted that answer very badly. Still, there was a part of me that wanted to resist. I could feel my mouth loosen. I could speak again, and speak I did:

"Now let me make sure I understand this. If I were to write the question in the style you taught me, you'll answer my question?" I got no response, yet I could sense his strong presence lurking over me in an overbearing, demanding fashion.

"Okay," I thought. "Someone's got to give. I'll try it." I placed my finger on the screen. I framed my question in my head. I allowed my finger to move. To my astonishment it began to write out my question.

"WHY ME?" Only it didn't come out like that. It came out in alien hieroglyphics. I recovered and made my demand again.

"Okay. There it is. You promised to answer my question."

They answered the question, all right, but not in the way I had expected.

# CHAPTER ELEVEN

# Family History

I'm afraid the aliens' answer to that fateful question left me with even more questions.

Why me?

Why had these creatures from some other star system, or some other dimension, at least from somewhere else far beyond my comprehension, zeroed in on Jim Sparks? Why had they focused in on an ordinary real estate dealer for their obscure and, quite frankly, bizarre purposes?

I guess that's what I meant when I said, "Why me?" and I suspect that unless you're a NASA official or George Noory, King of Nighttime Radio, you'd be asking that question of aliens as well, if you'd found yourself in my position.

I had a burning need to know, though, even sitting there, uprooted from my North Carolina booze binge. I guess that question was the over-riding thing in my mind.

The aliens did not answer the question with language or telepathy, writing or anything symbolic.

I'll describe what happened next in the best detail I can remember, so you can draw your own conclusions.

"Tell me!" I demanded again. "Answer my question, like you promised. I've written it out, just like you wanted."

Now imagine you're sitting there with me and right out in front of you is empty space — air and alienness, fortunately breathable and temperate enough for survival. This air just kind of frizzles and grows opaque. Then it lights up, with a black border. I guess you can imagine what it's like when you're watching something like this in a movie or on television and you're thinking — cool — these are some great special effects! But when you're actually there, believe me, it's nothing like anything cinematic.

It's like a portal opened up in that room, a large passageway into somewhere else.

A holographic scene appeared, complete with full motion about three or four feet in front of me. It was rich in detail, complete with dimension and color. Yet there was no sound and the scene was faintly transparent.

It looked like a World War II scene. I say that because it was definitely a war scene, with humans in military uniform. Why do I say WWII?

Well, I may not have had any media exposure to extraterrestrials, but I have seen pictures of Nazis before.

These Nazi officers wore dark uniforms, and there were soldiers posted at the doors of a room. The group, I came to see, was not merely Germans — there were men in Italian uniforms as well. Maps and clipboards were strewn across the table, along with cups of coffee and espresso, and these officers were talking and pointing. The Italians were speaking animatedly with lots of gestures.

I sat there in that alien room, staring at this scene suspended in the middle of the room, and a slow shiver went up my back.

This scene was hauntingly familiar. I felt déjà vu stronger than I'd ever felt it before. It was definitely as if I'd been in this place before.

As I studied it carefully, I could almost taste the espresso and smell the stale, male sweat from those uniforms. My gaze fixed on one of the Italian officers and electricity ran up and down my back.

Cripes! This guy looked like me!

"No way!" I thought, but as I studied him closer as he argued with a Nazi commander, I couldn't help but see that chin, that nose — those dark eyes and eyebrows — they were formed just like mine! The hair was even curly in just the way mine is, only shorter. He was my height, my weight, and the way he was wagging that finger and using his arms was just like me!

I wondered what my captors were trying to say with all this? As you know, I'm from Italian stock, but why were they sticking me in a World War II scene?

Surely this couldn't be an actual historical scene. It had to be some kind of visual trick, just like that morphing of the drones into human cops.

Still, as I watched this military meeting, I couldn't help but have strange emotions indeed. World War II? These were some of the darkest days of the 20th Century! While looking at my image working with the Nazis, thinking about all the death and destruction, I started feeling impli-

•FIG. 14: I FIRST SEE THE WW II STREET SCENE

•FIG. 15: DETAILED IMAGE OF THE WW II HOLOGRAM I SAW

cated somehow. I started feeling guilt and shame for being a part of the human race that would inflict that kind of horror.

I had to forcibly remind myself that there was no direct involvement on my part. I was born years after the end of WWII, right? Why was I being shown a guy in a uniform that looked like me?

This suspended scene dissolved, to be replaced by another scene fading into view — the gates of a factory.

Surrounding them were the ornate hallmarks of Victorian masonry. Beyond the gates I saw smoke stacks and a dark grim haze of clouds. A group of men in long coats and hats stood outside this factory, talking to one another. A horse and buggy trotted past. The scene tightened in focus and the viewpoint moved in closer. From what little I know of historical costume, I'd say that the scene was placed in about the mid-nineteenth century. Again, although the scene was vibrantly colorful, and I could almost smell that smoke. There was a translucency about the image, and I could vaguely make out the details of the corner of the room through it.

Why a Victorian factory?

Again my eyes were drawn to a figure in the scene. It was a man, again, who looked like me, only dressed in a black suit, a shiny black top hat and muttonchop whiskers! He had a bluff and proprietary sense about him. I sensed that he was the owner of the factory.

Yes, this guy looked like me, I thought, but he sure wasn't me!

More quickly this time, as though realizing somehow I was getting a grip on what was happening here, this scene faded and another took its place. The new scene depicted a small village on a green hillside, which was a pleasant place along a seashore. Gulls swooped on a breeze. From the style of the houses in the village and the total lack of technology, my best guess was that this time period was around the 15th or 16th century. The scene swerved, and I noticed a man and a woman in a field, working a crop with crude farm tools.

•FIG. 16: POSSIBLE ANCESTOR: A VICTORIAN-ERA FACTORY OWNER

94

Again, there was a familiarity to the looks of the man, although nothing as similar as that World War II scene.

I had another question. Rather than go through the rigmarole of vocally or even mentally requesting an answer, I just went straight to the screen. Again, I got a thrill as my fingers seemed to know the proper characters to express my question.

"Have you been following my physical family line?" I wrote.

As soon as I finished scribbling this out, I got an answer.

"YES. LOOK."

As the village scene faded away, another scene appeared, this one depicting the interior of a medieval inn. Men and women surrounded a large, roughly built wooden table drinking what looked like wine from pewter goblets. I'm no history expert, but the time period seemed earlier than that village scene, perhaps anywhere from the 6th to the 12th century. And yep, there at the table was a guy that had a resemblance to me.

•FIG. 17: POSSIBLE ANCESTOR IN A 15TH- OR 16TH-CENTURY FIELD

Or at least I felt a kinship to him. Maybe these resemblances were more of a visual translation of a sense of genetic kinship, or maybe this was the way the aliens were highlighting individuals in these scenes. I find this to be a more logical explanation.

The guy that looked like me was wearing some kind of cloth or leather hat, which was slightly pointed and drooped to the side. He was drinking lots of wine and laughing.

I can't tell you how bizarre this was. I couldn't help but laugh, and it felt good to have laughter come out of my unparalyzed mouth. Our shared laughter sounded odd, echoing in that alien room, but it was a human sound, and I cherished it.

The medieval scene disappeared, to be replaced by another. I saw buildings, white buildings with classical lines. Buildings of a city on a series of hills. I knew it was early Rome!

The scene shifted to one of columns, steps and beautiful statues.

•FIG. 18: POSSIBLE ANCESTOR DRINKING AT A MEDIEVAL INN

This scene seemed to be of the Roman senate. A large hall or reception area was populated by about twenty men wearing togas or white robes of other sorts. Some were standing, and some were sitting side by side on multi-leveled benches or bleachers. These men seemed to be having a debate of some sort, and from their facial expressions I could tell the topic was important.

I examined the men's faces, and sure enough, there was a guy that looked like me. He was just sitting and listening to others speak.

I shook my head and then put my forefinger down to the screen. Again, in the written alien script I wrote out my question:

"Have you really followed my family line that far back?"

"LOOK."

When these Star People communicate, they don't waste words.

Another scene took the place of the Roman senate. This time I saw an African savannah with patches of trees. I could almost feel the heat,

•FIG. 19: POSSIBLE ANCESTOR LISTENING IN THE ROMAN SENATE

and smell the stink. The scene pushed in to focus on a group of apelike creatures, and as the picture cleared I could see they were actually closer to humans than apes.

Thank God none of them looked like me!

Just because I didn't see a temperamental Italian didn't mean I didn't get the message.

My anger flared.

"Bullshit!" I shouted. "Bullshit! You guys are trying to tell me that you had something to do with human evolution?"

I got no response.

I was so pissed, though, I sure didn't feel like writing out the question. I just sat there and stewed.

They seemed to sense my rage, and they left me alone for a little bit. I was clear-headed but angry.

•FIG. 20: POSSIBLE ANCESTORS LIVING ON THE SAVANNAH

Then, instead of answering any questions, they made their presentation again, though this time in written form, in their language. I watched it and found that, again, I could comprehend it, and it all underlined their message:

"WE'VE BEEN AROUND FOR A WHILE. WE'VE BEEN WORKING ON YOUR PERSONAL FAMILY LINE. WE KNOW YOU WELL. HUMANS ARE OURS."

Then acceleration, and I was whooshed back to North Carolina.

# CHAPTER TWELVE

# The Watchers in the Lincoln

Getting pulled into a lesson again was no easy thing for me, and as soon as I woke up back in my North Carolina hotel room and thought, "I'm not safe anywhere," I crawled right back into the bottle. I stayed in North Carolina two more weeks — drinking. When I got back to Texas I continued drinking about three more months, but then one morning I woke up after an abduction, and I thought, "That's it." Drinking alcohol is no solution. I knew I wasn't an alcoholic. I didn't need the booze physically, I was just trying to escape. So there and then, I made a decision: I have to face all this cold sober — stare it down — live with it. It was an important step. Drinking was probably hindering my ability to cope. I don't feel guilty about resorting to alcohol, I just feel smarter now. My advice to my fellow abductees is — alcohol does not help you, drugs do not help you, running does not help you — only other human beings can help you. Getting understanding and compassionate people around you is what helps. I guess that's true with everything, and I guess that's what I was looking for then, but I sure wasn't finding it.

When I got back from North Carolina in June, 1989, I was a wreck. Teresa was gone. She'd taken a leave of absence from work and simply wasn't around. I thought this was probably a good idea. I thought it may also have been a leave of absence from our marriage, which was good. I needed to work all this mess through, figure out what was happening and learn to deal with it. You may be thinking at this point that all this was deadly serious and without a shred of humor, but it wasn't.

As soon as I got home, I shocked the local security guard and mailman, and I don't blame them. I'd weighed 160 pounds the last time they'd seen me, and I was probably down to 130 or 125 pounds. I was haggard, unshaven, and scruffy as hell. I probably looked a little like Howard Hughes in his last horrible years in Las Vegas. As I was getting my mail, my neighbor, a gregarious guy named Larry, came out and took one look at me and just stared, with his mouth open. I looked back at him.

"Aliens," I said. The ludicrousness of the whole situation was juxtaposed against my suburban home and the everyday arrival of my mail, so I just told him the reason, pure and simple.

"What?"

I shook my head, astonished at myself. "Never mind."

Larry was the accountant type who enjoyed conversation with me because I was more of a chance taker or rebel than he was, and he was curious. Our first conversation had been short, but it didn't take me long before he craved conversation with me to learn my skills of marketing and selling.

"Really," Larry said, "Tell me what's going on!"

"If I tell you, you're just going to think I've gone crazy."

"No I won't. I promise."

I shrugged, too tired to object.

"Well you asked for it! Come on in and I'll make us some iced tea." I figured after about ten minutes of my story he would probably leave. I filled his ears with 40 minutes' worth of summarized alien abductions. I even walked him into the guest room and presented one of the featured props, the guest room window that the aliens walked me through. I went into some detail as to how the acceleration worked, and how it felt. Larry honestly seemed to pay attention and accept what I was saying. Most people either got frightened or got a "Yeah, sure, goofball" look in their eyes. Not Larry.

When I finished I asked the golden question, not knowing what to expect: "Well? What do you think?"

"I believe you. The same thing happened to my cousin."

You could have knocked me over with a feather.

"Are you serious?"

"Not only am I serious," Larry said, "but I can help you."

"What do you mean by, 'Help me?'"

"I know how to make all this stop," he announced.

"How?"

Larry smiled. "Don't you worry about it. I'll take care of it. I'm off duty at work just before dark. When my shift is over I'll be back, and I'll take care of your problem."

I think he patted my back comfortingly. I was open to anything but still it sounded too simple.

"Just like that?"

"Yes, don't worry. I know what to do."

I just sat there, stunned, thinking, "Could it be this simple? Have I actually found someone who could put an end to this?"

As the day wore on, I made listless stabs at trying to get my business back into order, periodically wondering if maybe Larry was humoring me. Maybe he was off to get a paddy wagon and professional mental experts. On the other hand, he was a pretty reliable, steady guy. He'd always been a good subdivision security guard and had helped me out before. Larry was a police officer and a good one, the kind you could trust. So maybe he really meant what he said. And if he came back with a good shrink — well, I was open to just about anything.

Thirty minutes before dark, Larry the cop was knocking at the door. I opened it, and he was there, smiling sympathetically, alone. In his arms he held a carton of eggs, a cloth doll with a crucifix around its neck, and a bottle of water.

"It's always best to do these things just before dark on a Sunday," Larry announced as he brushed past me.

"What things?" It didn't look like things I'd like much, but you know, how can you say no to a burly, cocksure cop?

"First of all, Jim, take me to your guest room window," Larry said confidently.

"What for?"

"You'll see."

So, I led him to the guest room. He set the doll on the windowsill, facing it and its crucifix toward the outside.

"What did you do that for?" I asked.

"To ward off the evil spirits coming through the window," he said with a determined "Of course!" emphasis.

I'd pretty much figured that Larry was up to some kind of voodoo hoodoo, and the thought of what my drones and supervisor would make of all this kind of struck me as damned funny. I wanted to burst out laughing, but I managed to contain myself. Larry was so sincere about this, that I was sure either I would hurt his feelings if I laughed, or maybe even get him angry.

"What's the little bottle of water for?" I asked.

"It's holy water," he explained.

Larry started sprinkling that water all through the house. As this ceremony proceeded, I just stood there thinking that I was witnessing an example of precisely why extraterrestrials just don't land on the White House lawn and say, "Hi! We're here!"

So Larry drenched the house with water and grabbed that carton of eggs. "Let's go outside," he said. I followed him, not saying a word. On the lawn, he walked around the perimeter of the house placing eggs one at a time right up against the walls. Can you picture this? We're talking about a guy who looks like "The Night of the Living Dead" warmed over, following a cop placing eggs — eggs — around a house!

Then Larry said in a serious, confident tone, "The eggs should deter evil spirits from walking through the walls. The doll with the cross should stop them from coming through the window. Now if they are still determined enough to somehow get in, they should leave right away because they can't stand the holy water."

I didn't want to offend Larry, so I acted interested. I asked him where he got the idea to do something like this. He told me that his family heritage was Mexican Indian. These sorts of remedies, he claimed, had been in his family for generations. Well, I'd said "aliens." Obviously, he interpreted "aliens" as manifestations of evil spirits. If I said that they were "extraterrestrials" now, he probably would have just nodded his head sagely and said "Of course they're extraterrestrials! They're from Hell!"

Now mind you, I have no intention here, or there with Larry — or anywhere for that matter — of demeaning anyone's beliefs, because I realize how important a person's spiritual philosophy is. On the other hand, I don't have a problem with distinguishing religious entities — including superstitious critters — and ETs. I'll tell you, humans would far prefer to believe in anything other than the fact that there is advanced non-human intelligence secretly interacting with us! Still, just because I knew my tormentors were extraterrestrial didn't mean I was dealing with it particularly well. I must say, I got a chuckle out of Larry's performance, and more than that, I appreciated his help.

Maybe those eggs did keep the evil spirits away, at least for two days. Then a disturbing thing happened that did not feature extraterrestrials, but had everything to do with them. If you've read other writings about UFOs or aliens, or even if you only see movies or have watched "X-Files," you'll know about the Men in Black. Well, let's just say here that I've met some guys that are awfully similar! Two days after Larry put his strange barrier blessing on my house, I was looking out of my window. It was morning, and for some reason I had a strange sense that there was something out there.

Parked across the street from my house was a late-model Lincoln sedan. Two men sat inside. I had the unsettling feeling that the two men were watching my house and watching me.

I immediately caught myself. "Whoa, guy!" I thought. "You're getting kind of paranoid here, aren't you?"

Still, I felt uneasy. I went back to trying to get my business back together, but I looked out every hour or so to see if that car was still there. It was. Eight hours after the first sighting, the car was still there, complete with its men, and I still felt weird about the whole thing. I mean, just because I was paranoid didn't mean these guys weren't after me, to paraphrase a joke. I figured that if these guys were really here for me, the most logical thing to do next would be to go to the store to see if they would follow.

Sure enough, when I headed for the store in my car, they followed, hanging behind about a half-block. I went to a store that I figured would be a safe place. I went in and bought some groceries. Back outside, I saw the car again. The men were definitely watching me. Being on edge didn't help me, and I shouldn't have let my temper get the best of me, but I guess I just snapped. I walked right up to the guys.

"What the hell are you watching me for?"

They didn't answer. They just looked at me, as though they were studying me, and taking mental notes. Exasperated, I cursed, spun on my heel and went back to my car. The men followed me back home. I thought about calling the police, but were these guys doing anything illegal? Besides, calling the cops wasn't how I'd find out who they really were. They'd probably planned for that and would either split at the first sign of a bubble top or, worse, already have the police in collusion.

"No," I thought, "They have me where I want them."

I would watch them, too. What with the outrageous things happening to me in the past year, this was just another oddity that I could add to the list. They'd make some sort of move soon enough. Calmed down, I took careful notice of the car. It was a white four-door sedan. It had Texas plates, but the car was unmarked in any other way. They didn't look like what I thought your prototypical government men should look like. They were crew-cut middle-aged men in dark suits, and they didn't even wear sunglasses! Both of the guys seemed thirtyish. One of the odd things, though, was that they didn't seem to take breaks. I didn't catch them eating once any of the times I checked.

Toward evening, I heard a car starting. I peered out the window. Their Lincoln was just pulling away and heading down the street. In its place, though, was a white sedan, with two more different men. A change of shifts! I got little sleep that night, because I was determined to keep watch on the new car. I checked every hour or so, but all it did was sit there! (I always wondered why the neighbors didn't notice and call the police.)

In the morning, I was tense, worn out, and agitated again. Maybe if they thought I was about to run for it, they'd do something and I'd be able to understand what was going on. I found the automatic garage opener. I opened the garage door, but I didn't go out. Sure enough, that got a response. There was a knock on the door. I guess I panicked, because instead of answering the door, I went out the garage. I didn't get in my car, I just looked around to see who was out there. The two guys from the day before stood on my front porch. As though he knew I was watching him, one of the men turned and stared straight at me.

"Jim!"

"Yes," I found myself saying.

"Look. We know what you're going through," he said in a reasonable tone. "But you have to stop talking about it."

"Who are you? How do you know my name?"

They just whispered to each other, which got my goat.

"If you're not going to identify yourself, I'm going to call the police," I threatened.

The other one spoke in a low voice. "Jim. You have to stop talking about these experiences of yours, or we'll have to make it so you can't talk at all."

"Who the hell are you?" I demanded. "And how do you know what I've been through? You want to explain what I've been through? Hmm. That would be great, because I sure would like to know myself!"

My anger bolstered my courage, because I walked right up to them. They just stared at me. "If you don't stop talking about it, we will hurt your wife and family." That did it.

"You bastard!"

I grabbed the guy and pushed him against the door. The guy did nothing to defend himself. The other did nothing to help his partner out.

Seeing red, I snarled at the guy I was holding, "If you even so much as touch my wife or family, I'LL KILL YOU!"

Believe me, even though I have a good bit of Italian temper in me, I'd never behaved like this before. I was like a maniac. Shocked, I let the guy go. He just nodded to the other and they started walking back to their car. At the car, they stopped, and the guy I'd manhandled spoke.

"You must stop talking to others about it!" he said.

# CHAPTER THIRTEEN

# Graduation

Yes, I was upset. Again, though, my anger focused me. Was I foaming at the mouth? Maybe. Fuming and wanting to kick something? Perhaps. As the sight of those guys driving away lingered in my head, I tried to calm myself. Nonetheless I was thinking clearly enough to be aware of something — something important. I was crazy mad, yes, but I wasn't crazy.

The fact that these guys — government goons, alien pawns or whatever — spoke to me about what was happening to me, was an acknowledgment that something bizarre was happening to me, even when everyone I knew would not accept that what was happening to me was real. And the fact that they did this in broad daylight, in the consensus reality of cars, a suburban neighborhood and a food store, meant someone was confirming to me the reality of these abductions!

In a strange way, even though these fellows fell far short of being friends, they were doing me a favor. Men in black, princes of paranoia, whatever the hell they were, they'd given me a gift. Even though I had no answer to my question, I was somehow less alone, to say the least.

A couple of hours later, a couple more guys in a white sedan showed up. That was enough. I decided that I should do something. I almost liked this particular mystery. I looked up the closest address for the Federal Bureau of Investigation. I couldn't do much in the matter of my alien tormentors, but I sure could do something significant in broad daylight! I was going to go to the authorities, to the people sworn to protect common Joes like me. I wasn't sure what would happen, but at least I could see if they'd follow me! More than that, I'd be able to see how determined they were to keep tabs on me!

So into his car goes Jim Sparks. Out goes Sparks into No Man's Land, determined to see just how determined this new batch of guys were! Sure enough, it didn't take long to find that white sedan in my rear-view mirror. First I sped down some farm roads at 80 m.p.h., and that white sedan just kept up with me. Back to the highway went I, back to the highway went they. Onto the freeway I led them, driving like a maniac, passing and twisting and turning through the traffic — and they paced me.

Miracle of miracles, I wasn't stopped by cops. Maybe I would have been eventually, but we hit a major traffic jam, the bumper-to-bumper variety. Everything indicated an accident up ahead, nothing uncommon on this freeway. As I sat there, smelling the exhaust and feeling the anger and uneasiness accumulate around me on that hot Texas highway, I thought, "Let's see how serious they are!" Without giving any warning, I floored the gas pedal and turned onto the shoulder. With tires screeching, I kicked up lots of dirt and gravel back onto their car. I felt clammy with perspiration. The guys were still on my tail! I sped down the shoulder about half a mile and drove through a shallow ditch onto the service road that ran parallel to the freeway.

I found my way out of that mess and navigated my way back toward the address I'd found for the FBI. That sedan followed me straight there. Sure enough, the place looked official enough: a government-style building, with a chain-link fence and parking lot. I pulled up in front of it, stopped and looked. They weren't behind me. They'd stopped a bit back.

"Okay, Jim." I asked myself. "What now?"

Well, I was here. Let's see what would happen. I went inside that F.B.I. building into a standard issue Reader's Digest and cheap furniture waiting area, smelling of floor wax. Behind a glass partition was a woman. I wasn't sure what to do, so on the spur of the moment I devised a plan. I called myself Bob Jones. I told her I was being harassed by a religious cult.

She seemed to take this in stride. I don't know, maybe they get people every week who claim to be abducted by aliens and then followed by guys dressed in black, but at least they wouldn't think I was nuts if I told them this. I'd get to talk to someone. I wouldn't get brushed off with a form and a "Please call this number if you see these aliens again."

Politely, she asked me to sit down. She'd get me an official. Sure enough, soon a man came out, conservatively dressed, with close-cropped hair. He was obviously an authority, but a relaxed and very kind authority. I explained that I thought my wife and I were being targeted or stalked by some sort of cult members. I tried to sound reasonable and logical — and above all, sane. His response was simple.

"First of all," he said, with a gentle but firm tone, keeping a sincere eye contact. "Religious cults are perfectly legal, unless of course they break the law, in which case you would have to take that up with the local authorities. Then upon the authorities' request the F.B.I. could take action."

He was considerate, but didn't spend much time with me. I didn't get any kind of sense that he or the F.B.I. was involved in any kind of conspiracy with me as its subject. I felt a bit deflated. I'm not sure exactly why I didn't tell him the truth and then run out and point at those guys in the car. Maybe I thought he'd just have me locked up. Or worse, if I dragged him out, the guys might be gone. I thanked him for his help, and he showed me to the door.

What happened next I've shared with very few people, but I feel I should mention it here in my book. Those guys in the white sedan weren't gone. They were still parked outside the fence. I was about to point them out to the FBI man, but the direction of his gaze indicated to me that he already knew who was there. Moreover, as he spotted them he lifted his hand — and waved to them.

I almost fainted, I was so scared. Was this my imagination? It certainly opened a whole can of worms! Although the FBI cars in the outside lot were different from this one, it would seem that the agencies were working together. I tried to say something, but nothing came out. I'd lost all my fighting spirit. I just let them follow me home. I was bone tired, with this and the abductions, so I just decided to let them watch me sleep for a while. I managed to sleep for over ten hours.

When I woke up, I peered out the front window. The men and their sedan were gone. It would be several months before I would see any other sign of them. To this day I have never solved this piece of the puzzle. Had my visit to the F.B.I. discouraged them? Had higher authorities pulled them off my case? Or was it all arbitrary? And, who were those men?

All this happened in mid-1989. For a while things were quieter, save for strange noises and thumps and odd lights. Teresa would check on me from time to time, but I encouraged her to stay away. I tried to keep my business going, and make some money, but even so, I still was not in the best mental shape.

In the last four months of 1989, I was abducted four to six times a month. Always I found myself in the same room, always being taught — but now I could communicate with the creatures better, clearer, and much faster. The reward sessions became more complex and interesting, and the semen extractions much more pleasurable. The Visitors seemed extremely interested in sex — my sexual drive and my libido. Oddly, I started to build a sense of trust with the creatures. I saw that they didn't want to kill me, and some of my instinctual fear was dying down. Still, on a regular basis I would request to be allowed the freedom to move around and explore. This request was always denied or ignored. I knew in my heart that it was really my fault. I still felt a lot of animosity towards them. They felt this, and they didn't trust me. During this time, I also noticed other aspects of the phenomena, and I experienced it directly. I began to understand the whole nature of the interdimensionality of these things.

The following experience explains exactly why it's so hard to pin these creatures down with the rules and laws of everyday reality. You'd think with the UFO reports coming down to us for fifty years, the general populace would have enough evidence by now to know if this was really happening or not. Well, the truth is that much of what happens simply doesn't fit the day-to-day, nine-to-five, car in every garage reality that we live by. There's so much interaction that's reported about the Visitors that's so dream-state-like and confusing, but I experienced all this in a waking state, and I remember it exactly.

111

It's late 1989. I'm lying on my sofa at night, sometime between 3:00 and 4:00 A.M. and I'm feeling a little jittery — anticipating something. The air just has that metallic taste... the atmosphere... that creepy feel.... I'd just been awakened from a deep sleep. Usually I have the overwhelming urge to go back to sleep. Then, acceleration... whoosh... disorientation... Lesson Time with my alien buddies.

This time, though, it was different. I fought that return to sleep. I wanted to be consciously aware of exactly what happened. Difficult stuff. However, as you may have concluded by now I'm a willful bastard at times, and I clung to consciousness. The sitting position helped. I concentrated hard, and the first thing I noticed was a crackling sense of static electricity all around my body. Fear jabbed me hard. My heart started thumping, and my breathing got labored, then paralysis took over. My head started to pulsate so hard it felt as though my brain were going to burst out of my eyes. Then the sights and sounds of acceleration hit me. "If you don't have a heart attack," I thought, "you might be able to tell someone about this — so don't have one!"

The living room furniture started turning transparent. My television, chairs, sofa, then the walls themselves started to fade away. I discovered that I could turn my head to the right, left, up and down. The whirling sound became so loud I almost blacked out. I could feel the soft fibers of my carpet against my bare feet. I could also feel my rear end sinking into the foam rubber sofa cushion. Slowly my feet began to feel cold as though they were dangling in the air. At the same time I could feel cold hard metal under my butt. I looked down. My feet were dangling in the air as if propped on a hospital table. Yet at the same time I could see my feet firmly planted on my living room carpet. How could this be? Then I glanced down at my lower torso. I could see and feel myself sitting on a metal table, and I could see and feel myself still propped on my sofa. Somehow, I could also feel the cushion of the sofa at the same time that I could feel cold hard steel under my rear end.

"Damn!" I said. "I'm half here — and half there...."

But where was there? I certainly didn't seem to be on the alien craft. All about me were my furniture, my walls, my television, lamps, and pictures of my living room, yet they were almost invisible. As I continued to stare I could see that I was in a large facility. The walls were painted white. The ceiling was much higher than normal, perhaps 30 feet high or so, and there were no windows. I recognized fluorescent light fixtures. On the Visitors' craft, the lighting seemed to spill from everywhere.

Around me now were human military guards with their backs against the wall, spaced about 20 feet apart. I couldn't tell their service branch, but they looked like military police. Now, this could have been some sort of trick or screen imaging, or the interpretation my brain made of what was going on. However, the fear had left me. I could tell their magnetic field or whatever was still buzzing me — my heart thumped, electricity fuzzed all over me. My living room was completely gone now. Jim Sparks was 100% elsewhere... but where?

It looked as though I'd been allowed to transfer consciously... but instead of putting me in front of their teaching tools, I was in some sort of underground facility. I say "underground" because it had that bunker feel, that subterranean texture. The walls looked like something humans would construct, only higher than usual, and, as I said, the lighting seemed fluorescent. From my perch on that metal table I could see that I was in one of many rooms separated by dividers. The divider to my right was clear glass or plastic. I could see activity... humans, not aliens. These humans wore white lab coats with ID tags. They were too far away for me to read their ID tags, but perhaps they were some sort of radiation detectors, because as they got closer I could see there was no writing on them at all. I also noted that they were of different colors. I tried to shout, but nothing came out — paralysis.

A military officer approached the entrance to one of the lab rooms. Somehow, I felt I knew him. As he stood by the entrance, the men and women in the lab coats filed out one at a time — maybe 30 of them. My head cleared of acceleration effects. A man from the group stepped forward and stood about three feet from me. He was of medium build, about five feet eight with dark hair and glasses. He was definitely Asian.

He held up what looked like a high-school graduation cap, with a tassel and all. "Congratulations."

113

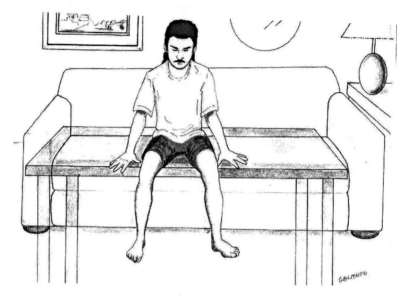

•FIG. 21: I AM AWARE — HALF HERE AND HALF THERE

I could suddenly talk again. "For what?"

"You graduated."

"Graduated what?"

I had déjà vu. Big time. I somehow recognized the guy, but I didn't know how the heck I could have known him. It wasn't like any memories came along with the recognition. Nonetheless my emotions were swinging from fear to comfort. I say comfort because somehow I felt safe with my own kind — and people I knew who wouldn't hurt me. Nonetheless, I felt anger at being kept in the dark.

"I know you!" I blurted. "I don't know why, but I know you!" I was excited, and when I'm excited it's hard for me to keep things close to my chest. I looked over to the others and got the same associated feelings. "I know you. I don't know why I know this, but I know."

They all smiled. Then, one by one, they came up to my table and congratulated me. Not a one looked at all alien. This was bizarre, yes, but although it had a dream's bizarre logic, it sure didn't feel like a dream.

114

When the last one was finished congratulating me, I asked again, "Congratulations for what?"

No answer. They all left, save for two or three. They stood there whispering to each other, but I couldn't understand what they were saying. These people seemed as amazed as I was at the fact that I was there — as if I were some successfully conducted experiment, the results of which they were very happy with. Oddly enough I felt a strange pride, as though I'd somehow helped them. All sorts of thoughts passed through my mind, most as usual leading to more questions than answers.

Then as one of them waved good-bye, that familiar low-pitched whirling sound sprang up again, and my heart began to race. Acceleration! Heart pounding, breathing difficult, I nonetheless kept my focus. I stared at the Asian man, who had the friendliest feel. Again, no blacking out — and the walls, rooms and lab equipment slowly faded, and my living room started fading back into place around me. Everything was the reverse of the previous experience, but holding in that half-there, half-here moment. This time, I had no fear, just fascination as I experienced the blending shift of dimensions. There was something wondrous and amazing about the experience, I guess I could compare it to a caveman's first flight on a 747 jumbo jet.

They kept me in between for several minutes. I liked it. It was peaceful. Yes, this was strikingly different than the accelerations I experienced before. I was in slow motion. It felt good, euphoric, as though someone had a hand on a rheostat controlling pleasant feelings inside me. Then, after about a minute of holding this freeze in transit, the underground facility faded out and my living room came in stronger, bolder — filling out into reality. The rooms and hard hospital gurney where I'd been sitting faded totally. Slowly, the whirling sound subsided and my heartbeat slowed. I sat back on the sofa, totally exhausted. At first my muscles were wound tighter than a rubber band; then suddenly they relaxed.

I looked around. Home sweet home. Funny thing, though. Usually, after this sort of trip I feel disoriented and traumatized. This time I just felt exhausted. I took a few deep breaths, and got off the sofa. I paced and I thought. What did all this business mean, then? This just made it stranger. Who would believe me? I almost wished those guys in the sedan were around. I'd ask them. "Look, tell you what. I won't tell this to anyone, but you have to explain to me what the hell is going on!"

Was that last incident an indication that I was part of some human experiment? Had some previous Jim Sparks volunteered, agreeing to have his memory taken? Or, and I was leaning toward this more heavily, was all that just an odd fabrication set up for me by my alien abductors to confuse me or to see how I would respond?

But I seemed to know those people!

Questions, questions, and damned few answers.

# CHAPTER FOURTEEN

# My Daughter

In late 1989, I took stock of myself: One thirty-something Homo sapiens of Italian descent, caught up in something he didn't understand. Feisty, but overpowered. My mirror did not lie to me, I looked rough. However, this latest experience gave me a better sense of control. And the fact that I'd stopped drinking, made me feel like there was still hope.

I wasn't going to let this thing get the best of me. I started to eat regularly, exercise, and take every opportunity to sleep. Yes, the abductions continued, and yes, I was not a smiling Jim Sparks — but my physical health improved and my weight shot back up. Plus I probably smelled a heck of a lot better, too. Still, I didn't socialize. Teresa checked in on me and even stayed for periods of time, but I didn't want her at the house long. My father would call me from Florida. "Hey Jim," he'd say. "Come and visit me and your Mom." He didn't exactly buy my aliens story, but he thought that getting out of Texas for a while might do me some good. Dad was convinced I was sick. I'd refuse, but something deep inside told me it might be a good idea and one of these times I might just do that.

The abductions continued. I won't bore you. They got to be routine, but around this time something else happened of note. I was there in alien zone, sitting with the teaching thing. The workers were working, and the lesson was spinning along — then everything halted. The machine went black, and the workers froze.

In came the Supervisor, and he froze too! A queer feeling came to my gut as the light in the room began to dim. My head and eyes seemed pulled to the left. Five feet away was a hologram: a tall, quite steep, jagged cliff, rising up to a sharp peak. The light that projected from this hologram was intense, its clarity astounding. An intimidating figure appeared, perched on the peak of the cliff, a magnificent sight! It radiated power and shone with glory. It was a birdlike figure, but not just any bird. I recognized it from pictures, though it outstripped those pictures.

It was the mythical phoenix, glorious in gold and silver plumage, with flashing blue, blue eyes. I was awed and overwhelmed. There was something terrifically spiritual about the thing that just pierced me. My pulse pounded, and I stood transfixed as this phoenix spread its large wings, almost as though ready for flight. Just at the point that the blinding light was too much to bear, and the bird-thing seemed poised to fly straight at me, with a sharp implosion, the thing was gone. Normality returned. The teaching continued, the workers moved, and the Supervisor left. I couldn't continue interacting with that machine. I was just emotionally drained.

"What the hell was that?" I asked them. When they didn't reply, I got some of my angry emotions back. I yelled at them and called them mindless drones. "You have no souls!" I screeched. The magnificence of the thing I had seen fed the rebellion in me. The workers turned. In those almond eyes shimmered what seemed awareness. It was as though the phoenix plus my outburst had knocked them toward an attempt at examining their own existence. This made me wonder again if these workers weren't artificially constructed. Then I felt the presence of the Supervisor. I turned and, sure enough, the boss was there.

"DON'T SAY THAT TO THEM."

Somehow, I felt guilty for a moment, but then my outrage returned. I wrote out my question on the screen, as they'd requested. "What was that bird?"

No direct answer. Nonetheless, an image formed in my mind. It was an outline memory of my classroom in elementary school. I saw myself as a child standing among my classmates, gazing at the American flag and reciting the Pledge of Allegiance. I got it. That bird symbolized whatever their society or government or alien equivalent was. They were paying

some sort of respect. Why it had shown up then is hard to say. Maybe it was part of my education. All of this the aliens neither confirmed or denied, but I was satisfied that this was the case.

I felt a twinge of remorse. Maybe I shouldn't have shouted such abuse at my captors. I had every right, and these angry spoutings were helping me to keep sane, but still, I had a twinge of guilt. They were showing me something of themselves. In a sense, the experience with that phoenix bridged a small gap. Recognizing and respecting the symbol of one's nation — for us, the flag, for them, the phoenix — was something we had in common. They seemed somehow a little less... alien.

After the phoenix experience, things were quiet and I recovered physically, if not totally emotionally. Larry the cop dropped by a few times to see if his anti-hoodoo was working. I told him it must be helping some. The rest of the neighbors, and my other friends ignored me.

As for my business, all I can say is thank God for Jim in North Carolina who took up the slack. I paid him a fair commission, but he went above the call of duty. I'm sure Jimmy thought I was on a major drug trip, or that I had just lost my mind. But if it weren't for him and his wife Peggy, both excellent real estate brokers, I would have gone completely bankrupt.

At this point in my life, the only thing that seemed to matter to me was to survive this abduction phenomenon. Christmas of 1989 was around the corner, and Teresa was coming home to spend it with me. My relationship with her was distant at best, mostly because although there was a three-week lull in abduction activity, the paranormal stuff continued: strange lights, noises, and things flying around the house. If not for my alien experience I would have thought the place was haunted by a poltergeist. Worker aliens appeared in transparent state to observe my daily activity. At other times they would make their appearance more obvious, in which case I would yell a few obscenities at them. Mostly I was tired of fighting and just allowed them their odd communications.

The aliens seemed to be extremely interested in spontaneous human reactions and emotions. I got the impression that they were somehow recording or storing the information. Sometimes I would even hear them when they got into solid mode, bumping into things or knocking things down. In 3-D reality, they were clumsy guys! They were masters of their spacecrafts, but clods in Jim Sparks's house!

They had me happily sequestered in isolation. No one believed my stories... and they knew it. However, I was thinking clearly enough by now (thanks in large part to the return of my health) that there were others besides Teresa and myself who had encountered them. Did they have the same residual effects as me? Did they feel as though their dormant telepathic muscle was being worked? I now longed to meet these people, but when?

Teresa and I had a relatively nice holiday and fell into the easier-going aspects of a relationship. Our bodies and minds were, after all, ultimately used to each other's company. The traditions of the season helped lull us into the illusion of normality. Then, just a couple of days before New Year's Eve, I was "pulled" the hard way. There, before that teaching machine, I felt I'd hardly left, as though my real life were the abnormality.

On this particular trip, I was taught a lesson on some rather complex symbols that were difficult to learn because as I duplicated each stroke, I could feel motion from the stroke throughout my whole body. For example, if I moved my stroke to the left, I could feel that same flow move through my body to the left. The same sensation applied for up, down, angles, circles and so forth. I got the sense that I was learning the basic principles of telepathic communication.

I began to understand. Could this be a tool in communicating messages between extraterrestrials and humans? This could even be an experiment to see how much we could actually communicate. One thing was certain — the only way I had any hope of getting answers to questions was to address them with writing in their symbols. This understanding gave me incentive to learn because it was easier to interact with them. It helped make my abduction experiences go a lot faster and more smoothly.

In the midst of this lesson the word "LOOK" appeared on the table screen. Beside the table screen was a girl, a human girl, I thought at first. Then I had to look closer, because I wasn't so sure. She was young, maybe twelve or so. She just stood there, staring at me, and not one time did she blink. A real cute girl — frail, with a slightly pointed chin, thin short, dirty-blond hair. However, by human standards her nose was too small, her lips were too thin. What stood out the most were her eyes. They almost looked like human eyes, but rounder and larger. I wasn't frightened. I couldn't stop looking into those eyes. I sensed love and at the same time a mental strength. My impression was that she was half human and half alien, but there was something else. Something hauntingly familiar. Then it hit me. She was my daughter.

"She's mine!" I found myself saying. Of course, I had no daughter I knew of, but I couldn't deny that some of her features were similar to mine, though definitely blended with the alien characteristics. Before I could think too much about this, one of the new symbols flashed. Next to it "TUG OF WAR" appeared. I thought to myself, "TUG OF WAR? You mean, like the camp game?" Then the girl's eyes started to move. The symbol was duplicated, and I could tell that the girl was doing this with her mind. I could sense her telepathic activity with my own newly acquired ability. Only she was doing it wrong. I tried to tell her this, with my mind — and she seemed to understand, but she ignored me. Once again on the wall screen the words "TUG OF WAR" appeared. I formed the symbol properly for her, with my finger, repeating it to her with my mind.

She didn't like that. Struggle showed on her face as we went forth in a kind of tug of war indeed, altering the symbol. Oddly at the same time during this game, I felt I was communing with my newfound hybrid daughter. The experience was almost like hugging a child, yet without touching. I caught the meaning pretty quickly. It was a game. I could feel the radiation of strange energy from her.

Had this been the destination of my sperm? Was she a reproductive hybrid of me and some extraterrestrial biology? Anyway, the tug of war was oddly enjoyable, once I realized it was a mental game, and I got involved with it. I drew a new symbol, one that I'd just learned, and we went back and forth with that. It was an interesting interplay, and I felt a kinship, a bond. Then I could sense it was time to go. Acceleration. Living room... sofa, paralyzed, of course. I sat there, thinking about the implications of the little girl I'd just been with — my little girl? Yes, I was sure of it. It was unsettling, yes, but I also wasn't as upset as I usually am after an abduction.

I got some sleep. In the morning, I decided to make breakfast for Teresa, who was sleeping in. I needed eggs, so I headed off to the store. I had a good feeling inside of me, as though I'd reached a turning point and maybe the rest of the way on this strange journey would be up. Outside though, who should be waiting for me but the guys in the white Ford sedan, just sitting there watching. I recognized them, all right, and my benevolent mood vanished. I lost my temper and screamed toward them and immediately canned the expedition. They'd follow for sure and I'd be so pissed off, I'd do something like run into them. I headed back into the house. Cereal and toast would have to do for breakfast. I also came to a decision.

GALANTE

•FIG. 23: MY NAMELESS DAUGHTER

As we ate, I told Teresa about my father's invitation. I told her that I wanted to accept it and sincerely asked her, in the interest of our relationship, to go along with me. We didn't have to stay long, I promised, just long enough for me to get myself back into order. She didn't have to think long. She could see I was really struggling, but succeeding. She knew that maybe this would be the best course for me. She agreed. In fact, when I told her that, as she was still on an indefinite leave of absence, I thought maybe she should leave a few days ahead of me, to get my parents ready for me and to get our living arrangements set up. I checked with Mom and Dad. "Yes, certainly," they said. "The sooner the better."

When Teresa was ready, I drove her to the airport, but I didn't point out to her the guys following us in the white sedan. I didn't tell her anything about what was going on, just that I was working hard on getting better. I kissed her good-bye and for a moment, as I held her, there seemed to be a moment of a brighter future. I might not be able to shake the Visi-

tors, but maybe I could shake my flesh-and-blood trackers. I didn't particularly want to encourage those guys in the Ford sedan to find out where I
was going. Yes, they probably could, but it was worth a try to avoid them.
Instead of sleeping at home that night, I checked into a downtown hotel.
In the room, I thought about the past two years. I was through running
away trying to seek denial and oblivion. I was onto something new. I
didn't really consider going to Florida as an escape. The Visitors surely
had me tagged in some way; they'd proven that. No. In Florida, fortified
by family, a relaxing by-the-sea climate, and a resolve to understand, I
was going to face what was happening to me.

When I woke up the following morning in the hotel room, I was
pleased to find that I hadn't been abducted the night before. After washing
up, I packed my belongings and headed for the airport. Sure enough, waiting for me outside were my two "friends." I stopped at my house long
enough to grab a few more things. My buddies followed me. At home I
just hoped that going to Florida would shake these bozos for a while. As I
packed, I felt in a way I never could have before that I could see a future,
and it was a future in which I would never live in this house again. Alien-
gifted precognition or simple gut feeling? Who can say?

As the two sedan boys followed me to the airport, I had another
feeling. Anger. Paranoia. Tears stung my eyes. But almost as though I was
calming myself, I had the feeling, the strong precognition that even
though they probably had the wherewithal to follow me, going to Florida
was the best way to ditch these goons. I was sad, too, because I loved
Texas. I loved the home I'd built and the sense of place. But I had to move
on. I just had to. It was the right feeling.

Since that day, I've never again seen any of the guys who watched
me from those white Ford sedans. Although I never knew exactly who
they were, I didn't really care. That was a mystery I didn't want to work
on.

I had other mysteries to concentrate on.

# CHAPTER FIFTEEN

# Beach Puzzles

I was born in the Miami area and lived there until I was eighteen, when we moved to the west coast of Florida where I spent a good deal of time. The humid air, sunshine and palm trees, and fetid smells was home, but now Florida seemed far, far from Texas or anywhere else in the United States.

This was a good thing, I thought, as I got a smack of tarmac smell in my face, and an urge to put on some shorts as soon as I got off the plane. Certainly the first thing I should do was to buy some sunglasses. A Florida winter was a lot brighter than a Houston winter!

My father and mother had turned out to greet me along with my younger brother. It was good to see them. The kiss from my mother, the hearty handshakes from my father and brother felt good. Their presence made me immediately realize I'd done exactly the right thing.

Teresa was at the house when we got there. We didn't say much to each other. There wasn't much to be said. I was glad to be there, though, and looking around the comfortable house all I could wonder was: How long before the Visitors come for me again? And how would they go about it, what with a house full of people? I had almost made up my mind at that point not to talk about the abductions. This was not the time or place for traumas, but it seemed reasonable now to venture out a bit. I mean, they were my family, right? If I was here long enough, they'd be able to see I wasn't drinking and didn't show any effects of drug abuse.

125

So after I got settled in and the small talk got a bit strained, I asked Dad to go with me on a long walk. As the wind blew off the Atlantic and fluttered the palm leaves, we walked along the beach and I tried to tell him what was happening to me. He just kind of shut me out, as if he simply didn't want to hear it.

When I approached my mom, she was sympathetic but she couldn't grasp any of the concepts I was dealing with. My brother simply figured I'd flipped my lid. These people had always considered me to be stable, logical and down to earth, but this out-of-this world Jim just didn't fit them.

However, my sister-in-law, Janet, did believe part of what I was saying. She told me about a friend of hers who had gone through almost the same thing, with a few slight differences. My ears perked up, and I asked her for specifics.

"I have no idea where she is now," she said. "She moved several years ago and we didn't keep in touch."

Janet considered this friend stable and intelligent, so she thought it was worth listening to me and remaining open. It felt so good to have someone who didn't think I was three engines short of a jet airliner.

I settled down some, and everybody seemed to approve. Jim was becoming his old self again.

Hooray.

The move to my family's home in Miami slowed down the abduction scenario. In fact, month after month passed with no sign of the things. Were they leaving me alone because they were giving my mental faculties a rest? Probably they didn't really care. They hadn't shown any consideration before. Why now? Maybe my living with a bunch of people slowed them down. Still, I had my own private room. No one had spotted them in the hotels they whisked me from. Were they finished with me? Probably not. I wasn't sure what the reason was, but one thing was for sure, the thought of going back to Texas scared the daylights out of me. More and more I felt that I might never return to live there again. As time went by, I got even more of my mental and physical strength back, and my confidence returned.

I was stronger all around. What's more, I was ready for the Visitors when they returned for me. I felt further abductions would not waste me like the previous ones had.

Also, unsympathetic ears simply were not worth my words. I decided to wait until I could find the right person to tell everything to. Otherwise it was a waste of breath.

Four months had gone by, and it was April 1990.

I was still at my parents' house and I was getting restless. Although I wasn't ready to go back to Texas, I felt it was time to move on. When I was eighteen, my first apartment was on the island of Fort Myers Beach, off Florida's west coast. Those were good days. I saw no reason why I shouldn't move there again. So, I headed out there for the weekend and put a deposit on a rental apartment about a hundred yards from the beach. I was scheduled to move the first of May. I was excited about this move because I always did like the beach. When I got back to Miami, I informed my family about my plans.

A few days after I got back from the Gulf Coast, I was sleeping alone in my parents' guest room. I woke up. The clock said 3:30 A.M.

The owl was hovering in the room, in phosphorescent shimmer. Time for School.

I thought I was ready. I wasn't.

I jumped out of bed and scurried into the kitchen. I had made enough noise to wake the dead. The house was dark and I was banging into things. I disturbed no one. I even went into their rooms and shook them. They just simply couldn't wake up.

I felt that strange yet familiar static electric buzz around my body, and the overwhelming urge to go to sleep. I fought this urge and the willfulness tore through my automatic reactions. Wait a moment, I said to myself. Remember. You've been through this before. "Take it in stride," I said out loud. "Why do you bastards come for me in the middle of the night? You know it scares me!"

I got back in bed, still tasting fear. Sleep came, then the acceleration. Again, the familiar yet alien environment loomed before me. On the
screen was the last symbol I'd been working on, as though I were there
yesterday. I had plenty of questions, and I knew not only how to ask them
but that the style of my asking would please them. But I thought it would
be best to just go with the flow to see what was in store.

Something new was in store this time. After a few new symbols, I
got puzzles, which were a combination of alien symbols, numbers and
memory. I had to place symbolic combinations together into a certain
form. I got the feeling that if I functioned well on this, they'd be more than
happy to answer any questions. Over time the puzzles became more difficult, but once I got a grasp of the basics, the more complicated symbols
were easier for me to put together. This whole learning process seemed
easier this time. I'd adopted a new attitude of acceptance, although sometimes I still felt animosity and had to check my anger.

I was still curious, and I wondered if I stayed cooperative and doc-
ile, would they turn me loose to see the rest of the ship? You have to
understand that when I was in that teaching position I was at the very least
partially paralyzed and it would be quite nice to be able to get up and have
a look around.

Reward time. This time I got strange projections of a possible future
— whether it was a forecasted future or a look into an actual future, I
couldn't say. In any case I don't remember the scenes per se, but I do
remember the pleasure and contentment. The lab rat gets its cheese.

Then — wooosh! — back to the guest room. It was almost daylight
and instead of being traumatized, this time I was calm. I awoke late, but
refreshed, with a sense of moving forward with the whole experience.
Sure, the abductions would disrupt me, but not as much. I can't tell you
what an important step that was for me.

Teresa and I moved to the West Coast of Florida to the apartment I
had rented. Staying with my parents had been extremely helpful, but we
were ready to be on our own again.

I liked my new place. Here was the beach life, a relaxed and, thanks
to the income from the business, an almost carefree life. A complete turn-

around from the hell in Texas. It wasn't easy for Teresa. She missed Houston's bustle, her old home, even her job. She frequently mentioned wanting to go back. Although our differing attitudes toward the abductions had put a wedge between us, I wasn't upset by much since my mental faculties had returned. "Sure. Go back if you want," I said. I guess the leisure, sun, and surf had its charms for her too, because she decided to stay for a while and make the decision later.

Our income was low, since mine had lowered and hers had stopped, but things didn't seem to cost so much here and the price was worth it to me. In Florida, for some reason, the abductions had reduced in number. And the laid-back relaxation of sun, shorts, and sunglasses certainly was a balm to my nerves.

After living in the beach apartment for several months, we moved to a beach house. The place had gotten developed since my former days here, and I wanted to be in a little less congested area. Isolation didn't seem so scary to me now. If the aliens wanted me, they could get me anywhere. In 1990, I got abducted far fewer times than in 1989. Why was this, I wondered idly? Some sort of base in Texas? Hard to say, but mostly I think what I had at first was "Alien Boot Camp" and the training helped me deal with my new life later on.

Nothing happened out of the ordinary — if you can count regular programming in alien symbols ordinary — until early 1991.

And when it did happen, it was pretty bad.

# CHAPTER SIXTEEN

# An Adventure on Board

This relaxed time probably made me less eager to search out other contactees and abductees. Probably I was just recovering and lying low for
a bit. In any case, when I did finally start going to the meetings in 1994,
I realized I could help lots of people with fragmented memories simply
because mine were pretty complete. Conversely, I found people there
who could help me with my experiences. There were solid people in this
group — people like Don Watkins, a law enforcement state supervisor,
and Daved Rubien, an engineer and investor.

Don Watkins is a short, cocky guy — a muscular fellow in his fif-
ties who looks like a cop in every way — steely eyes, short hair, and
hard-looking. From the first, I could pretty much peg his main fault.
Don was the high-machismo sort — heavy on ego and personal power.
However, around me he was pretty much a puppy dog and we got along
great. We both knew the alien abduction phenomenon was real. His
memories of it all were fragmented. Sometimes they were clear, but
mostly he found in me a way to get in touch with what he couldn't
remember. He became one of my best friends.

If God is the master of the Universe, Daved Rubien is the soul of
the Earth. He's a tall guy, filled with health and compassion, love and
comfort. I guess you could say that Daved was the emotional stabilizer
for all of us abductees. If we called any time day or night, he was there
for us. A financial success in a big way, Daved's smart and sharp as a
tack. He is a very caring guy who has made a real difference in my life.

Two years after my rough experience in 1992, I found support in that group for my grief and shock. A couple named Courtney and Steve Wood had had a similar experience. They were a good-looking couple with Southern drawls in their mid-forties. They were both in the banking business — very responsible, solid folk. Courtney was blonde and lovely, and everything about Steve spelled strength, both physically and emotionally.

The bad thing for Teresa and me was that while we still were married, we were not as close as we had once been. In early 1992, she missed two periods. Now this was odd, because while we did have sex, it wasn't that often. Plus, when we did get intimate in this way, we used birth control. Pregnant? Surely not. Still, she went to the doctor, and it didn't take long to determine that yes, indeed, she was expecting. My first thought was that she must have been having an affair. As we had serious marital problems, I almost half-expected this, but my Italian jealousy was checked by practicality and compassion. She assured me, though, that this wasn't the case. I must be the father, she stated.

"Well," I thought, "I could always check the DNA later." Still, with my having seen both Teresa and my "daughter" on the alien craft, I got a sick feeling about the whole thing. So I just took it day by day. A part of me said, "Be cautious."

At the end of her third month, Teresa went for a check-up and was just fine. That evening though, she woke up in great pain. I rushed her to the emergency room at Lee Memorial Hospital in Fort Myers. I waited with her in one of the small examination rooms for a staff doctor. He asked me to leave so he could run some tests, so I waited in the hall. An hour later, he came out to say that Teresa would be fine. There was only one problem, though. While she definitely had been pregnant, with a fetal sack and all, there was now no fetus inside. He held up an ultrasound photograph with a uterus, a sack, and no fetus.

He explained that although this was a quality picture here in his hands, the fetus might not be showing for some reason. It had happened before. "If your wife was still in pain, I would take more intrusive and extensive tests. These tests are a little riskier and quite expensive. She seems to be doing just fine, so I don't see the point in disturbing her any further. If the pain happens again, bring her back in here and we'll do other tests."

My stomach sank down to about ankle level. The baby was gone. I was convinced that the aliens had taken it. I was absolutely sure that this was all a part of their plan for her. My wife had a miscarriage, sure enough, the next day in fact, and there was no actual fetus in the expelled material. The doctor assured me that this sometimes happened, that the body sometimes absorbed a faulty fetus. The first trimester was the riskiest part of the pregnancy span, and I researched the situation. Everything he said was true. It did happen. This could well be perfectly possible, but I had a gut feeling that the aliens had taken it.

Indeed, when I mentioned this feeling at the meetings I went to during 1994, my friend Courtney mentioned that she'd had several pregnancies where she was positive the aliens abducting her had taken the child just at this point. Even as she declared this, another woman named Hillary said she'd had the exact same experience. Another abductee, Shirley, said, "I wouldn't be surprised to find this is a common phenomenon among female abductees." In these cases as well, although there had been sex, there was surprise at the pregnancy. I was heartbroken about the miscarriage. Although we hadn't planned on a child, the idea of me being a father had not seemed to be a bad one at all. In fact, I'd rather liked the idea. I felt a real loss — a real sadness. Eventually, the pain for both of us wore off.

Two years crept by, with only occasional abductions. Then on March 7, 1994, everything changed. That was the day I took that walk on the beach with the alien in the 1940's suit, and the day I got my wish to roam about one of their craft, which is where I started this book — on the ship, free to roam, having been brought on board the easy way — that is, the way you or I might board a passenger jet. I was still pretty awestruck. I thought I would have been prepared, but I really wasn't. By now you probably understand why, although I was frightened at finding an alien in human disguise making like Humphrey Bogart, I wasn't totally surprised.

With the Visitors you expect the unexpected. But I must say, I was pretty shocked to find myself with free rein of the ship that night.

After that walk to the beach, though, with all the sensory aspects of reality — the breezes, the sea oats, the vivid sea smells — there could be no doubt that this was indeed all truly happening, including that ship hanging there above the sea. It was real as real can be! As you may recall I was left alone in an examination room with the door open. I walked and explored, and I was stunned at what I found in the room where I ended up.

I'd been hoping for just this opportunity for years. Now, though, with what was spread out before me, I wasn't so sure I should have ventured out into the ship. There were creatures, things, fifteen or twenty of them. I don't know the exact number, because I was too shaken up to count. They were on the kind of examination table that I'd just departed, on their backs, covered by thin blankets or sheets pulled up to their necks. They were like the worker aliens but a little more human, which actually made them all the more alien. Their heads were bigger than the workers'. They had no hair, no eyebrows or eyelids and smooth faces. I had the sense they were female, although they had no breasts. They were just lying there, not looking so much asleep or dead, but more like they had been turned off.

I don't know what came over me, a surge of horror, or an incredible realization of what I was involved with. Routine had turned into raw dread and fear. As soon as I got my voice, I started screaming. I backed up against the wall and just let it rip. My terror was suddenly mitigated by the perceived presence of a Supervisor. I could feel him behind me, and I almost welcomed the arrival of this familiarity. My body became paralyzed, and I felt a river of calm flow over me from the alien. Then, my reality altered. Something reached inside my mind and — click! — a projection of a different view of the room developed. It was screen imaging. It rippled over this screen image, and suddenly the strange beings lying on the tables were beautiful women. This image somehow relaxed me. They turned and looked at me, but these women I also thought were shut down or dead. They all had exactly the same kind of makeup and hairstyles, sort of ludicrously glamorous. One spoke to me.

133

"We're not dead, Jim," she said.

I was still frightened, but not in any kind of panicky way, and then, mercifully, I just blacked out. When I got back my consciousness, I was on an examination table myself, lying on my back, propped up at a forty-five degree angle. A worker stood by, and a Supervisor stood right next to my leg.

I felt no paralysis. A thought occurred to me that I could just kick the bastard because he's so close, but it was just a whim. I realized immediately that I wouldn't do such a thing on purpose. Although I was angry, I didn't want to harm anyone or anything, and I sure didn't want to get myself in trouble with these things that had such power over me. I realized then that I was naked, even as one of the workers put a too-familiar apparatus over my groin. Oh, boy! Semen extraction again. I was far from thrilled. It's difficult to tell you how abusive this felt.

The Supervisor sensed my apprehension and I could feel the screen image percolating. He looked over toward a doorway, and two very attrac-

•FIG. 24: I VIEW THE ALIEN HYBRIDS FOR THE FIRST TIME

tive young women entered the room, petite with beautiful dark hair and skin-tight blue jeans. The mere sight of them bore a shock straight to the old reptile brain of Jim Sparks. They were almost a parody of what I liked in beautiful women — clearly these beings could read every centimeter of my mind. One even wore the kind of silver and turquoise jewelry I find attractive on women. They seemed so real.... One of them ran her fingers through my hair and stroked my face. She turned to the other woman who was staring down adoringly at me and said, "My, isn't he handsome!"

Well, that proved they weren't real! Still, it was easy to fall into the illusion. They stroked me and gave me pleasure and then a warm mild electrical shock coursed through my testicles and I ejaculated. This shook off the spell, and the sense of abuse came over me again.

"This isn't natural!" I yelled.

Almost reflexively, I jerked away and tried to get away, and my leg kicked up hard into the Supervisor beside me. This startled me as much as it did him. The two women beside me vanished into thin air. I fell back onto the table, upset and maybe even contrite, but I noticed that all signs of any kind of reality overlay had been smacked away. Gone were all the false images. The Supervisor suddenly seemed frail, atrophied. His large head was a mass of wrinkles, like those of some very old man.

And I got an incredible jumble of thought beams projected at me from him! How could you do that to me? You know better! You should have known better. I trusted you. You betrayed my trust in you. You betrayed my trust in you. You disappointed us. Did you try to disappoint us? You did this on purpose. You tried to hurt me. Why would you want to hurt me? Don't you know this is bad? On and on in a gush, a stream, a mind-blast.

A hundred of these phrases ripped out, complete with emotion. I felt and heard each and every phrase clearly — all in one second! I was numbed. Laying back on the table, I knew I'd never forget how those ancient, strange eyes had looked at me. Acceleration. Why the hard way again? That, after all, was the way they'd brought me here this time. Onto the moonlit beach, then directly on board. Maybe they just couldn't deal with me.

Back in the quiet pre-dawn hours at my beach home, I felt exhausted, overcome and of two minds about this whole experience. On one hand, I was elated. I'd been able to explore their ship a bit. I was moving forward. I'd had a different experience. At the same time, I felt depressed. Maybe I'd blown the whole thing. Maybe I'd failed a test. Of course, even if I'd hurt the Supervisor, it wasn't badly. And since they knew me through and through, they must have known I didn't intend to hurt him. And even then, they knew they were doing things to me that I felt were abusive and I was simply reacting to them. Still, I couldn't shake the feeling that although there was a strong possibility I'd taken a big step forward after six and a half years of confusion, there had been a bit of a slip. The big relief at this point was that it was 1994, not 1989. I had someone to share all this with — Tim, and the group. Maybe I'd share it with them later, I thought, as I eased off to sleep with those images of the creature-things on the examination table fading away into dreams.

"I was taking these changes better," I thought, as I finally fell asleep. It was still culture shock, yes, but something inside me was tough now and trained to take this mental and emotional punishment.

# CHAPTER SEVENTEEN

# This Way, Please

Pine resin. I smelled the sharp smell of trees and the bitter taste of dead leaves, moss, weeds and ocean, with a touch of swamp. I was in the woods, a deciduous forest of some sort, it seems, with just a touch of a cool breeze. There were oaks and pines beneath an overcast night sky. I stood in a large clearing. What was I doing here? I didn't recall at first... but then I remembered the whirl and rush of acceleration. This was an abduction, but I had been brought here instead of on board a craft. "Details," I told myself. "I have to remember details."

By now, of course, I realized how important it was that I cling to my memories, as most abductees I'd met had had a hard time with that. If my experiences could help others, or accomplish something, then the pain of my experiences would count toward others' learning — maybe even help humankind. This kind of thinking wasn't actually purely altruistic. Frankly, it helped me keep my sanity. Okay. Details....

The clearing where I stood was maybe half the size of a football field. There was more than the breeze sighing through the tree branches, though. There was the dreadful sound of people crying and moaning. Alarmed, I looked down. There were maybe fifteen people sprawled on the ground around my feet. I turned at another sound, and saw that there was also a young man standing to my right. The people on the ground were both men and women. Most of them were in their nightclothes; a few were nude. The guy to my right, though, wore a short-sleeve white dress shirt, dark dress slacks and leather shoes. He had dark hair and medium build. Although he was standing, he was paralyzed, except that

137

he could speak. He was panicked, and he murmured, "The last thing I remember was driving home in my car...." The people on the ground had clearly been abducted from their sleep. They lay paralyzed, disoriented but completely conscious. There was an exception: a blonde-haired woman in the group was in fetal position, rocking back and forth on the ground and screaming uncontrollably, only partially paralyzed. For some reason, I was calm.

As my eyes adjusted to the dark pools around me, I could see that about twenty yards to the left, another dozen people were sprawled on the ground. Above them stood an alien. Twenty yards to the left of that group were another dozen or so people. Detail: Three piles of disoriented people in a clearing, barely dressed or naked. I was determined to remember this. The young man standing by me was losing control, shrieking terribly. An alien appeared beside me, and I heard his telepathic communication: "CALM HIM."

"Me?" I said. "Are you giving me a job?"

Again the alien said, "CALM HIM."

As he seemed truly bent out of shape and I certainly understood what that could be like, I figured I should at least try. Although I doubted my efficacy in the matter, I grabbed his arm and said, "You'll be okay."

"I feel sick," he said. "My stomach is... sick!"

"That's normal after just being transported," I told him, trying to sound reassuring. "It happens to me all the time, but it quickly passes."

"I'm so scared," he said.

"Yes. I know how that feels. The same thing happened to me. Try hard not be scared. You'll be just fine. You'll be okay."

I continued my soothing words. He began to calm down. I was truly astonished that I could do this. The blonde woman on the ground seemed to be even more distraught now, though, rocking back and forth. Then the alien said, "CALM HER."

I could move. I realized then what was happening, I was being trusted again. I hadn't blown it when I'd freaked and kicked the Supervisor alien. I leaned over and placed my hand on the girl's shoulder. "You'll

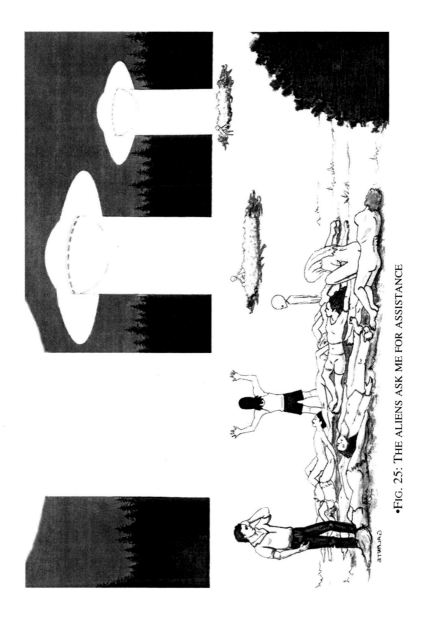

•FIG. 25: THE ALIENS ASK ME FOR ASSISTANCE

be okay. They'll take you aboard their ship and teach you things. A new alphabet. Numbers. Symbols."

"NO! YOU ARE TELLING HER TOO MUCH. JUST CALM HER!"

I continued to do my best to soothe her with calming words. As I talked to her, I heard others on the ground moaning and crying in fear. I felt overwhelmed. One of the people cried, "Look! The ships! They're coming!" I looked up. Above us were three balls of light, glowing within the low clouds. One streaked from the horizon to hover just above us, as though on cue. The others followed. Then, majestically, one descended.

For all the stuff you see in movies or pictures, being there in the flesh makes all the difference in actually experiencing them. This was the case with this vessel, this thing that others might call a UFO. Silently and gracefully it descended in gorgeous, magnificent splendor. Its beauty took my breath away. It was a large metallic sphere with a streamlined dome. The egg-shaped bottom, slightly out of proportion with the rest of the ship, lowered. I saw windows containing the silhouettes of humanoids. Some figures stared down at us, others scurried about. The most astounding thing of all was the light radiating from the bottom — intensely bright white with a bluish hue.

I was witnessing some sort of mass abduction in process. I was spellbound by the sight. I walked forward a few feet, trying to get closer. The second ship came down and hovered further down the field. The third ship did the same, hovering above the final group. I thought maybe I'd been trained for just such a moment. I tried to signal the ships in the symbology I had learned, tracing it in the air. I blacked out.

When I awoke, I found myself in a large foyer. Beside me was the group of people I'd stood among, totally zombied-out.

"LEAD THEM."

There was only one way to go. I headed down a corridor and sure enough, these people followed. The hallway felt like something on a ship, it felt familiar. At the end of it was a huge room buzzing with activity. Inside there were rows and rows of computer monitors, each fronted with

140

seats and a work desk. There were already some people in the front. Each of the monitors displayed the same picture. It reminded me of a NASA control room or a TV salesroom.

"SEAT THEM."

I did my best. It seemed automatic almost, the way I was familiar with this whole set up. These guys were a class of many, though, and I'd always been a class of one. Even as I put them into their seats one by one, I noted the monitors going blank. It was rather nice knowing exactly what I was supposed to do and performing my function competently. Soon my group was all seated. As soon as the last person was down, I blacked out again. I reawakened to discover myself in a chair. "Gee," I thought, "all they needed to do was to tell me to sit, and I would have done it." Or maybe not. I had been scanning the whole room, getting curious again.

On my screen and the screens of those around me erupted a color image showing a vibrant green forest with old-growth trees, backed by mountains in the background, with a clear, crisp blue sky. All this was majestically beautiful, as were the following images: a clear lake, a fantastic waterfall, a rain forest, settings of nature here on planet Earth. I lost my objectivity and became mesmerized. I felt the intense fabulousness of it all.

It was like an amazing slideshow. We all got a few seconds of each image and then it moved onward, like a View Master experience supreme. But then, the scenes began to repeat. Blemishes began to appear in the scenes. Brown foam in the lakes and rivers. Blackened waste in the forest. Skies became nasty and gray. I felt a depression weigh upon me. Then: dead fish, bloated and floating in the turgid mess in a lake. Such was the change from elation to depression that I couldn't look any more.

"YOU ARE KILLING YOUR PLANET!" said the Voice inside my head. "YOUR PLANET IS DYING."

At the bottom edge of each image was a symbol. To combat the depression I felt, I started trying to translate these alien symbols — cataloging symbols, I supposed.

"NO!"

I can't tell you how emphatic and truthful this environmental message was. I felt it with every fiber of my biology. True, so true, and yet I tried to deny it, focusing on the symbols as the images spun out their awful story. I blacked out.

On the other side of unconsciousness, I was in a smaller room, rather like a locker room, complete with benches. My group of people surrounded me, all naked, all showing fresh scars from surgical procedures, usually concave pieces of flesh removed from forearms or calves. These wounds, I remembered from the support group and my own experience heal, often showing no lasting scar, but the people in the group were whimpering with terror. An alien walked in and told me,

"CALM THEM."

I did the best I could. but my words did seem to help. Then another alien entered. "FIND AND PUT ON YOUR OWN CLOTHES." You'd think that, as orderly as the aliens are, the clothes would be neatly folded and stacked. Alas, no — they were mixed up and thrown all over, but the great task of finding and covering their nakedness helped put aside any panic. That was it. My job was done, and soon, after acceleration.

I was back on my familiar sofa, but this time I felt different, even good. I felt an odd enjoyment of the experience, and an accomplishment. I felt as though I had a place in whatever strange scheme was happening. Unfortunately, there was one problem: My right eye was sore. I didn't remember bumping it, but that meant nothing. I'd conked out a lot on this last abduction and could have hit a few things, but there were also those bright lights. My next thought was about Tim, and how glad I was that I was going to be able to share this with him.

My eye was still hurting when I saw him, but we were too excited about this whole experience to discuss my eye problem or go to a doctor. Tim was so thrilled with my story that he insisted that I let him hook me up with Budd Hopkins. "You have to meet Budd," he said. "This is much too important."

I agreed. I was starting to see more of how I fit into all this, and how I had to share with more people other than just the group. There was a reason behind all this. My eye continued to hurt. I saw a doctor. He gave me

142

eye drops, which helped to soothe and heal the eye in a matter of days. But I'll never forget his question after examining me.

"Has this eye been exposed to bright lights recently?"

# CHAPTER EIGHTEEN

# The Gift

I'd heard of Budd Hopkins, of course, from other members of the group. I didn't read his books, as people suggested I might, because even then I had the sense that I had a unique mission and view of the whole alien scenario, one that I was just working out. I honestly feel, and still feel to a lesser extent, that reading too much other material will sully and confuse my memories. Mary Anne, one of the members of my alien support abduction group agreed with Tim that I should talk with Budd. More than that, she knew an easy way to contact him. She had a summer home in Cape Cod, close to where Hopkins spent the month of August each year. She knew him well and invited me to stay with her and meet Budd there.

Hopkins had spent 17 years studying alien abduction phenomena and had figured importantly in Whitley Strieber's exposure of the whole business to national media attention through Communion. He had written the best-seller Missing Time. When I agreed to go, it was fairly quiet. The summer of 1994 saw no abductions. Rather than compromise myself totally, though, instead of actually reading it through, I just perused passages here and there to get the gist. I must say, even this reading process turned up some amazing similarities to my own story. Well, maybe not so amazing, since it merely confirmed to me the veracity of my own memory.

A few days before I was to head north, though, I was pulled. I found myself in the same teaching room as before. This time, however, there wasn't a bit of me that was paralyzed, and I was unattended. I

144

made no effort to explore like last time. I'd wait here to see what they had in mind. Sure enough, in a little while two Supervisors appeared, holding a black box — a perfect cube. The psychic radiation of their presence was a little upsetting, but I got a hold of myself and didn't panic.

"LOOK. A GIFT FOR YOU."

One of the aliens took the black box and laid it on the table, and I noticed again how long and slender his fingers were.

"A gift?" I said. "What do you want me to do with it?"

"DO WITH IT AS YOU WILL."

They turned and left me with that box. I remember that although I was free to move around, I did feel a little foggy-headed. I had no sense of danger from the box, and I was curious, so I tried to open it. Alas, it seemed to have no lid. I tried to wrest it open, but no luck. I thought about banging it against the table, but I didn't want the aliens to think I was tearing up their ship. After pushing and pulling didn't work, I just put it on the table and stared at it. Then I realized the one thing I hadn't tried was a

•FIG. 26. THE ALIENS GIVE ME A MYSTERIOUS GIFT

145

gentle exploratory method. Sure enough, I gently grasped the lid and played with it, pulling it toward me. It slid off. Well, I just hope that wasn't an intelligence test, because I probably scored pretty darned low!

I noticed a foul odor rising. In the box were about 6 or 7 upright, long glass tubes. Each tube was about an inch to an inch and a half in diameter. In the bottom lay a thick, dark brown, sticky, smelly fluid, about two inches deep. The alien returned and stared. I broke eye contact, not because I was frightened but just to be safe. "What is that dark stuff?"

"IT'S YOUR GIFT. WE EXTRACTED IT FROM YOUR LUNGS."

"From my lungs? This trash was in my lungs?"

I really didn't know what to think. Could this really be true? It's possible because at that time I was indeed a smoker. I didn't know what to say.

"FOLLOW US," one instructed me.

They took me into another room and instructed me to stay. I just stood there in the dark — then I blacked out. When I awoke, I was in another room, this one well lit. I could move, but only in a kind of slow motion. Peripherally, I noticed that there was another woman in the room. It seemed to be Teresa. Then, I was aware of the slender fingers of an alien touching me and guiding me to another part of the room, so that the woman was out of my range of vision. The alien, definitely a Supervisor, led me to a wall. There stood a full-length mirror that seemed to be the sort they have in dressing rooms.

The alien stood me in front of this mirror and said,

"LOOK."

The figure in the mirror was me, only altered and not distorted, like a funhouse mirror. My hair is dark brown, full and thick. The image showed me with thin dark brown hair, mixed with blond. My chin seemed pointier. My image had no eyebrows, and my moustache was gone. My eyes were slightly larger, and my body more frail.

"What is this all about?" I asked. I got no answer, and I didn't push it. Baffled, but happy to know that I'd be able to talk about this with an expert like Budd Hopkins, I just paid attention as best I could. Soon I was

146

transported back. I found myself back home, and the clock read 5:30 A.M., safe and sound. The whole thing had been somewhat of a gift — after so long, a refresher abduction to remind me of details, just days before my trip to Cape Cod! I'd be able to report things absolutely vividly!

Cape Cod was gorgeous in August, with the Atlantic breezes smelling clean and the sun giving off a much more pleasant kind of heat than muggy old Florida. Mary Anne was a splendid hostess and showed me the places in the area where she'd actually been abducted from her car. One of her abductions had been especially harrowing. In general, however, she dealt with the whole experience well, using them to help others cope. I learned that one of the reasons she'd done so well with this whole thing was that she'd had a very supportive family who actually believed her and did the things to keep her together in the first harrowing experiences. I felt a little bit envious.

Although my main purpose here was to meet Budd Hopkins, Mary Anne wanted me to talk to another contactee to whom the aliens had shown their symbols. I'd shown very few symbols to my group and generally kept them to myself, reasoning (perhaps faultily) that if I found another person knowing the same alien symbols without having me disseminating them beforehand, it would be 100% rock-hard evidence that my experiences weren't just extremely vivid hallucinations.

Sure enough, the person Mary Anne wanted me to meet kept a meticulously sketched record of the symbols she was taught during her abduction experiences. Mary Anne knew this, and thus linked me up with a terrific lady whom I'll call Sandy. We met, and we were both quite excited about the symbols. She invited me to her home so we could go over some of her experiences and view some of the symbols she had seen.

Sandy is very fastidious. Most of her experiences were kept in diary form, and any alien symbols she remembered, she kept logged and filed. We both became quite excited about one particular abduction experience in which the similarities were astonishingly similar to one of mine. I'll never forget the shock that coursed through me as I looked at two of those symbols, exactly as I remembered them. It was emotionally satisfying, and it made me feel so much less alone.

The next night I was to attend a meeting of alien abductees from the New England area, where I would meet Budd Hopkins. This was such a special meeting for me. Budd Hopkins is such a pleasant gentleman. He's graying, avuncular, soft-spoken and best of all — he listens carefully to you. An extra treat that night was the attendance of David M. Jacobs, author of the book Secret Life. I shared some of my story and listened to those of others. There were similarities, but also differences, which confirmed my opinion that quite a wide variety of alien races are visiting Earth. Afterwards, Budd invited me to come by and talk further. Sipping cold drinks that next day, we focused completely on my story. He was such a pleasure to talk to, and it was gratifying to see how amazed he was by my memory for detail. He asked if I'd had anything odd happen to me before 1988. No, I replied. However, there was one exception...

One day in the mid-1950s, my mother and I were visiting relatives in New York City. I somehow got lost. I remember a strange man in a suit who offered to help. He took me to his car and we drove around for what seemed at least an hour. We found my mother, and all ended well. However, the odd thing was that to this day my mother swears that I was gone only for a couple of minutes. She'd panicked, looked around for me — and there I was, holding the hand of a man in a dark suit. As I told Budd, my mother was quite overprotective, and it's hard for me to see how she had let me get lost on my own. Also, my memory of that car ride is crystal clear. Besides, I know a car ride would have taken much longer than a few minutes.

"This could be a case of missing time," Budd said. Although I couldn't quite see how it related to my experiences, it did pique Budd's interest. He mentioned that in most cases, encounters with aliens begin in an abductee's childhood. He thought it would be a good idea to explore this further through hypnotic regression. The process could uncover gaps or lost memories. I was a bit nervous about the idea. I'd never been hypnotized before, and I didn't really need it to recall my experiences. I felt I was unique and wanted to keep it that way. Budd understood. He explained that there were myths about hypnotic regression. Debunkers claimed hypnotists lead the individual into believing or recalling events the hypnotist is suggesting. He assured me that this wouldn't happen. He just found that the hypnotic state was a relaxed environment that allowed recollections to occur. Of particular interest to Budd was the "Gift" I had been given. "It's a fresh abduction experience," he said, and he wanted to work with that a little bit.

I agreed to undergo the hypnotic regression. Budd led me to a small room, just big enough for a comfortable, single bed. Budd instructed me to lie on the bed while he sat in a small chair. There was a small bookshelf against a window with several books atop the sill. I felt relaxed. Budd asked me to close my eyes, to think of a place where I enjoyed being, one that made me feel good. For me, that place has to be on the Gulf Coast in the morning, when gulls are feeding on baitfish that chum the glassy water. After a few minutes of relaxation and soothing words, Budd asked me to talk about my memories of childhood, between the ages of three and four. I did. He asked me to linger there and stand in front of a mirror and tell him what I saw.

I must say now that I had the totally wrong idea of what hypnotic regression was. Maybe I had visualized stage hypnotists making people bark like dogs, but there on that bed I was completely conscious and totally aware and I knew I could end the session at any time. Once I was ready, Budd simply asked me to share the story again, the story of how I was lost as a child. Although I was under hypnosis, I pretty much said the same thing and told the story with the same detail as I had before. However, there was one big difference. As Budd asked me questions, and I watched the whole thing unfold again, I described everything. I was watching people through the square window of the vehicle I rode in.

"What do you see?"

"I see lots of people walking on the sidewalks. I see cars and buildings and I can see the tops of the men's hats. I am saying to the nice man as I look at the women, "That's not my mommy, and that's not my mommy."

Then it hit me! I almost jumped off that bed. I was viewing the city streets filled with people and traffic all right, but obviously I was up in the air! I was looking down! We were moving, and I was in some sort of craft.

The implication here was that the aliens had been keeping track of me since childhood.

When the session was over, Budd and I discussed the whole thing. I would like to emphasize that in no way did he plant this memory. It was just there. You have to understand that I did remember the craft — it just apparently never occurred to my young mind that I was flying.

That evening at Mary Anne's house I had the chance to go over all this again. I had a true feeling of discovery, achievement, and belonging. I felt good. I felt validated.

The next day at Budd's we immediately used the regression therapy to get into the alien-gift scenario. And thanks to the hypnosis, I got into an area where I had previously gone blank. All of the business up to the dark room was the same. Then, instead of losing consciousness (or feeling that I had) I lingered in that dark room for quite some time until I heard a voice in my head. This voice, followed by other voices, lectured me.

The gist was that they wanted me to take more responsibility when I spoke of them and my interactions with them to other humans. In other words, this was a duty — bearing the message of what I learned to others. I understood, but I didn't like the tone or method, so I guess I was being a little stubborn. They left me in pitch black.

"STAY HERE AND THINK IT OVER."

They wanted to ensure that I would tell my story accurately, not adding anything of my own, just what I remembered. In retrospect, standing there in the gloom, this didn't seem unreasonable. I suppose I reacted in that way because of my natural stubbornness and resistance, which had given them such a hard time before, but in turn helped me maintain my memory.

I told the rest of the story. Budd shook his head. He didn't see that regression was really useful with me because I wasn't coming up with that much more. I remembered almost everything consciously. Down the road, I might want to retrieve a lost memory with it, but for the time being it didn't seem that useful. My conscious memory aligned pretty well with my unconscious recollection. Budd gave me his thoughts on the matter.

"Let's go back to the beginning. First of all, they gave you a gift. When they left you alone in another room, you felt you were being chewed out or lectured. I would have to call this a 'good-cop, bad-cop' scenario." Secondly, Budd said he felt the reason the aliens had me look in the mirror was to make me believe that I was also one of them. I was surprised to hear that. "Why?" I asked. He thought this way I would feel more a part of them and be less reluctant to take on the duties they were bestowing upon me. He seemed to have great insight, and I gained a great deal from it as we spent a little more time going over his investigations and theories.

Later that evening, Mary Anne and friends dined with Budd. When she returned, she told me that Budd said that in all the years he had worked with abductees, I was the individual with the most conscious recall. At first that had seemed a curse. Now, it was becoming more, at least I hoped anyway, of a blessing.

# CHAPTER NINETEEN

# Human or Alien?

"I believe that the aliens are embarked on hybridization experiments," I told the group. "Semen and eggs are extracted from us and, by utilizing alien DNA and biology, new beings are created. I think the worker aliens are a product, and may even be a commodity they trade in some sort of galactic business. But there's more to the alien agenda, and much that I've observed and theorized jives with what I heard from Budd Hopkins and other analysts I spoke to in Massachusetts."

The Florida Alien Abduction Support Group listened carefully as I reported my new experiences, and the news from my visit north. The group was growing. Its membership was gaining not marginalized folk, but solid, everyday, upper-middle-class citizens — Democrats, Republicans, bankers, lawyers — a cross section of the community. Also, these people weren't just locals. Some had traveled several hundred miles, because they'd heard that I was going to speak! I seemed to be gaining notoriety. Again, as I remember the woeful isolation I'd felt all those years, I could see a reason for it now. I not only could help others with their experiences, but it was also helping me. So, I agreed to let Tim schedule a few speaking engagements for me, hoping, as I do now, that I could help people. I also tried to do as the aliens requested and be as accurate as possible in my reporting. It was as though they approved of my spreading the word of their activities to those who would listen and be open to what was happening.

In December of 1994, after a stretch of peace, I was pulled again. I lay flat on my back with the effects of acceleration still buzzing around my head. I had the sense of a large echoey space, and sure enough, this was not the normal room in which I usually found myself. I was on a hard table. I pried myself up and, although I could move, it was slow. My eyesight was blurry and my peripheral vision limited, but I could pretty much tell where I was, as I pulled myself to a sitting position, legs dangling off the edge. I was in a huge rectangular room perhaps half the size of a football field. The walls seemed to be corrugated metal. In fact, it looked as though I were in the interior of a jet hangar. As my eyesight cleared and I looked around, I saw something I didn't like much — human military guards. They were lined up, backs against the wall, spaced out at 20-foot intervals.

Outside I heard the roar and scream of jets taking off and landing. I looked around. On the other side of my table was a rectangular platform, 20' by 15', surrounded by tiers of steps. On this platform stood two barrel-shaped transparent containers made of glass or even some sort of magnetic field, perhaps. These were maybe 15' in circumference, about 8' high. Each case held one male and one female human. The female had a certain resemblance to Teresa, but I wasn't sure.

Two men in lab coats appeared, walking with an alien. Humans fraternizing with aliens on an equal basis was pretty upsetting to me, of course, but I had to remind myself that I'd seen humans before who had been the result of screen imaging — aliens messing with my brain. Nonetheless, the longer I watched, the more I had the sense that these really were humans. I also seemed to sense that these containers were some sort of transport system, and that they were man-made. But if this indeed were a human facility, why was the alien here? Why was I here? Had I been transported here using one of these things? Was the U.S. military in league with my alien abductors?

One of the men had some kind of metal rod or wand. The three turned their attention to the woman in the chamber who was still too blurry for me to identify. He started prodding her. A tremendous sense of outrage filled me. I felt I had to stop them from doing whatever they were doing because it was abusive. As though in slow motion I struggled off the table and wobbled up the steps. They didn't hear me coming or expect me, so I was able to dart between them and grab the arm of the woman, who I could tell by this time wasn't Teresa at all.

I pulled hard, and the zombie-like woman didn't budge. The alien stepped back. The images of the men in lab coats wavered and they became aliens as well, but this seemed to me to be just a ruse to confuse

•FIG. 27: I SEE BARREL-SHAPED CONTAINERS OF HUMANS

or frighten me, and I was far too angry to be put off from my mission. I heard the pounding feet of the guards by the wall, coming forward. Another rippling and the alien images faded. Again I was with a woman, an alien, and men in lab coats. The man with the rod motioned to the guards and they stopped in their tracks.

"I'll handle this!" he said right out loud, without telepathy, in good old brusque, American English.

He touched my hand with the rod, and Ouch! did that sting! I yanked my hand away from the woman, but I was still out of my head with anger. I tried to pull away again, but again that rod flicked down with unbearable pain. I staggered back, and things got very fuzzy. Then I was on the table again, with the impression that time had passed. The canisters on the transport platform were empty. I could see this as my head was tilted in that direction. I looked up. Hovering over me was a figure, examining me in some manner, and this figure kept changing back and forth between alien and human. I felt quite drugged.

Usually during these abductions I'm wide awake. This time I was filled with fogginess with only intervals of clarity. The human/alien was lecturing me in a fatherly fashion. I could comprehend everything he was saying, yet my mental state was such that I couldn't retain it. The sound of jet planes kicked up again. The man/alien left me. The jet activity stopped, and dead silence descended. Then there was a rolling sound of a giant hangar door opening! I looked up and sure enough, this door was slowly moving, revealing a night sky. I could see lights and runways, and past them the dim forms of a starlit desert.

The smells and feels of cool desert night air rolled in, and I could smell the sage and the cactus. I recognized the sight and feelings, and it felt like Nevada. There was every sign that I was in the Southern Nevada desert. I used to vacation in Las Vegas several times a year, and I would always take trips out to enjoy the unique air and sensations of the Nevada desert. That was what I experienced now. Out on the desert landscape, I noticed, on the horizon to my left, a bright stationary light, just hanging in the sky — a spacecraft! It did not make a sound, but just hung there as though waiting for me. I sensed it was time to go, and not through the transport cylinders either. Realizing this, I felt relieved. Then, almost from nowhere, a man walked up to me. He leaned over the top right side of my head and began to speak, telling me to read a book. He said it was The Roman by Mika Toimi Waltari and that it would aid my understanding. Then the whirls and whirs of acceleration began.

I returned home remembering only this much and no more. More startling though was the fact that I had many cuts on my hand where the man had hit me with that wicked stinging rod. Any wounds I'd ever received on alien abductions before usually healed amazingly quickly — the process was almost finished at the end of an encounter. These wounds were quite fresh, and didn't look anywhere near healed. They weren't deep, but they were quite painful. I didn't resent them though as they confirmed the reality of what had just happened to me.

At the next UFO meeting, my friend Don, the law enforcement guy, noticed the cuts, healing but quite red and obvious. We'd gotten close, and it felt good that he trusted me, because he didn't want it to be known to the community at large that he was a UFO abductee. I told him the story, and what bothered us the most was the idea that the U.S. military was involved in this whole business. Government officials have routinely denied any knowledge of UFO or alien activities, all the way back to the late forties and Roswell. Don just suggested that I not read too much into anything, but just roll with it, and let it play out. I hadn't mentioned the book I'd been told to read. I didn't even know if it really existed, and I was afraid to go to the library to look for it. Maybe I was afraid it was an illusion, that it would show that I'd been fantasizing all this — that my cuts were some sort of strange stigmata.

Maybe, though, I was even more afraid that the book might actually exist. Finally, my curiosity got the best of me. Almost three weeks later I was staring at a library computer monitor, typing in the title of that book and the name of its author. Sure enough, it popped right up on the screen, and there was a copy available. I was so shocked that I even started to faint. I grabbed onto the monitor and held on, as though to my sanity. When I recovered I did manage to check the book out and take it home. It was a 600-page historical novel about a man who held tremendous power about 2,000 years ago in Rome.

Remember the bloodline business I spoke of before? I was convinced that I am descended from this man who claimed to get his knowledge and advice from Godlike creatures whose dwelling was the "Stars." It seemed pretty obvious to me that I had some sort of tracking gene, something that came down the ages in my family, that the aliens could follow, manipulate and work with. Even though this book helped me understand a good deal, I was still pretty unsettled with the business that took place in that hangar. But what could I do? Journey to Washington, D.C., pound on doors, and demand to know what exactly was going on? I would just have to wait. Later, though, I got my answer.

# CHAPTER TWENTY

# Diamond in the Sky

I continued my work, sharing and helping others, continuing to spread the word. After the hangar experience though, I started seeing things in a different light, particularly when I heard reports on UFOs and government reaction.

I continued to talk to small groups sometimes. I attended various UFO group meetings, including the Tampa Project Awareness Conference, where I had the good fortune to meet Linda Moulton Howe. I was also invited to do a few radio talk shows, including the Mutual UFO Network, the Kathy Fountain Show in Tampa and the Brad Collins Show on WINK 1200 AM in Fort Myers.

Initially, this widespread exposure made me nervous. I guess I really wasn't that comfortable with the idea of coming forward publicly with weird stories and opening myself up for ridicule. But then when I considered the things that I had experienced in the last years, I figured I could handle radio.

I kept my story simple and down-to-earth (no pun intended!) After the first few shows, I was surprised to find that the public at large was more receptive than I had anticipated. In fact, I was astonished when the calls came in. Many shared abduction experiences. Many respectfully just wanted more information. I was also amazed at all the UFO sightings!

It was now March, 1995, and I had not been abducted lately. I was feeling pretty good, so I decided to attend the annual "Shrimp Festival" at Fort Myers Beach.

The county-fair-like festivities take place on the beach just a mile from my home. It was late morning as I walked there, a clear and beautiful day, without a cloud in the sky. I had such a good time eating and drinking and watching the people and the parades, that the time whisked by. Before I knew it I had less than a half hour before sunset. I wanted to be home before dark, so I started to walk down the beach to a more isolated area. That day though, a young man and woman were wading in the water, waiting to watch one of our gorgeous sunsets.

As I approached them, a strange thing happened. My heart began to beat hard and adrenaline began filling me.

"Not here!" I whispered, thinking I was about to be abducted again. "Not now!"

An extremely loud voice inside me said, "WATCH US ENTER THE ATMOSPHERE." So strong was this voice that my entire body vibrated and swayed uncontrollably to every word. I attracted the attention of the woman, and I managed to get a hold of myself. "You're about to see something fantastic," I said.

"I know," said the woman. "The sunsets here are beautiful."

I felt sheepish. Why had I said that? But then as I turned to hurry away the woman cried out, "Oh my God! Is that a UFO?"

I turned, and for some reason I knew exactly where to look. Right there, hanging stationary in the sky in broad daylight was a diamond-shaped ship. It looked as though the sky had partially opened up to let it in because directly behind the ship was a streak of bright white light with a hue of blue. It was beautiful, just hanging there. We stared at the magnificent thing. "Remember what you are seeing here today," I said. "There are people who spend an entire lifetime investigating these things and never see one." Then, in a flash, it disappeared.

"It's not gone yet," I said to the woman. "Keep watching. It will come back."

"How do you know that?"

I hesitated for a moment, and then said, "I seem to have some sort of connection with these things." Sure enough, it came back and performed

•FIG. 28: WE WATCH A UFO ON THE BEACH

quite a splendid show. When it was over the guy started to jump up and down, yelling "Yahoo, Yahoo!" Then he ran away down the beach.

The woman just shook her head. "No one will ever believe that we really saw a UFO," she said.

I stayed a moment and made conversation with her. This was an exciting moment, but frightening as well. It was exciting because I'd just shared a UFO experience in broad daylight, straight out of everyday reality, with immediate feedback from others. It was frightening, because this was a new way they had contacted me, and I was always frightened when they reached that deeply into my life.

I asked the girl a favor. When she got back home, would she please write to me and tell me exactly what her experience was here, in her own words? She didn't feel that she could. She didn't feel that she could tell anyone about this — that people would think she was nuts back in her small town in Minnesota. I asked again, and gave her my address. I didn't tell her I had decided that I should start writing the book you're reading now.

Alas, I never heard from her. I had the feeling, though, that I would hear from the aliens again — and soon. A few days later, late on the evening of March 23rd, I awoke suddenly, intensely feeling their presence, yet it was different than before.

"WE ARE ALMOST THERE."

It got to me, this different feeling. I was used to acceleration now, but not this. I became very frightened, and the energy was so intense that I curled up into the corner of the sofa in a fetal position and said aloud, "I'm too scared. I can't do this. Go away! Just go away, please!" I was almost wailing in fear. "Why do you bastards insist on creeping up on people in the middle of the night? I'm not ready yet!"

The energy level radically dropped. I felt tremendous relief. I couldn't believe it. They had actually honored my request!

This was all very strange. It made me wonder if I were now dealing with a different crew of aliens entirely. I could feel their presence fade and disappear.

The next day I was invited back on The Brad Collins Show. I almost didn't accept, because the topic was the US government's involvement in the UFO phenomenon. Collins felt that involvement was heavy. I wasn't so sure. But still, it was a chance to communicate again and maybe even learn, so I accepted.

On the morning of the show, which was scheduled for 6:00 P.M., I had to run down the road a long way to get a part for my pick-up truck. Since moving back to the Fort Myers beach area, I had managed to settle down enough to acquire two beautiful and large dogs — one was a black Lab and the other a blond golden retriever. They loved riding in the bed of the pickup. On the 60-mile trip that morning, they rode along, as usual.

On the way back I was preoccupied, thinking about that evening's radio show. What was I going to say? I was in a pretty desolate area of highway, headed for the Gulf of Mexico, deep in thought when a telepathic voice in my head proclaimed loudly "JUST SAY WHAT YOU KNOW."

In the back, my dogs began to whimper with fear.

"That's it!" I said, and it suddenly all seemed very clear.

"DID YOU THINK YOU WERE IN THIS ALONE?"

If I didn't know better, I would have sworn these guys had a sense of humor, but I didn't have long to laugh before a huge diamond-shaped space craft appeared in the sky in front of me.

Yanking myself out of shock, I looked at the clock. It was 11:10 A.M. I looked back and yes, it was the same vessel I'd seen on the beach, just closer. Now I could judge it as maybe being 100 feet in length and about 50 feet wide. My truck rolled to a stop. It took me a while to realize that I'd stopped right in the middle of the road — not a good place! Still, there was no sign of traffic. There's always some kind of traffic hereabouts, but that day there were no cars or people either! The dogs behind me continued whimpering.

The craft began to move away. I hurried to get closer, but it eluded me. Finally it dropped right into the Gulf of Mexico without a splash, confirming to me its interdimensional qualities.

I raced down a side road to check it out, getting to the place where it had disappeared in the water. I got as close as possible and then I stopped. The clock read 11:42 A.M.

"Bullshit!" I thought. It had been no more than three minutes since the craft had appeared, not 32 minutes. The dogs had stopped whimpering. I tried to look around a bit longer, but I finally had to accept that the ship was long gone.

When I got home, I called Don. "Jim, you lost time. Do you think you were abducted?"

•FIG. 29: I DRIVE ALONG THE COAST AND SPOT THE UFO

I wasn't sure. "Everything about their behavior this past week has been different."

After chewing this over with Don, I felt better. Eventually all would be revealed. Was I dealing now with a different set of aliens, creatures with a different methodology? It was hard to say, but then everything about this whole business is tough to deal with.

162

That evening the radio show went without a hitch, and I was pleased with the way it turned out. Whenever I was asked or pressured about the U.S. government's involvement, I didn't speculate, I just said, if pressed, "That's possible, but I don't know for sure."

This technique seemed to ease the host, and at the same time it afforded me the opportunity to share my experiences as fact instead of speculation, which gave balance to the show.

In our UFO discussion group meetings, we often discuss the possibility that there are indeed different alien species involved in this whole interaction with humans, a kind of coalition.

I began believing this because of the different descriptions and behavior patterns described by other abductees.

I had a new attitude to all this by then, though. Before, I wanted the aliens out of my life. Now, it was as though I couldn't wait to see what was next.

What was next was an acceleration in the evening — a low-pitched whirling sound, then, waking up....

Only this time it didn't speed up as fast or get loud. The gut-wrenching part was still there, but not as strong, and it took longer than usual for me to black out. When I awoke, it was earlier than usual and I could see where I was going!

I was high above ground, descending slowly into an abandoned carnival park. I was floating over a large old-fashioned neglected wooden roller coaster. I also saw a few empty concession and gaming booths, shabby and falling apart.

It was night, but I wasn't frightened for some reason. In fact, I was so calm and relaxed that I was enjoying the ride. Twenty feet from the ground, I started to rock slowly back and forth several times like a pendulum, almost as if I were being guided to a target and this was the final adjustment. The transport method was the same, but the technology was notably much more gentle. When I was a few feet from the ground, I saw the profiles of about a dozen large creatures standing in a semi-circle, and then I blacked out.

•FIG. 30: A CIRCLE OF BEINGS GATHERS IN THE CARNIVAL PARK

"WE WOULD HAVE GIVEN IT TO YOU, BUT WE KNEW IT WOULDN'T HAVE MEANT ANYTHING UNLESS YOU EARNED IT. IT WAS THE ONLY WAY YOU COULD POSSIBLY UNDERSTAND WHAT YOU HAVE BEEN A PART OF AND WHAT YOU HAVE TO DO."

The message came to me loud and clear as I began to regain consciousness and opened my eyes. I later understood that by "IT" the Voice meant knowledge.

I found myself standing in that abandoned carnival yard, clearheaded and fully conscious. There were those creatures again, and I could see that holograms of human faces were cast over their faces, to disguise their true appearance and make me feel less apprehensive.

I noticed that each alien seemed to be concentrating and communicating or transmitting its thoughts to the creature to my left. They seemed to be of like mind, as though combining their consciousness into one tele-pathic Voice. They continued:

"THERE ARE SOME THINGS YOU NEED TO UNDERSTAND.

"YES, IT'S TRUE THAT WE HAVE BEEN IN CONTACT WITH YOUR GOVERNMENT AND HEADS OF POWER.

"IT IS ALSO TRUE THAT AGREEMENTS HAVE BEEN MADE AND KEPT SECRET FROM YOUR PEOPLE. IT IS ALSO TRUE THAT IN THE PAST SOME OF YOUR PEOPLE HAVE LOST THEIR LIVES OR HAVE BEEN BADLY HURT TO PROTECT THIS SECRET.

"OUR HANDS HAD NO PART IN THIS.

"WE CONTACTED YOUR LEADERS BECAUSE YOUR PLANET IS IN GRAVE TROUBLE. YOUR LEADERS SAID THE VAST MAJORITY OF YOUR POPULATION WASN'T READY FOR ANYTHING LIKE US YET, SO WE MADE TIME AGREEMENTS WITH YOUR LEADERS AS TO WHEN YOUR PEOPLE WOULD BE MADE AWARE OF OUR PRESENCE. THIS PART OF THE AGREE-MENT HAS NOT AT ALL BEEN KEPT.

"IT WAS ALSO AGREED THAT IN THE MEANTIME STEPS WOULD BE TAKEN TO CORRECT THE ENVIRONMENTAL CONDI-TION OF YOUR PLANET WITH OUR ADVICE AND TECHNOLOGY. WE SAY 'ADVICE' BECAUSE WE RESPECT THE FACT THAT THIS IS YOUR PLANET, NOT OURS. THEY ALSO BROKE THIS AGREE-MENT."

I felt an awful wave of emotion from them — the feeling of aban-donment. To feel any emotion from them at all was amazing, but this was quite overwhelming.

"You aren't giving up on us, are you?" I asked.

There was a long silent pause and I received the transmitted feeling of tremendous loss.

"Well, are you?" I asked.

"NO."

I felt an immediate sense of relief, straight from my own emotions!

"YOUR AIR, YOUR WATER, ARE CONTAMINATED.

"YOUR FORESTS, JUNGLES, TREES AND PLANT LIFE ARE DYING.

"THERE ARE SEVERAL BREAKS IN YOUR FOOD CHAIN.

"YOU HAVE AN OVERWHELMING AMOUNT OF NUCLEAR AND BIOLOGICAL WEAPONS, WHICH INCLUDE NUCLEAR AND BIOLOGICAL CONTAMINATION.

"YOUR PLANET IS OVERPOPULATED.

"WARNING: IT IS ALMOST THE POINT OF BEING TOO LATE, UNLESS YOUR PEOPLE ACT.

"THERE ARE BETTER WAYS OF DERIVING ENERGY AND FOOD NEEDS WITHOUT CAUSING YOUR PLANET ANY DAMAGE.

"THOSE IN POWER ARE AWARE OF THIS AND HAVE THE CAPABILITY OF PUTTING THESE METHODS INTO WORLDWIDE USE."

I let this digest for a moment. I definitely had the feeling that these creatures were speaking as one.

Then I asked, "Why aren't we doing that now?"

Silence. I was willing to wait. I had come a long way to be treated like this by them, to have this kind of meeting. Apparently, I had earned their respect and trust. The best part was that I was getting direct, truthful answers to my questions. I decided that I would milk this rare situation to its fullest, asking as many questions as I could get away with, even personal questions.

I repeated my question, and they answered.

"THOSE IN POWER VIEW IT AS A MILITARY AND SECURITY THREAT."

That upset me. "You mean to tell me the people in power have the ability to save and better this planet, and they aren't doing it?"

"AMNESTY."

"What do you mean?"

"COMPLETE AMNESTY TO THOSE IN POWER, GOVERN-
MENTS AND LEADERS WHO HAVE BEEN SUPPRESSING THE
TRUTH. THEY CAN'T BE HELD LIABLE FOR ANY PAST WRONG
DEEDS. IT IS THE ONLY WAY THESE LEADERS CAN COME FOR-
WARD WITH THE TRUTH. IT IS NECESSARY THAT YOU DO THIS
IN ORDER TO WORK TOGETHER AND SURVIVE."

Of course, they were suggesting forgiveness. My anger at all this
faded, as I thought about it. It made sense. Heads roll whenever cover-ups
are exposed, and this was a cover-up of galactic proportions. No pun
intended.

If anyone had a good reason to hate their government for covering
up this information, it was me, and others like me. Most abductees still
consider themselves victims who constantly suffer ridicule. When your
government's policy is to say, "You're just plain crazy," it only deepens the
pain.

I let my intelligence rule over my emotions and calmed down.

"How do I fit in all this? What can I possibly do?"

"WHAT YOU ARE DOING ALREADY. WE WILL SHARE
MUCH MORE KNOWLEDGE WITH YOU IN THE FUTURE.
ALTHOUGH YOU UNDERSTAND A LOT, WE WILL SHOW YOU
MUCH MORE.

"CONTINUE TO WORK WITH PEOPLE THAT COME TO YOU.
WE ARE AWARE OF THE SMALL GROUPS THAT ARE FORMING
AROUND THE WORLD AND WE HAVE ADVICE. YOU WILL
RECEIVE MORE KNOWLEDGE IN THE NEAR FUTURE."

These were not the exact same aliens who had worked with me all
those years — but there was a link between them, and the pain and learning I went through all led up to this.

I asked my questions and they continued to give me some personal
advice. They also said:

"CONTINUE TO WORK WITH PEOPLE WHO COME TO YOU.
THESE GROUPS FORMING AROUND THE WORLD ARE PEOPLE
WHO ARE PREPARED TO LEARN. CONSIDER THEM THE CORE.

THEN YOU WILL HAVE THOSE WHO WILL SEEK YOU OUT, WHO ARE STILL IN FEAR. ONCE THEY ARE OVER THE FEAR, THEN THEY WILL BE READY FOR THE CORE GROUP.

"MOST IMPORTANT IS THE CONDITION OF YOUR PLANET. THE FIRST STEP IN SOLVING THIS SERIOUS PROBLEM IS AMNESTY."

I asked them about fellow abductees I knew personally. First, I asked why they had chosen Tim.

"HIS NATURE MAKES HIM SUITABLE FOR FIRST CONTACT. HE THEN EASES OTHERS WHO ARE IN FEAR."

So true. I asked about Don and what he could do to deal with the problems he'd had lately.

"HE NEEDS TO CONTINUE TO WORK ON HIS EGO. TELL HIM THAT. HE'LL KNOW WHAT THIS MEANS."

(In fact, he knew exactly what they meant, although he'd never shared any of this with me, and he was deeply affected.)

I asked them about Daved, the state director for M.U.F.O.N. in Rhode Island. To everyone who had met him, though, including me, he was much more than that. As I stated earlier, he has a heart of gold. He was really calming and emotionally supportive to me and I know, for others. I have grown to have a tremendous respect for this man.

"WE HAVE LOVE FOR DAVED."

Boy, that caught me off guard — love?

The one that was speaking to me was sharing the collective consciousness of this entire group. They were different from the greys, because all of a sudden they had all these emotions. (The greys for the most part had no feelings.) I said nothing though, because I remembered that these guys weren't the Ice Corps that had put me through my routines for years. They seemed more attuned to human emotions, and I guess I figured I should appreciate that.

It started to rain. I don't mean just raining, it was pouring!

The semi-circle of aliens didn't budge and I felt no urge to either. We weren't getting wet. Although we were all standing outdoors, with no roof whatsoever, not one drop of rain touched us. We seemed to be protected by some kind of electrical field. I, of course, should not have been amazed, I'd seen so much alien technology, but still I was.

I was still thinking about Dave's question that he always asked me when he had the chance and he knew I'd recently experienced an abduction: "What do they look like?" Should I ask them?

Instead, I asked other questions, which they answered — questions and answers which I'll not go into here. Finally, though, they said,

"IT'S TIME TO GO."

A rare courtesy — a closure.

Then Daved's request flashed into my mind. "Wait. Please, I don't want to go yet! I want to see what you really look like.

"IT WILL STRIKE FEAR IN YOUR HEART."

I promised I wouldn't be frightened and said that it would be a privilege to see them. However, I did request that they make a peaceful gesture

•FIG. 31: I SEE WHAT THESE ALIENS REALLY LOOK LIKE

169

in the midst of this frightening exposure, just to reassure me. A wave, perhaps?

A spinning white light with a hint of green began to radiate over their faces and upper bodies. The intensity of this light slowly got brighter. It radiated from no detectable source.

Then I saw what they truly looked like. They were big, all right. Their upper bodies looked like football linebackers. As the light became brighter and the details clearer, fear and shock did course through me like lightning.

They had scales, and their faces were sort of snakelike, or lizardlike. Nothing at all like the smaller aliens.

I felt an odd, deep-down instinctual shock, but I told myself to calm down.

Their eyes were small like ours, but diamond shaped. The pupils were reddish. Their heads were big, and their brow stuck far out from their eyes to various degrees, giving them all some kind of individuality. I was surprised that I was deeply upset by them.

"Hey," I said feebly. "You promised to…uh…wave."

Wave they did. Each and every one of them slowly lifted their arms and waved them in front of their faces — a sight to behold.

This relaxed me, but I was surprised by a feature I didn't expect — their hands. Their hands were huge, with thick club-like features, which appeared too thick by my estimate to work fine instruments.

Once again, though, I had to remind myself that their technology is thought-activated, and anyway, I was judging by my limited human experience.

The acceleration commenced. I regained consciousness back at home as usual, but the experience still gripped me. What a message! What an important communication! These creatures had a vantage point that no one else had. They were able to see a totality that many of us refuse to see.

As the sun rose over the horizon, it felt as though it was a dawn of promise and possibility, and my fear was totally gone.

I drifted off to a peaceful sleep.

# CHAPTER TWENTY-ONE

# State of the Earth

"YOUR PLANET IS DYING."

It doesn't take an alien from another planet or dimension to prove this — there's plenty of evidence in the daily papers, the TV news, scientific journals, and magazines. We are all aware of the pollution, imbalances, global warming, and ozone layer depletion. What can I say that hasn't already been said?

What I can say is how this affected me. I started noticing the reports on news shows. I started realizing that global warming due to pollutants and ozone screw-ups was affecting me now, but more to the point, it would affect the whole human race in the future.

I think the average citizen, like me, just goes around with blinders on. Most of us are totally immersed in just getting through life, dealing with personal and professional crises that we just ignore the bigger picture. Even if we do pay attention to what's going on, we just feel so insignificant that we don't feel we can do anything. Or, feeling upset, freaked-out and frightened, we just stick our heads in the sand, ostrich-like, and ignore everything.

We can't afford to do that.

The next morning after this incredible advancement in my relations with extraterrestrial life, I woke up with fresh excitement. I had been approached almost as an equal. I mattered. I wasn't just a pawn in some obscure ET agenda — there was a cause, a reason for all that I'd gone through! I had the final proof I needed, and I was elated.

These creatures were neither evil nor benevolent. They were just different. It simply does no good to try to use human measurement and morals to embrace their ET designs. That said, though, there were physical laws we had in common. A polluted Earth, a dead planet, the human race a memory — these are clearly states that don't suit their purposes. Obviously they had a use for us and an odd, if ET, respect. They needed us. But why? For reproductive materials to create hybrids? Well, that's been my experience, so that's what I believe, but who knows what else? The human race has imagination and potential genius to spare, but what makes humans of particular interest to these visitors? From my experience, they are certainly interested in our emotions and sexual energy. Could that be how we differ from other beings in the universe?

In any case, the ETs consider us some kind of crop or harvest, and I say that in the best sense. Again, they are neither evil, nor particularly benevolent. They've been around, using us this way, for thousands of years. I believe this to be so because they have followed my family line and many others as far back as apelike creatures. But I wonder if their intention for us isn't actually something more than this? Is there a cosmic destiny that they have in mind for us and wish us to continue toward? Of course, this would involve using us along the way. Or are they a part of us and we a part of them?

But whether it's in their interest, or ours, the fact remains that this planet Earth is plenty messed up, and they seem more concerned about that than we are.

Talk about synchronicity. While I'm writing all this here in Fort Myers Beach, the television set is on and there's just been a news flash. Eighty-four manatees, and several dozen porpoises and sea turtles washed up dead on the shores of the Gulf of Mexico here, almost literally in my back yard. I would not have to go far to witness this. I don't want to, though. I'm feeling ill.

However, it does indeed remind me of the mission and purpose I've been selected to pursue. The ETs I've spoken with obviously don't feel they can just appear on television. There must be slower ways of mainstreaming this river of awareness. Just call me Jim Creek for now, dribbling some truth into the big mass of information that flows through us every day.

So, if the visitors wish to assist us with this problem, let's examine their possible motives. Is it because they have a great love for humanity? Destiny and possibility aside, I don't think so. In my opinion, it's simply to protect their investment. And is that investment linked with both of our future survivals?

True, we do have an excellent species-insurance policy. If we do destroy our environment and ourselves, the Visitors could conceivably recreate us somewhere else, on some other planet. They doubtless have collected every conceivable seed of life that there is on Earth.

Needless to say, I personally would prefer that we buckle down and fix our environmental mess. If the ETs are willing to help with technological aid, all the better.

Then there's the amnesty business, which is vital.

The more I think about it, the more it makes sense. Everything points to a grand conspiracy on governmental levels around the world to keep the truth of the ETs away from the covers of mainstream newspapers and the network evening news, podiums that people believe and pay attention to. This has been going on for over 50 years. Unless it is agreed that the people who have been responsible for this cover-up, this subversion of truth not be prosecuted — why should they confess? Would you?

However, if we work to understand why all this happened, and forgive, then we too might be forgiven, and we can work together with the ETs to build a better world.

Is this far-fetched? I don't think so. In my lifetime, I've seen the Berlin wall come down. I've seen the fall of the Soviet Union in an amazingly short time. These changes all seemed impossible just a few short years ago. I've seen things that no human being could even imagine with these ETs.

Amnesty? Not long ago, I would have said that it was impossible, too. Does a major tragedy have to take place first? Do uncounted millions have to die first to shock us into action? Or worse yet, do we continue down this road of self-destruction until it's too late?

Allowing the leaders who still keep us in the dark the legal right to disclose their information without penalty seems to be the proper choice here. Amnesty and forgiveness for them, should they come forward, seems the only way.

Just a few days after the experience in that carnival yard, I was in my car driving down the highway to meet Daved, with those incredible events still fresh in my mind. It was a nice day and I was pleasantly cruising along. From the corner of my eye I noticed a flock of birds to the right of the car — only they weren't flying.

Then as I looked closer, I saw that they weren't birds either. What first had seemed to be a flock of birds, had been a screen image. There, in broad daylight, were three huge diamond-shaped ships in a triangular formation. Just hovering there, not making a sound. It was an awesome sight indeed, and I took my foot off the gas pedal and just coasted to a stop, not afraid at all, just lost in wonder… what is next?

Then the ships began to rotate, revealing every angle of their surfaces. Excitement flooded through me. I knew somehow, that they were doing this for me. Then they stopped rotating and without warning, in the blink of an eye without losing formation, all three of them streaked to the right just a few hundred feet. I continued to sit there in awe. Then once again they sparkled in the sunlight and slowly began to rotate. Once more they came to a complete stop and hung motionless.

My body began to vibrate and a loud telepathic voice said:

"GOODBYE FOR NOW."

In the blink of an eye, all three ships dashed from the right horizon to the center of the sky and just hung there. Then I remembered that I was supposed to meet Daved. "I want him to see this!" I mumbled. I pressed on the accelerator and wove through traffic (to whom presumably the UFO looked like a bird flock). I kept track of the ships. "Don't go yet!" I said. "Please don't go." Daved needed to see this sight!

Then as I approached my turn-off, they suddenly streaked to the left horizon. I realized then that they would be gone before Daved could see them. However, in my enthusiasm I wouldn't give up. I feverishly sped through the parking lot. Seeing Daved, I jammed on my brakes and slid next to his car. I jumped out of the car and ran towards the highway waving my arms, looking like a complete madman, no doubt.

"What are you doing? Is there some accident?" Daved asked.

I wheeled around, pointing, but, alas, the ships were gone.

Breathing hard, I sighed and lowered my arms. "ET ships. They were just up there, communicating with me."

"What did they say?"

"Good-bye for now," I sighed.

We looked some more and I tried to concentrate whatever psychic powers I have, all to no avail. Those guys were gone.

"Always the bridesmaid, never the bride," said Daved, sighing. "I guess it was just for you."

This courtesy, this communication was the final part of my realization of a new attitude toward the Visitors. This particular species even made an honest attempt to visit on my own terms and when I was frightened, they respected my fear and left. When I was confused about how to handle that radio show, they advised me. Then they gave me the truth of it all — a comprehensible message to bring to others. They always gave me the opportunity to examine their ships at close range.

All this left me with the feeling that one day very soon I'd have the privilege of watching them land, greeting them face to face and walking on board. I was aware, though, of the duty I had been given, and of the serious, clear message.

"YOUR PLANET IS IN GRAVE TROUBLE."

And now, this courtesy — this privilege — the chance of a farewell and yet the promise they'd see me again.

"GOODBYE FOR NOW."

And I believed them.

# CHAPTER TWENTY-TWO

# What I Have Learned

I have often been privileged to connect with special individuals who feel as I do. We feel we have been altered in a positive way. This chapter covers some of the peculiar and paranormal activities that took place as a direct result of this phenomenon. I feel these events are as important to share as anything else written thus far. This information will help explain some of the oddities that take place as a direct result of being exposed to alien culture and technology.

Truly more things exist in this universe than meets the eye, or can be seen by the normal five senses. I have found most abductees have been given the ability to see and interact in other dimensions. Also they receive contact from what appear to be "normal" people, but who, in my experience, are not. I fondly call these strange people walk-ins[1].

In my opinion (gained from experience), our government is deeply involved in interdimensional human transport. We learned this technology from our alien friends. This advanced technology allows aliens, as well as humans, the luxury of working in more than one dimension at a time.

I learned that when I am transported in this manner, I get a glimpse of other life-forms that seem to exist naturally in these other dimensions. It took me almost eight years to finally accept these ines-

---

1. Some people may have a different term for walk-ins, but this is my definition. Since we are attempting to adapt our limited vocabulary to a vast universe that we are only beginning to glimpse, there may be differing terminology.

capable conclusions. I have a saying: "If you show even a dumb dog something 300 times, he will finally catch on and learn." So far I have been the dumb dog.

Remember, I am not the only person who has seen and experienced these things. I believe I speak for many abductees, but I come from a different perspective. I was fully conscious.

## The Man in the Black Robe

By now you are familiar with the details and sensations that are consistent with the acceleration, a method of transport I call, "going the hard way." When this method is in progress — as a rule, but not always — an abductee is completely paralyzed. After a few moments, I would slowly regain normal motor ability. The first part of my body to come out of this paralyzed state would be my eyes. After they would open, a few seconds later my body would follow suit. This pattern was consistent. I practiced time and time again before and after the acceleration to force my eyes open sooner than normally allowed. This was always a struggle, but over time I gained a few seconds.

Usually, after opening my eyes a few seconds early, I saw nothing strange. Once, I managed to open my eyes several seconds early. This time, I was returned to my guest room. As the acceleration wound down, I could feel the softness of my bed against my back. I was completely paralyzed. The loud whirling sound was winding down, and my heart rate was fast, but slowing down also. I struggled with everything in me and managed to open my eyes. I was shocked at what I saw, as was the being standing over my bed, an alien that looked human. He was wearing a black robe, with a black hood covering his entire head, but not his face.

I tried to scream, but I couldn't move my mouth. The alien had blond hair, a light blond beard, and a moustache. Some of his hair was out of the hood, resting on his forehead. He was holding a thin, silver metallic rod or wand, about eighteen inches long. When he saw that my eyes had opened, he leaned forward and started waving the wand around my face in a circle. As he did so, I started to lose control of my eyes. It was as if they were being forced shut by some invisible energy that apparently was coming from the wand. I was also losing consciousness. I yelled mentally "No! No!" and struggled to open my eyes again. When my eyes opened, he looked even more surprised. He leaned in closer to my face with his wand, and waved it even faster until I could no longer fight it and finally blacked out.

Having been exposed so often to alien technology, I am no longer confused by most events like these. During or after the initial shock of an experience, I learned to condition myself. Instead of being scared, I tried to figure out what they were up to. As far as I'm concerned, any unusual wonder they are capable of is simply advanced technology, and this approach keeps me centered and focused. This formula enables me to learn and share, instead of wading in the stagnant waters of fear.

Using this approach, I put a few facts together in an effort to make sense of what I saw. This was the first and only time I saw any alien or person wearing a robe. I usually do not pay attention to what any of them wear. However, on this occasion his clothing stood out clearly. I couldn't be sure he was human, because I only saw part of his face. The little I could see looked fairly human, including his expression of surprise when I opened my eyes. I have seen humans working with aliens on more than one occasion, so he could have been human.

The rod or wand he held really fascinated me, because I have seen it too often. When I was in the hanger in the desert, one of the men held the same kind of device — thin, metallic, thick on one end, perhaps a half inch to an inch in circumference then tapering to a point. You may recall, in that experience he kept tapping and stinging the back of my hands with this rod. Later, I realized every spot he touched left a small cut.

Sometimes when aliens were taking semen, one would hold the same kind of wand, touching my testicles with its tip, instantly causing an unnatural erection and ejaculation. I think this wand is a thought-activated tool with miniaturized components and wondrous capabilities, but it is simply technology. These individuals are not wizards.

I have come to believe that ETs have been secretly involved with humans for hundreds, if not thousands of years. On those rare occasions in the past when they found it necessary to reveal themselves, perhaps

•FIG. 32: THE CONTROLLING ROD USED TO EXTRACT MY SEMEN

ancient man saw them with this wand. His mind would no doubt have concluded that this was a magic wand. It's a wonder all right, but it's not magic, or mystical. It's in our nature to make a religion, so to speak, out of anything we don't understand, but it is simply advanced technology.

## Out of Phase

I have personally seen other life-forms in other dimensions. I believe they are not extraterrestrials. I'm not certain what they are or exactly where they come from, but they do exist. I used to have trouble with this aspect, and it can be very confusing. Our five senses (unless artificially altered) are not set up to grasp the concept or to have awareness of these things. I believe every human being possesses the ability to see in other dimensions. We can call this a sixth or seventh sense. These extra senses seem to be dormant, like an atrophied muscle. However, if this muscle is exercised and artificially stimulated (from exposure to alien technology or other means) it becomes active. There is no doubt in my mind that other dimensions do exist; one just needs the tools of technology to tap into them. In my case exposure to alien technology heightens the senses, and if exposed long enough and often enough, it renders one slightly out of synch.

Being slightly out of synch is a part of the residual effect, and it is usually temporary. However, in some cases (mine for instance) it may be permanent. When one is transported from point A (your home) to point B (on board their craft) a large part of this process includes matter, aliens and people passing through several dimensions. In these dimensions, I have gotten a glimpse from time to time of other strange life forms.

On first impression, these interdimensional travelers look like spirits or ghosts. Some look frozen in time. Others look like the spirits of the deceased trapped in a movie loop. Still others appear to be alive, with a sense of self and purpose. Some are as curious about me as I am about them. This aspect of the phenomenon used to scare me to tears and confuse the dickens out of me. However, if you are exposed to something long enough to see it for what it may be, it's not so scary.

Fortunately, depending on your point of view, (at times I have mixed feelings), this uninvited new ability an abductee acquires lingers for a while after an abduction. In addition, if one chooses, this effect doesn't have to fade away. If I keep this muscle exercised, like any other conventional muscle in the body, it will continue to serve me.

I don't understand everything, of course, but this I am certain of: This new-found ability enables me to see into other dimensions, and I know that other life-forms exist. They seem to occupy the same space as we do, but in a different dimension. Without the aid of technology, our five senses are not aware of these other dimensions. You can't see air, but it's there.

Advanced alien cultures have mastered time and can travel great distances. This technology enables them to tap into other dimensions, and so when they use this technology on us, we gain the ability to see into those other dimensions.

## Dimensional Blending

Star People have a technology that can split matter, including themselves and their ship, between dimensions in any ratio they choose. I have no problem accepting this, simply because I have seen it with my own eyes on several occasions. It has become second nature to me. However, to the inexperienced eye, witnessing this technological feat calls up a host of possibilities, such as angels, demons, and spirits. This is not to say that such things do not exist, but in this case, it is clearly humanoid-type beings using "magic" technology.

For example, they can take a plate and make two plates out of it. The original plate might contain 95% of the original matter and the second 5%, or the ratio might be 50/50 or 60/40 - whatever they choose. Here's the scary part: They can break themselves down, and us as well, in whatever proportions they see fit, which is what leads to the trauma most abductees suffer. I hope this information can help other abductees cope. Aliens make no effort to explain anything, in most cases. They simply use these advanced technological tools without regard to our feelings. It leaves poor unsuspecting humans at a loss to figure out what the hell is going on, just as we probably confuse the elk that we tranquilize, poke, prod, and leave in a different location.

The thought of non-human intelligence in itself boggles the most advanced minds, to say nothing about alien technology. Aliens do not explain anything to us either because they want to keep us in the dark, or they're just plain indifferent. Once anyone has grasped the concept or root understanding, things start to make sense. Aliens are seen walking through walls or floating in thin air. Ships are seen appearing and disappearing. It's not magic, demons or angels. It's just advanced technology.

## Alien Healings

What do aliens really want from us? I have a pretty good idea, and I say more about that in the next chapter. At this time I will discuss another pattern that helped me to discover what these creatures are up to. They have invested a great deal of time and effort in us abductees, even to the point of periodically maintaining our health. I am not suggesting, by any means, that they take care of every little ailment or sickness, or all life-threatening diseases. I am not exactly sure what motivates them to intercede in an abductee's health. I know for a fact that from time to time, they either adjust or correct abductees' ailments because it has happened to me and to other abductees I know. Let me tell you about "The Doctor."

In late 1995, I contracted a terrible flu with weakness, coughing, fever, chills, and nausea. I felt like hell. I don't get sick often, and when I do, it's short-lived. This illness was different, however. It dragged on for a month, and I was not getting better. Then, one evening, I had an unconventional doctor's visit. I was asleep on my sofa, when I suddenly woke up paralyzed, except for my eyes. I was turned sideways, facing my living room's front wall, through which walked two aliens. I remember thinking, "Here we go again!" I was more angry than scared.

I telepathed to them, "Why am I paralyzed? I thought I was past all this junk! Besides, I am real sick, and I am in no mood for this!" (as if my mood would make a difference!)

They walked toward me, and the nearest alien manifested a screen image over his face, an image of a close doctor friend of mine whom I will call Dr. T., who treated me for several years after a terrible car accident. I had grown to love and deeply respect this man, whose wonderful bedside manner is a real pleasure to experience. I am sure that the aliens were aware of my fondness for this doctor, from their probing of my memories. They also knew that this created image would make me feel less apprehensive. They were right. I didn't fight the false reality of that particular alien appearing as Dr. T.

As he approached me, I asked, "What are you doing here?"

He responded, "Don't you remember? I am here because of our agreement."

"To what?" I asked.

"You remember," he said, "we agreed that if ever you were to get real sick, I would come."

His face looked very friendly. Even though I knew that he was not Dr. T., I felt happy imagining that he was. Suddenly, I remembered our agreement.

"Yes, I remember now. Whenever I get real sick, you said that you would come. And now you are here."

"That's right, and now I am going to examine you."

They both leaned forward and proceeded to do just that — examine me. They took several minutes poking, prodding, and turning me around in different directions. I felt an assortment of instruments making contact all around various parts of my body.

When they were finished, they stepped back, and the one who looked like Dr. T. said, "You have a secondary upper lung and throat infection as a result of the flu."

I said, "Well, did you heal me?" I got no response, so I asked again. "Did you heal me?" Again no response, so I said, "Should I go see a regular doctor, or what?"

They never responded, but simply turned and walked back out through the same wall through which they had come. A few seconds later, I passed out. When I opened my eyes, it was morning. I sat up on the sofa and stretched my arms. I suddenly realized that I was not sick any more.

While I resist believing that the aliens would do something as helpful as healing, I cannot argue the fact that I was miraculously healed.

## Black Helicopters

During their visits, aliens seem to frequently create interdimensional fields that alter matter for travel, duplication, invisibility, and passing through solid objects. I am sure that these fields have countless other uses that we have not yet observed. In my experience, a special traceable signature or residue lingers during and after the use of one of these interdimensional fields. This signature is unique and is clearly distinguishable from anything else, using appropriate monitoring devices. Without doubt, it's the most dependable way covert government agencies can monitor alien activity.

This residue can linger for quite some time on anything, including humans, with which it comes in contact. It is my belief that there is not a single abduction, cattle mutilation, or other alien-related event that takes place without the knowledge of certain government agencies that monitor these activities. If this signature is particularly strong, it indicates frequent or extended activity. In that event, black unmarked helicopters are dispatched to check it out. Not every event warrants an investigation. I have noticed that usually several events take place before a helicopter is dispatched to inspect more closely.

I understand to a certain degree why ominous black helicopters show up from time to time. A high percentage of abductees claim to have seen these black metallic birds. Usually it's after an abduction or sighting. Sometimes it's after cattle mutilations or the appearance of spectacular crop circles. I feel certain that I know one of the reasons that they appear, and I have a good idea who pilots them. And it's not aliens.

In my July 1995 encounter with "The Doctor," the aliens worked with me, in our dimension, for the entire evening. They conducted what I believed to be experiments and medical procedures. Because this session was of such long duration, the lingering effects of the field were very strong. After the aliens left, I felt as if I had been irradiated. My senses were extremely sensitized, and my developing sixth sense was especially sharp and clear. I felt magnetic. The residual effect of being exposed to their field was extremely strong.

I am no longer traumatized by alien visitations. In fact, I was enjoying the "Doctor's" visit, and I tried to take advantage of its strong residual effect as long as possible. I knew that it wouldn't last very long.

I had made a commitment a few days earlier to take my seven-year-old niece to school on the morning that unexpectedly featured "The Doctor." I also had some items to pick up at the K-Mart, which was near the school. After dropping off my niece, I arrived at K-Mart 30 minutes before opening time, so I waited in my car, which was the only customer vehicle in the lot. As I waited, I felt a strange sensation course through my body. It was the same feeling I had felt a few months earlier, just before the diamond-shaped ship appeared in broad daylight on the beach. I exited the car, knowing somehow to look north. It was clear, and at first I saw nothing, but I knew I would, because the residual effect was very strong and all of my six senses were extra keen.

Then it appeared — a black dot that gradually grew larger, until it became recognizable as a black helicopter. It emitted a deep, thundering roar as it made a beeline in my direction. (I have on other occasions seen silent black helicopters.) I had no doubt that it was looking for me. I felt it! It approached fast and suddenly stopped, hovering over me and my car. It seemed to be hovering at about 150 feet in the air, and its color was pitch black. The windows were opaque black, and I could see no occupants. I stood staring at it for 20 or 25 seconds. I made a few very noticeable obscene gestures, as many as I could think to create. Finally, the aircraft slowly looped around and headed back in the direction from which it had come.

I was radiating a strong residual signature that morning. I feel certain to this day that the reason for this close encounter with this black helicopter was my residual signature from my experience with "The Doctor."

## Diet

Six months before "The Doctor" healed my flu, I had had another medical visit that was very uncomfortable. It changed my eating habits in a profound way. I had been a heavy meat eater. My diet included a rare steak at least once a week, hamburgers for lunch at least twice a week, meat loaf, pot roasts, roast pork, you name it.

I was a true carnivore, but not anymore! Since this event, my diet has consisted of a minimal amount of chicken and fish, some bread, and of course, vegetables. Anyone who knows me knows that this change in my diet is not like me at all. "It would take an Act of Congress for Jim to stop eating meat," people would say. But I did stop, and I'll share the reason. Some of these alien medical exams, unfortunately, include anal probes - Yuck! - a subject I do not enjoy talking about, writing about, or experiencing. Of course, not everything I write about is comfortable to relive, and in this case I feel it is necessary.

I was asleep on my sofa when I was escorted to the ET craft the easy way, and I found myself face down on an examination table, in tremendous pain. They had inserted a deep anal probe into me, and I could feel it churning about in my guts. I felt so miserable that I cried out, "What the hell are you doing to me?"

One of them responded, "An examination of your system."

"The pain is awful! You're hurting me," I yelled.

Then I blacked out. When I regained consciousness, I found myself face up on the table, sore inside, but not in pain. Two aliens were present, and it appeared that they were just finishing up their procedure.

One of them said telepathically, "It is necessary that you stop eating animals. Your system is overloaded with trash." (The word "trash" surprised me.) "Intelligence dictates that you do not have to kill to survive."

I blacked out again, and later I found myself at home. When I sat up, my insides were extremely sore. I was accustomed to a little discomfort from my encounters with these creatures, and I knew any discomfort caused by them would pass relatively fast. I went into the kitchen, made some coffee, and started making breakfast. As I opened the refrigerator door to reach for the bacon, these words rang through my head: "You must stop eating animals." I could not bring myself to cook the bacon.

At lunch I stopped for a fast-food burger, but I couldn't eat it. This pattern continues to this very day. I can no longer eat red meat. I like the change in my diet, and I feel better.

Exactly 30 days after this diet-changing visit, the aliens returned and I suddenly awoke to see them walking through my wall again. I had thought that they would be working with me again in my living room. As they approached, I passed out and found myself on my side on the examination table. They were poking and prodding me again and I hated it!

"Damn it!" I said, "Why are you doing this again? I stopped eating meat!"

"We know," they said, "we had to make sure that it was helping you, and it is."

I blacked out, and when I regained consciousness, I found myself at home again. My insides were sore for a few days, however, but I have not eaten red meat since that time. I have done many speaking engagements across the country, and I have met many fellow abductees. The bulk of them are vegetarians. I find that odd. Do you?

## Hybrids

The alien-human hybrid life-form is neither a created worker, nor a human, nor an alien, but a combination of human and alien. It is part of the aliens' insurance policy. They are creating a being that is more alien than human, at least more alien than we are. This way, if we fail to turn our environment around and we die off, after the dust settles, they can repopulate the Earth with hybrids that could possibly be more adaptable to the Earth's changed environment. They need far less food, water and energy, yet they still have enough human raw material to be useful to the aliens.

## Walk-Ins

"We come in many different shapes and sizes."

To me a walk-in is an alien who appears in human form and contacts abductees on our turf. In my experience, there are two types. A type-one alien walk-in screen-images himself to look human. He is physically alien, but he simply projects a human image.

The type-two walk-in looks human in every way. This type is extremely perplexing, and I have great difficulty accepting that they exist. However, I know from personal experience they do, which can also be verified through other abductees. We have experienced these beings while being alone, or in a few cases with other abductees.

Type-two walk-ins pop in on us from time to time and talk in riddles. They may start a conversation with you out of the blue and speak on a topic you shared with someone else in private. They exhibit the same behavioral patterns as alien doctors, appearing only when really needed.

I am very uncomfortable with type-twos because it is hard enough to deal with aliens on board their craft, without having to interact with them in my own space. Also, I feel safer not relating too many stories regarding my face-to-face contact with what I call walk-ins because I'm not sure what my involvement is with them or how much information I should reveal. I believe there aren't very many of them, and their appearance is rare.

I don't believe the men who followed me around in Texas were aliens. I think however, they were government people. In what capacity? Who knows? Budd Hopkins theorizes that they were human all right, but possibly born and raised by aliens.

Here is a personal example of the type-two walk-in that involves another abductee and me. My close friend Don, his daughter, her fiancé and I had rented a van and drove 600 miles from south Florida to Mobile,

Alabama, for a UFO conference. On the way, over we talked about everything under the sun to occupy twelve hours of driving time. At one point we talked about recent movies, in particular, "City Slickers." For hours none of us could come up with the name of a popular actor in this movie. We struggled and strained our brains to the point of exhaustion, and at times it was at the tip of our tongues, but none of us could come up with his name. Finally, we gave up.

About ten minutes later, out of a dead silence, Don's daughter and her fiancé simultaneously shouted, "Jack Palance!" We all laughed. Stay with me, and it will start to make sense.

The day after arriving in Mobile, Don and I walked around the downtown area looking for a place to eat lunch. We paused for a moment across the street from a few restaurants, talking among ourselves and deciding where to eat. As we stood there, an odd middle-aged man in house-painting clothes walked up and said, "Come on in, because in here, you can have anything you could possibly want!" It was an innocent enough statement, nothing really out of the ordinary, except for some oddities.

He didn't come from inside the restaurant; he came from down the street. It wasn't as if he had just eaten there, and was walking out complementing the place. Also, after making that statement, he didn't go into the restaurant. Further, we had been across the street from the restaurant, talking alone, completely out of earshot of anyone. We could have been discussing anything, not necessarily restaurants.

The events so far really didn't get my attention until later, but they piqued Don's attention. He commented, "How odd!" We looked at each other, shrugged our shoulders, walked across the street and ate. As we were sitting at the table, our friend (whom Don and I now fondly refer to as "the painter") walked up to our table from what seemed like out of nowhere.

He looked at Don and said, "Do you know who you look like? It's on the tip of my tongue, give me a second, um… um…" He continued to act in this manner repeating the same words over again. Don and I looked at each other with a strange smile as he rambled on. Suddenly he shouted with emotion, "I got it now. You look like that actor, Jack Palance." Being in law enforcement and thinking like an investigator, Don processed the facts of the case: "He quoted and expressed our conversation in the van, word for word! How can anybody do that? Unless the van was bugged. However, we rented this van out of the blue; no one had any real time to prepare. First he said, 'Come on in. You can have anything you want,' and remembering a conversation word for word the way he did! Jim, I think this man is a walk-in." At the time I didn't agree or disagree with Don's conclusion.

After lunch, we went back to the hotel and attended the conference. The idea that this man was possibly a walk-in did briefly run through my mind, but I dismissed it. Early that evening after the conference was finished for the day, I met a young abductee woman who was very nervous about her experiences. I felt led to help her cope with some advice. Although there was a lot she wanted to say, she was hesitant to speak, primarily because of not wanting to be overheard by any of her conference-attending friends. I assured her there would be no pressure from me, and perhaps we could find some out of the way place to talk, where none of her friends could possibly run into us, and she agreed. We searched and found what we thought was the perfect spot, an old-fashioned bar and grill. After a few minutes of talking, someone tapped me on the back. I turned and was shocked to see our friend, "the painter."

Before I could say anything, he looked me in the eye and said, "You should know, we come in many shapes and sizes." He turned and walked out. I sat there with my mouth open and watched him walk away. The young woman said, "Wow, it felt strange when he was standing next to us. Who was he?"

"Oh, he's a painter, just simply a painter." I replied. She sensed I didn't want to talk about it and didn't ask any more questions. Later that evening, I caught up with Don and told him the story. It helped to confirm what Don believed. I still wasn't sure. However, it was strange.

Sunday afternoon the conference was winding down. Don found me in the lobby and said, "I ran into our friend again, or should I say he ran into me." I asked Don, "Well, what did he say?"

"He walked up to me," Don said, "offered his hand and we shook. He was wearing old shabby painter's clothes, so I asked him if he was attending the conference. He said no. Although I knew he wasn't with the conference, I asked him in order to dig for information. I asked him if he was doing some work here, like painting, etc. He answered in a riddle: 'No, I am not working here, but I have a few loose ends to tie up here, and then my work here will be finished.' Then he left."

Don continued, "The point here is this: He obviously knew of our conversation in the van. He knew what we were talking about on the street that day, and there wasn't anyone around to overhear our conversation. He shows up in that out-of-the-way place where you were the other night. Then he tells you, "We come in many different shapes and sizes." Then he shows up at a UFO conference in shabby clothes and talks in riddles by saying he is not here to attend the conference or do any work. However, he still had some loose ends to tie up and his work is finished. Jim, he must be a walk-in!"

Whether or not this man was truly a walk-in is unprovable. Don seemed convinced. As far as I was concerned there were many odd indications pointing in that direction and this will have to be enough for you to get the picture of what a walk-in is.

I will close this chapter with an example statement made to me by a person who made it clear he was a walk-in. These people are intergalactic or interdimensional travelers. The following statement typifies that fact. At one point in a conversation with one of these fellows, I asked, "How long will you be here?"

He said, "I will be here for two weeks, but I am leaving tomorrow."

# CHAPTER TWENTY-THREE

# The Nice Doctors

There's an interesting side of human nature of which we are all aware, but which still managed to surprise me, and it affects abductees all the time. The pain of this effect cut deep into my soul, but in the end, I learned a lot.

The majority of us thrive on a support system that makes us feel as if we belong, whether it's our family, place of work, or fans at a sporting event. These social boxes can be positive and give us that security we crave from family, community, and country. At the same time, anything we do or say that doesn't fit into the accepted "norm" of a particular box can be seen as weird. Therefore, we do our best not to step outside our boxes in order to avoid rejection, so we often keep silent, no matter what the cost.

Most abductees experience this first hand by being rejected by the very support systems that sustain them — family, friends, church, and community. I was no different. In the early chapters I wrote that my family was politely supportive of my alien abduction. However true this may be, it certainly didn't start off that way. Initially, I was flatly rejected. In those early months it was pain on top of pain when it came to the disorientation of the abduction scenario, and almost as traumatic was the initial rejection from my family, which was totally disheartening to me, because I know that I am an honest, logical, and truthful person. My father's initial reaction was total disbelief, not just in the abduction subject, but suddenly, for the first time in my entire life, he didn't believe a word I said. My brother, on the other hand, didn't seem to care. To him it was a concept that couldn't exist, and hence he ignored it. When I talked about my experiences to my normally very warm and compassionate mother, she stood there silently, giving me a blank, cold face.

As for most abductees, disbelief adds so much more stress to an already chaotic situation. The support system that knows you better than any one else can't believe or handle your experiences. You stand alone, and as I learned I was able to do that, it made my confidence grow. I now wonder if that is not part of the ET game to test us.

For me, time played a big part in changing all this, and over time my family became supportive. However, this, too, carried emotional pain of a different sort, because it was the way they changed that bothered me at first. Thanks to television, magazines and other media reporting abduction incidents, and the personal support offered to me by cutting-edge researchers such as Budd Hopkins and Harvard professor, Dr. John Mack - my family's attitude towards this subject shifted.

I was deeply offended and hurt that my own family had rejected what I was honestly reporting, but they began believing me when "professionals" with accepted credentials believed me. I kept this pain to myself, and came to understand it in a positive way when I accepted this deeper understanding of human nature - that the need to belong is a driving force in all of us.

As you know during my first 18 months of alien interactions, I was driven to no avail to convince anyone and everyone to believe that what was happening to me, was really happening to me. All I got was closed minds and ears. At that time, I made the decision not to speak of alien abductions. What a surprise it was to find that this strategy made everyone feel better! In fact, a friend of the family said to me and I quote, "Jim you are a perfectly normal person as long as you don't talk about that stuff." So I didn't, for several years. Again, it was when mainstream media began producing documentaries on alien abductions that family and friends started seeing me in a different light. Although I never said anything, it made me angry inside. Why couldn't they just believe me from the start? Why must my credibility depend on others?

Then one day my mother shocked me. I was sitting out in the Lanai at my parents' home one afternoon enjoying the good weather. My mother came out, sat down, and lit a cigarette. She started talking about a show on abductions she had seen the night before. Then she just said it: "I have been examined by those doctors all my life, and they are always nice to me. Every time I am there lying on that gurney, they say nice things to me. They want to make sure that I am OK. They are never mean to me, like the ones you talk about. I like them, and they like me, and this has happened to me all my life."

One would think at this point that I would have fainted. There sat the woman who birthed me, the same person who was so despondent when I came out with "ET world," and just like that she spills her guts, as if it were a natural everyday occurrence. I realized that even if someone is unknowingly experiencing something bizarre, they still can be in denial for quite some time until the conscious mind is ready to accept it.

I responded in kind with just a couple of words, knowing two things at that point: Mom was an abductee, and, thanks to media support and hopefully being forthright with my own experiences, she came out with it.

She couldn't relate to my story, because in her mind all along it wasn't the same thing. I was talking trauma, and she was experiencing kindness. Was it screen imaging? Perhaps. It didn't matter, because I now knew that Mom was also an abductee all her life, and to her it was pleasant, and that's the way I wanted it to stay. So I said very few words, and we never talked about it again. We didn't have to, because from that point on, we both knew, and we were both content that we shared a new social box together, no matter how bizarre it would seem to the rest of the world. It still gave me comfort.

# CHAPTER TWENTY-FOUR

# The Real Situation

In some ways, this chapter was the most difficult to write because of the complexity of the phenomena. On the other hand, the passing of much of the pain associated with the subject makes it easier now. My life and how I view things have been tremendously expanded. The knowledge and understanding I have gained are incomparable. Although I feel that I have paid a very high price, anything worthwhile has its price. This is a law I feel applies to the whole Universe.

We are not alone in the Universe: We play a major role in the universal life chain. Yet I feel that there is another universal law: Higher intelligence takes advantage of and uses lower intelligence, not unlike the way we use cattle. With the privilege of use comes the responsibility of care. A farmer tends to his animals by feeding them and taking care of their medical needs. He makes sure that all their survival needs are met so that he and his family can also survive. The cow, with its limited intelligence, lives out its life span completely unaware of its fate.

If, however, the pasture were to become contaminated, the farmer would take actions to protect his investment, either by cleaning the pasture or moving the cattle. If he had the technology, he might even take eggs and sperm from the herd and store them as insurance against the possibility that the pasture could not be saved, or that the cattle would be unsalvageable. Clearly, it would be easier to move cattle seeds than cattle bodies to cleaner pastures, and any such activity would take place right under the cattle's noses, without an inkling that anything was out of the ordinary.

Of course humans are not cattle, and the Earth is not a green pasture. Or is it? The Earth is too big to be a pasture, and humans are too intelligent to be cattle. Or are they? We know we are too smart to destroy our environment. Or are we? Our governments and scientists tell us that we are effectively alone in the Universe, and we believe what they say. Or do we?

Why do aliens take seed and raw materials from humans? One revelation that came to me is that the aliens are creating worker beings, much as ants do. Does this mean that the aliens are farming us? Yes, it does, but not to eat, fortunately. Farming humans for raw materials and spare parts is only part of the story.

## The Field

The alien field to which I have frequently referred may be electromagnetic, vibrational, or something for which we have no name. Light is sometimes associated with it. I have been exposed to it many times, and it makes my body feel magnetic. At times I feel static electricity. At other times everything it influences loses color and fades into black and white. This field enables the aliens to do many marvelous things, some of which I discuss below.

Invisibility. When the man in the dark suit escorted me from my house to the beach, you may recall that when we got to the water's edge, we stood there waiting, watching an obscure small light hanging not far away over the water. Suddenly the light formed into a large rectangle into which we stepped, and we were on board one of their spacecraft. The ship had been there all along, but it used the field to make itself invisible.

Interdimensional Travel. Interdimensional travel is the ability to go from Point A to Point B in literally no time at all. I know this, because I have been taken by this field from my home to and from their ships and to different points on the Earth's surface. The Star People, use this field both to travel across galaxies and to transport selected people to and from their ships any time they wish. Distance becomes inconsequential, and our laws of science are probably a minor and incomplete subset of their science laws.

Screen Images. The field seems to play at least a part in screen imaging. You might recall that once when I was out driving, I thought I saw a flock of birds, when in reality it was three ships in formation. It seems that they use the field to disguise themselves and to project perceptions that people see.

Scanning. The field seems to enable the aliens to scan us and to know ourselves better than we do. With it they can browse through every minute detail of our lives, including lost memories.

Technology. The aliens use thought-activated technology, and their machines are at least partially biological and can interact with us as if they were alive. Their ability to take in, process and project information is so vast that they can see the future coming.

## Spare Parts

With all that they can do, why do the aliens need us? What is the common denominator that links all intelligent life? It is the need to survive as long as possible. I suspect that if intelligent life could live forever, it would. I further believe that our alien friends come very close to immortality, but they need us to do it. I have seen and experienced many, many things to reach this conclusion.

Natural life dictates the inescapable need to survive for as long as possible. It is as natural for animals and humans as for aliens. We all seek all means to feed the yearning appetite that survival demands. An animal seeks food and shelter, knowing that if it gets too cold or doesn't eat, it will die, but its brain capacity limits it to hunting for food and shelter. Humans, with larger brains, have developed medicine and science and can even transplant spare body parts, if the tissue match is compatible.

What if we could successfully implant into animals significant portions of our genetic code, not enough to interfere with the animals' well-being, but enough to maintain a sustainable reservoir of human DNA, blood and tissue, to support human bodily repair needs? There would be medical teams to track, secure, tag and extract necessary materials. Individual animals and blood lines would have to be tracked constantly, so that they could be retrieved on demand.

You get the picture. Aliens have been taking advantage of us with their superior technology in secret for a very long time. They implanted portions of their genetic code in humans long, long ago, and their ships come regularly, in waves, to "abduct" (secure) and return tens of thousands of humans, extracting whatever biological materials they need. The donor is unharmed and completely unaware that anything is missing. The tiny wound is quickly healed by the "abductee" (donor). However, they transplant in ways we do not understand. With their field technology they can reduce extracted biological specimens to vapor and then superimpose it into the recipient, where the pattern is reproduced as necessary.

Consider: The Earth and the known Universe are billions of years old, life is abundant in the Universe, and countless intelligent cultures have developed, advanced, and died out. Flying disks have been seen and recorded throughout human history, from cave drawings to today's video recordings. Every year thousands of people around the world report being

•FIG. 33: ALIENS CAN HEAL BY SUPERIMPOSING PATTERNED TISSUE

197

abducted, many of whom report extraction of semen or eggs. Reports of alien abductions tend to follow family lines. I have seen and experienced these things with my own eyes.

We self-proclaimed intelligent masters of the Universe are not much more than a spare part inventory for aliens. That is humbling. It is hard enough for people to accept the existence of any intelligent life any-where else in the Universe without having to also see ourselves as main-tained organ donors for aliens. Even with this truth, however, I doubt that people would run in the streets in panic, or that the stock market would fall, or that the church would disintegrate. We are humans. We are resil-ient. We are survivors. We will get through this.

## Our Exopolitical Situation

Because of the intensity of the cover-up of information relating to these topics, we cannot know exactly what has gone on between the visi-tors and our governments. Let me speculate, based upon my experiences and perspective, about what really happened: Aliens made contact with principal Earth governments years before the Roswell crash. They explained to the Earth leaders that environmental disaster was imminent and that we had to do something about it. Our leaders, however, guessed that Earth populations were not ready for knowledge of aliens just yet. So a deal was struck: The aliens would supply certain technologies to us to help us clean up our environment, which would help ensure human sur-vival and protect their investment in us as an inventory of biological spare parts. In return, certain time guidelines were agreed to, during which our leaders were to carefully spoon-feed all Earth populations with informa-tion about the existence and role of non-human intelligent life on Earth. The technology duly arrived, but the appropriate time to disclose never did, leading to a long period of secrecy, disinformation, incarceration and missing people, most of which was done for the sake of national security. We took the technology and made money and weapons with it, and we let the disclosure timetables lapse.

It's also possible that the aliens may have delivered even more tech-nology in return for Earth governments destroying all nuclear weapons.

They clearly detest nuclear weapons. Once again, we failed to honor our side of the bargain, again because of international distrust and competition. Roswell and other crashes were covered up, not only to conceal the fact of off-planet life, but also to hide the depth to which our governments have been secretly involved with alien civilizations, and the reckless risks our governments have taken with the viability of continued life on Earth.

In order to protect secrecy and national security, information was suppressed using criminal acts, which is why individuals in the secret government sector do not come forward. The criminal justice system would simply crucify them unless they were granted complete amnesty in exchange for the complete truth. That way - and only that way - can the truth be told. Once it is out, we can use the technologies the way they were intended to be used and work together to fix the environmental crisis facing our planet.

If we continue to misuse our environment as we currently do, the human race will not be long on this planet, and life will not be worth living during our exit process. The possible end of human life on Earth deeply concerns the aliens, who have a large investment in us. They have taken great invisible steps to adjust our environment, but the task is too great for them to do it alone any longer, and they respect the fact that it is still our planet. The aliens and we need each other. We need their technology to fix our environment, and they need our governments to disclose the truth so that we can all work together to preserve life on Earth. Truly, we are all in this together!

# CHAPTER TWENTY-FIVE

# Closing the Gap

So much has changed since completing the first book that it would take at least two more books to go into detail. However, let me touch on a few highlights. Let's presume that what I am about to summarize is true — because it is — no matter how bizarre it may sound.

This world is filled with a lot of good people who give and keep on giving. On the other hand, the human condition as a whole is paranoid and selfish, and too often greed is God. However, there is good reason for the negative — we are mortal, and we die. There is no time to evolve. We have to eat at any cost, which means killing something. We must have shelter and a sense of security. This means we must use natural resources. The more of us that exist, the more we need to take from the planet. All of this forces us to compete with each other for all that Mother Earth has to give, and then we die. Truly, we are human animals and I'm damn proud of it. We have to scrape, scrap and fight for everything. I will take human beings over the most advanced alien culture out there, including people from the future.

At times I refer to most alien cultures as "assholes from outer space." I look at them face to face and say, "How come you aren't doing more to help us?" I have come to realize why they can't give a straight answer. It's because they are not human, they can't understand. As a whole we humans have the potential to be more advanced then they are.

The message I received from the ETs was that our planet was in trouble. In some ways things have improved, but with melting ice caps and extremes in temperature, it's minimal. We need to alter our consumption habits and reduce the amount of heat that we are allowing to build up in the atmosphere.

For me personally, my experiences with these cultures has expanded my mind and my interaction with them. They only occasionally abduct or pull me from my bedroom, living room or car in the middle of the night anymore. I have also had several encounters with people from the future. As far as I can tell, they are anywhere from a few hundred to several thousand years ahead of us. The types of people that come to me speak English and are from the good old USA. It's comforting for me to know America still exists in the near and distant future. These encounters have been fun, and to say the least, most interesting. I will summarize these encounters, which will only touch the surface, but this book had to end some time.

Future people always seem to meet you in the most unexpected places, at least for most people it would be unexpected. I'm much more comfortable being around near-future people — the ones that are a few hundred to a couple of thousand years out from now — because they are still somewhat like us. When the originating time frame gets out further — 10,000 to 50,000 years — we start to get a little kinky.

Within the next hundred years, time travel and much more will be as common as using a remote control. Time travel will be of no consequence, and for the most part boring.

Future people come on tours. I am not kidding. They love to have encounters with people of this era and other time frames to which they travel. They blend in and don't interfere — they just observe. However, the highlight of the tour is to talk to a person of the destination time period, which has been me on many occasions.

At times their clothes are funny or they do not fit into our current time period. They speak both verbally and telepathically. They carry conventional American paper money neatly folded and ironed in two-inch squares. Many of these bills from different time periods fit neatly into what looks like a wallet. When it is time to spend or make a purchase, it's funny to watch them unfold and inspect the bills in front of a merchant to make certain the bills are of the right time period.

There is a trust, so under any and all circumstances, you don't give them away, or ask questions. In time they will tell you what you want to know and then some.

I have learned that many of the visitors people call "aliens" are really "us" from the future. That's right, us! We become far removed from what we are today, and we look more like what we commonly refer to as Greys. We get smaller and thinner, our cranium becomes more enlarged, our eyes become much bigger, and our skin color changes to a grayish blue. Whether it's good or bad, we leave behind emotions. How else does one become far removed? I will site just one example. Ask any abductee how often he or she has seen a Grey sit down for a nice dinner of meat loaf with gravy? Answer — never. And their mouths are very tiny, and they don't seem to move. So I would say they don't eat food, as we know the term!

Think about what a social impact not-eating would have on our society — no more breakfast with the family, lunch with friends, holiday meals, etc. Everything in our world would change. There would no longer be a global food-based economy. At this point the impact is almost unimaginable, because our day-to-day life revolves around eating three square meals a day.

However, there are already some monks who are said to go without food, and "breatharians" who seem not to eat. More and more people are becoming vegetarians, so our eating habits are changing. So, as the generations pass, we can foresee telling our children what meals and tasting food was like. As more generations pass, it would become an old-fashioned fable. As much as I love eating, the good side of this would be a lot less killing.

Now some of the people I have met come back to our day after thousands and thousands of years have passed. Now maybe you can imagine that these future people find it impossible to relate to us as flesh-eating animals. To us they appear as aliens and to them, we are animals, which happen to be their ancestors. Get the picture? To make your heads spin even further, imagine that it is us traveling in time — no longer being emotional — no longer aging, eating or talking! What an alien world that would be! So, my friends, consider our descendents as the aliens of the future!

The river of time flows like the infinity sign, (a sideways figure eight). It just happens over and over and over. So how does one travel in time? In a sense, you just need a boat that's fast enough and you can travel the river any where you please.

This analogy sheds new light on an old childhood song:

> Row, row, row your boat
> Gently down the stream
> Merrily, merrily, merrily
> Life is but a dream.

It's best that it stays just that way for the most part. For the world isn't what you think it is, it's better.

# CHAPTER TWENTY-SIX

# The Message

My 1995 meeting with a circle of aliens in an abandoned carnival site was indeed a turning point. I knew then precisely what my task was — to help spread the message I was given by these ETs, but how and when, I wasn't sure. Most of all, though, I realized how much I as a human, an entity, had opened myself up to humanity, to a collective, and to reality on a universal level. Before 1988, I had been living like an ostrich with my head in the sand. I had my head pulled out, by no choice of mine, and was forced to take a long look.

In order to join the galactic neighborhood, we must first clean up our own backyard. Humankind in its present state is a poor galactic citizen, much too dangerous to be turned loose in the cosmos. However, change we must, if we are to join. Can we do it? I think so.

I am different now. Happier? That's hard to say. More aware? Incredibly. My previous senses have been sharpened, and I am aware of extrasensory aspects of existence here, existence in an intergalactic level, and interdimensional levels.

I have a purpose, and that makes life so much richer! I feel myself obliged to serve my family of humankind. I am particularly grateful to my friends who have also experience the ETs. Without the support and companionship of my fellow abductees, I would not have been able to survive these experiences and grow from them as well as I have.

I have had subsequent experiences with the ETs and many other odd kinds of paranormal experiences as well. At this point, it's all moot and beside the point compared to this issue. I have been given a unique purview of reality, and I can tell you: Our planet is in grave danger. We must work with the extraterrestrials to solve the environmental quagmire into which we have sunk.

However, because of all the intergovernmental conspiracies and foul-ups, to work with the ETs we must forgive and grant amnesty to all those who know about the ETs and have been trying to keep the truth away from the majority of people. Only then can a program for proper integration of ET thought, truth and maybe best of all, ET technology be brought to Earth.

Scary? Yes. It will be frightening, at first. However, how much more frightening is the death of our cultures and our civilization? Sure, maybe humankind could be resurrected on a planet of some distant star. But there would be no Gulf of Mexico sunsets, no fishing boats drifting by the beach, or Shrimp Fests. There would be no pasta al dente with extra virgin olive oil and tangy Parmesan cheese, no symphony orchestras playing Mozart or Beethoven, and no poetry in English, French or any language that we know.

No, I choose a continuity of survival, and I believe that this is possible even now. I suggest to you that once your fear is gone, the wonder, awe, and excitement will set in, and what the ETs truly have to offer will enrich the lives of our civilization.

This, I think, can be human destiny. It is a wonderful possibility to think that it may indeed happen, and it is worth all the confusion, disorientation and yes, the terror that I experienced all those years. When faced with the Unknown, it's inevitable that we experience fear, and there's plenty of Unknown out there, believe me. Facing it alone is worse, but we don't need to do that anymore. We can face the future together.

Now, I ask you to think about what kind of future we might have, with full contact with these ET beings that have been working with us secretly for millennia. Think about the ET technology that I have described: interdimensional travel, faster-than-light ships, thought activated technology, genetic tracing, genetic manipulation and incredible hybrids, thought-screen imaging, levitation and manipulation of gravity and electro-magnetism, wands with great power for pain or for healing, telepathy, and thought control.

As a person nowhere near a scientist or even with any grasp of science fiction, I have tried to explain as best I could the kind of powers of mind and physics I encountered. However, doubtless there were things happening, ET technology operating around me, of which I could have no comprehension.

This is just the kind of technology that humankind with its ingenuity could use not only to better the quality of life for all, but to fend off the dire consequences of pollution and environmental destruction that our heedless civilizations have wrought.

Consider the other implications of my story. I have contributed much evidence to the theory that the human race hasn't simply relied on evolution to develop our achievements and advancements. Although there are curmudgeons who would argue that humanity reached its intellectual peak with the civilization of ancient Greece, there can be no doubt that our race has developed incredibly quickly.

In 1869, the U.S. was building railroads to the West Coast of this continent. In 1969, the U.S. was landing men on the moon. What incredible things might be happening in 2069? Is this the result of ET manipulation? That's hard to say. What I can say for sure, for whatever purposes, the ETs have no desire to keep our development checked, except perhaps when it comes to nuclear destruction. Whatever their part in our destiny, they wish for us to continue toward whatever cosmic awakening may be part of our spiritual path.

I am no spiritual leader, but with what I have seen, heard, felt and experienced, there are things ahead of us just breathtakingly wonderful. The gifts of the ETs are not just technological. The ET gifts of the mind could truly take our sense of self into a healing and joining of humankind. This could break down the barriers that keep us apart with hatred and suspicion. This mental technology could take us into territories of discovery that we are only just now beginning to glimpse, and that our myths, literature and science fiction have only touched on. I now feel the language they so painstakingly taught me was not only common ground communication between us, but a basic foundation for telepathic communication that humans can learn.

I am no prophet, either. I certainly have no intention of trying to minimize the potential threats and dangers ahead of us. I'm half-afraid that it's already too late. The human race may indeed die here, with our biological echoes having been carried off to some other planet for inscrutable purposes. But if we can somehow survive, touch the sky and reach for our future, we can link with the vast minds and talents that walk among us.

I believe the ETs offer rapturous vistas of not just technological advancement, but also emotional and spiritual advancement, along with an expansion of awareness, longevity, and peace. Ah, that would indeed be a glorious future. A future that, if I live to see any part of it, I'll have the satisfaction of knowing that my voice, here in print and through other means of communication, helped bring it about.

My name is Jim Sparks and I have been contacted by extraterrestrial beings. I bring a message of grave warning. But most of all, I bear a message of hope for a future of joy and fulfillment for the human race, beyond our present comprehension.

# CHAPTER TWENTY-SEVEN

# Accepting My Mission

The main purpose of this second edition was two-fold: to answersome questions that I've received over the last few years, but first and foremost to further emphasize our most urgent need — saving our planet for future generations. Even though I reached a turning point in 1995, it took me many years to realize that conveying this simple but essential message from them to you was my purpose in working with them, a mission that I now understand, accept, and am acting on.

I am a down-to-Earth person who tries hard to be honest at all times. I am not perfect, but I find it most important, considering the subject matter we are working with, to honor the facts, as best as I can. We are sailing in foggy, uncharted waters, and I am piloting the best way that I can.

Since I was first "pulled" against my will, out of my ordinary life, my experiences with non-human intelligent beings, or ETs, have evolved considerably. In the last few years I have been witness to, and interacted with, advanced cultures in a way that is unlike anything I have previously experienced. In the early years they pulled me from my home, day and night, without warning. Nowadays, though, I usually get a bit of advanced notice, and in rare moments, I even meet with them face to face, which is a milestone.

As you know, my first six years of dealing with ETs was hell — what I refer to as "alien boot camp." Once I overcame my fear and anger and stopped resisting, I learned to cooperate, and then I was trained in elementary telepathy. The next 13 years was about learning. When I started cooperating with the ETs, it was not because I chose to, but because I realized that I could return home sooner if I cooperated. Once I started to follow their directions, things started to get even more interesting, and I have seen amazing technologies that can change our world for the better, if only we can take off our blinders, improve our ways, and work with the truth of the ET presence among us.

I've been asked a lot of questions; many I could answer, and others I can only offer my impressions, given my years of experience with these beings. Keep in mind, it's not as if the ETs offer me a time for Q&A; it's more like they give me information on a need-to-know basis. If I want to know something, they'll tell me when the time is right for them. I've learned that there may be plans of which I am aware and in which I am possibly even involved, but if it's not the right time for them, no matter what I do, my questions do not get answered. They have an agenda — this I do know — and they have their own timeline.

Many people have asked me about the alien alphabet I was taught and why, if they communicate telepathically, did they need to teach me this? As you know, a picture can be worth a thousand words. Within their symbols are contained volumes of information, like a computer chip. Their minds work perhaps ten to a hundred times faster than ours. It served their purposes for me to learn a faster way to communicate with them. Once I learned their alphabet and symbols, it became easier for me to keep up with them. I must conclude that the imprint of their three-dimensional symbol structure in my brain creates for them a framework that facilitates their telepathic delivery of information to me.

I will now address a subject that will, when fully revealed, without a doubt, change the face of the Earth, as we know it.

In the two decades during which I have been dealing with the ETs, I have witnessed amazing technologies that could eliminate our need for fossil fuel by creating free, nonpolluting energy. These technologies are not just pipe dreams — they are real, and they have been kept secret from humankind for thousands of years by otherworldly beings. However, today is quite different from ancient times. I believe that many of these advanced technologies are now in human hands, but they have been kept from the general public.

Perhaps some presumptuous Earthlings have accepted advanced technologies in exchange for the freedom to abduct citizens. Due to human greediness and thirst for political power, these technologies may have been used for war, power, and profit. In their defense, decision-makers still do not take into proper account the limitations of the Earth's capacity or the effects of our activities on her well-being. Hence, our governments, in the name of national security, begin and maintain many projects that have caused harm to the Earth. High-intensity naval sonar weapons, for example, seriously disrupt the sensitive sonar communications of whales, dolphins and porpoises that depend on sound to survive. Such technologies were used without considering the consequences to the sacred web of life on Earth.

We have powerful technology in our possession to stop global warming, but it's being held back. Automakers have had technology for years to greatly increase the fuel mileage. Why is it held back? There are those who know about it, have used it, or even reverse-engineered it, who want to come out with the truth, but they are afraid of reprisal, because people in government have discredited, maimed and killed people for the sake of maintaining secrecy. This leads into the concept of an amnesty program, an idea that was given to me by a group of Reptilian ETs. Because of all the secrecy around the UFO/ET subject maintained by humans, the ETs feel that the only way informed people will publicly come forward with their knowledge is if they are given full amnesty. I do not have all the answers on how to do this, but I am introducing the thought to you now. Perhaps if all of us put this into our intention, something positive may come of it.

Another question I get is why would they pick me — an ordinary guy — to help them? I've asked the same question. However, if you look back at history, it was almost always the ordinary people who made the greatest changes in civilization. They have little vested interest in the status quo. When enough of us make our voices heard, the governments will respond, only because doing so will preserve their vested interests. We're seeing this happen right now. A few years ago global warming was dismissed, and people who talked of such things were ridiculed as "tree huggers." With many people continuing to get the message out, and former Vice President Al Gore being a dramatic global spokesperson on the issue, the topic has become visible. Now we see the "green movement" taking hold everywhere.

I'm just one among thousands of contactees, but considering what I've seen and been told, the ETs began contacting ordinary people because the agreements they initially made with Earth governments had not been honored, and time is running out: Our planet is dying and needs help. Many contactees seem to be very environmentally focused. Is this because they are subtly brainwashed by the ETs, or do the ETs pick individuals whose focus is already where they want it to be? I don't have an answer to that, but I do know that I have always had a strong desire to preserve the Earth's environment, which I did as a responsible real-estate developer. I've learned first hand that you can still make money even while preserving the environment. Around the world one can see green "transition" communities being established. It's encouraging.

From what I've been shown of the future, humans do survive, so there is no doubt in my mind that at least some of us make it. You may then think, "Well then, let's relax. After all, the future is assured." In one sense, it is — humans survive all right — but the path we take can make the difference between widespread unpleasantness and a global, sustainable richness that the Earth has never seen.

Clearly the fraction of humanity that survives is a function of our choices. Currently there are about six billion humans on the planet; within the next 25 years there may be as many as nine billion if trends continue. Or perhaps only a few hundred humans survive. Do we want to keep polluting until Mother Earth kicks us off, or do we want to work with her? I choose the latter, and I hope that you will join me and urge others to join us.

I don't think we can just kick back and relax, because in this case, if you are anything like me, you would rather see more rather than fewer humans survive through the coming events. Imagine how much better of

an impression we would make as a species if we joined the galactic neighborhood with several billion robust and healthy Earthlings, rather than a
meager few hundred survivors. Indeed what a statement that would be:
We are Earthlings! We have survived, and we have saved our planet for the
future! Now we are ready to work with you!

We all know our world is in trouble, so in order for more of us to
make it into our future, we have to clean this place up, starting now. We
need to create an environment in which we all can live safely — including
Mother Earth. The ETs have given me an assignment, which is to help
save the Earth's rain forests — the very lungs of Mother Earth — that we
are rapidly destroying. These forests remove $CO_2$ from the atmosphere,
and deliver oxygen and water vapor into the global atmospheric circula-
tion system that waters our growing regions. As they decline, more of the
Earth gets hot and dry, and deserts spread.

First and foremost, we must stop the destruction of the rain forests,
so Mother Earth can, with our aid, rejuvenate. How can we do this? Where
do we start? I've been shown a plan — a way to stop the destruction of the
rain forest.

We need to start by asking what motivates the destruction of the
rain forest. Let's face the first formidable obstacle — human greed. There
are people, governments and corporations who control the rain forest
land. They use the land as they please, without regard for how this affects
our planet. This has to stop, but how?

First, we all begin just buying the land. Owning the forests would
then give the global community owners' rights and all the freedom necessary to defend the rain forest against all threats.

Second, the global community needs to determine who are best
suited to be the stewards of this land. It is clear to me that those who have
traditionally lived on the land — the native people, indigenous to the
property — are the most appropriate stewards.

Third, we consider the reason for the slashing and burning: There
are millions of people who need to farm this land simply to grow crops, or
to earn a living in some other way from the land in order to survive. The

212

global community must realize that these people need to be preserved and protected and cannot be ignored or wiped out, as has happened so often before on Earth. They need to be taught sustainable ways to maintain the land and to improve their communities.

I've been given this task, and I've been working on a nonprofit foundation to carry it out, which I will discuss in the next chapter. Sometimes life does not occur according to our plan, and it's taken longer for me to bring it together, but now it's happening. However, I believe that ETs contact many of us, because there are already many organizations out there who are making things like this happen. We are a global community.

For your information, on the following page is a short list of organizations that are already doing things to improve the condition of the rainforests and to preserve the life-styles of those living there.

Some things are worth repeating — if we want to join the galactic neighborhood, we have to clean up our own backyard. We have a serious problem on Earth, and we don't have time to waste. The baton has been given to us — the people of our planet. A change is happening all over the world and it is good, but we need to keep working.

We do matter, and one person can make a difference, but it takes a great number of us to make a permanent change. Remember, if you can't contribute money, you can always reduce your carbon footprint by reducing, recycling and reusing.

I believe we humans are geared up for contact on a level that no government will be able to deny. This contact will be so undeniable that nothing will ever be the same again, but I believe we have to do our part in showing "them" that we belong in the galactic community.

## Organizations that are making a difference

Rainforest Alliance
> 665 Broadway, Suite 500, New York, NY 10012
>
> 888-My-Earth;   http://www.rainforest-alliance.org/

Amazon Conservation Team (ACT)
> 4211 N. Fairfax Dr., Arlington, VA 22203
>
> 703-522-4684;   http://amazonteam.org/

Seacology
> 1623 Solano Ave., Berkeley, CA 94707
>
> 510-559-3505; Fax: 510-559-3506
>
> http://seacology.org/     Email: islands@seacology.org

Tropical Rainforest Coalition (TRC)
> 21730 Stevens Creek Blvd., Suite 102
>
> Cupertino, CA 95014     http://rainforest.org/

Nature Conservancy (NC)
> 4245 North Fairfax Drive, Suite 100,
>
> Arlington, VA 22203-1606
>
> (703) 841-5300;   http://www.nature.org/

CHAPTER TWENTY-EIGHT

# Your Earth

In this day and time most citizens of the globe who have the capacity to help want to do something to better the planet. Most people are concerned about the sea, trees, air and their own drinking water. There is no doubt that we have all the resources necessary to overcome all of Earth's woes, but how?

We must realize that some of the most complicated environmental problems can be resolved in simple ways. For example, the new president of Ecuador, Rafael Correa, announced that his government would keep the oil in the ground under the most precious and extensive Amazonian jungles on Earth. Such solutions to other problems could be possible with matching contributions from the international community, conservation groups, private donors, and investors. Correa has faced enormous resistance from just about everybody, except environmentalists, indigenous Indians and poor people, to start drilling oil on a one-million-hectare tract in Yasuni National Park, under which sits at least 300 million barrels of heavy crude oil, worth over $30 billion at today's prices. He has also taken the oil profits away from the companies and returned the profits to his country.

Did you know that it would cost less then $10.00 per adult American to save some of the most precious tracts of real estate on the globe? If we spread the cost around the globe, it could cost a few pennies per capita. The money is there. Where should we apply it?

Your Earth is a true global hands-on organization dedicated to saving the planet's rainforests. Advanced off-planet cultures know that the we must come to grips with ourselves before they would even consider allowing us "open access" to outer space. Your Earth involves people, businesses and governments on a global basis. With greater involvement, poachers will hesitate to destroy any land.

Your Earth's mission is to:

• Purchase as much rainforest and equatorial land as possible.

• Attract the most brilliant minds of the globe

• Enlist the cooperation of the inhabitants of threatened lands in order to preserve them

• Provide education for sustainable agriculture, housing, and subsidies for preserving forests

• Eliminate limits and barriers to preserving the planet

• Enable the human race to join the galactic community

• Include every human who wants to be involved in any way
With current technology, it could take many years to restore large tracts of rainforest lands. With the hidden technologies that exist, it could take as little as a 20th of the time.

In order to use these hidden technologies, an avenue must be created for a full disclosure of hidden information to take place. This can be done by assuring amnesty for anyone who reveals suppressed information about the present and past role, and activities, of ETs on Earth. With amnesty, knowledge of ET life and all the wondrous hidden technologies that could change the environmental and political face of the Earth as we know it, could be safely revealed by the     groups and agencies who possess that information.

One must remember the various levels I am discussing, and for simplicity's sake, I'll break it down into three levels.

1. The present federal government that we deal with on a day-to-day basis. Many feel that our government is hiding the truth from us, and that it lies by telling us that UFOs, ETs and highly beneficial technologies do not exist. This level of government doesn't have a clue about the truth.

2. The second level is the "back-engineering boys." These are the ones with the retrieved, crashed discs and a few captured aliens who have survived. They have reverse-engineered technologies

216

from these events. They know but cannot talk.

3. The third level is the "The BBB – the Black Budget Boys." Here you have the heart of the matter. They are the ones in the know, the top of the heap. They have all the technology, and in a lot of cases they are in league with various groups of intelligent off-planet beings. For the most part, the first two levels haven't a clue that the BBB exist. What I am about to say will be hard to imagine. There is a growing majority within these groups that want the truth to be told and to see technologies brought out, so long as secrets sensitive to the security of the USA and the free world are not revealed. Yes, there are first-rate people in these groups, and they are trapped. I have been advised that they need an avenue to release this information: amnesty.

What the nonhuman intelligent beings, along with humans in black-op agencies, want to see in place first is an all-hands-on global effort. An avenue of amnesty would be created during this time to protect them from being charged and prosecuted for crimes against humanity, and to protect their secrets. Crimes against humanity? Some of you may be asking, "Then why should we forgive them?" It comes down to a matter of importance of where we should put our energies: prosecuting people, or saving the planet? I choose the latter. We can't change what's been done, and amnesty would pave the way for those who choose to come forward with the truth. Complete forgiveness is necessary, not only for spiritual reasons, but for practical ones as well.

Your Earth clearly intends to help save the planet's rainforests and get an amnesty bill passed. One of our methods is to form a PAC — political action committee — a private group, regardless of size, organized to elect or defeat government officials or to promote legislation. Legally, what constitutes a PAC for purposes of regulation is a matter of state and federal law. Under the Federal Election Campaign Act, an organization becomes a "political committee" by receiving contributions or making expenditures in excess of $1,000 for the purpose of influencing a federal election.

If there is one overall issue that involves all of us, it's the health of our Earth. If there is one group of people on the planet who has put the Earth first and viewed her in a "bigger picture," it's the abductees, contactees, and those who know there are other existences that need to be integrated into our present reality. Twenty to forty years ago, we did not know how many of us existed, as we were isolated and afraid to talk to anyone. Many of us were told we were crazy. Times have changed, and with thousands of us joining together, our voice will become powerful, especially if we join with those already seeking to save the planet.

A PAC allows us to begin to have some power and to have our voices heard within our own government. A PAC gives us a legal vehicle to organize many people with the same goals in mind — saving the lungs of the planet and establishing amnesty in order to reveal the truth so that new technologies can help the Earth quickly heal.

Please write me a short paragraph at jimsparks888@yahoo.com and let me know how you feel led to get involved.

Visit us on-line at http://www.yourearthfoundation.org, or at Jim-Sparks.com

We at Your Earth are grateful to you.

# Supporting Comments

I have had many close friends along the way in the last 18 years, and I have lost a few close ones who passed on — my friend Don Watkins and Dr. John E. Mack. I decided to do something different and ask a few friends to write some paragraphs on what they learned regarding the phenomena. I figured it would be a good opportunity to publish what others have learned. I was clear when I offered this chance to these people and said, "Please write what you learned and not about me." So guess what a few wrote about anyway? Please enjoy the following....

### DAVED E. RUBIEN

Many of you who read this book will question if what Jim Sparks relates to us here is the truth. Some may think that he wrote this book just to make money. Others may think that Jim dreamed it all and just believes they were real experiences. I have known Jim now for over 15 years. I have found him to be a very honest, unselfish and caring individual. From what I understand, those who have written books on the subject of UFOs or ETs have not made very much money.

So why did Jim write this book? I can tell you from what I experienced with him — he has been driven to get the information out to the world. I can recall while he was writing that he would start early in the day and many times would go right through the night. I am not going to try to convince anyone to believe what Jim has to say, but I will tell you about some experiences about the investigation of UFOs and ETs.

I never paid much attention to UFO reports until 1954, two years after graduating from college, when I read an article about a UFO sighting in my local paper. It stated that two law enforcement officers in Connecticut had seen a silver disk very clearly in the sky during their patrol. Back then, if you had the nerve to say that you had experienced anything like this, you would be laughed at. The fact that these individuals were police officers, and were willing to go through that embarrassment caught my attention. About six months later, I read an article in the paper about a priest reporting that he had a relatively close sighting of a UFO. Again, I thought, "Why would a priest put himself in that position?"

That started me on an experience of over 50 years of investigating UFOs and ETs. The majority of the sightings investigated by me were explainable. Some were false reports, and about 15% were actual unexplainable sightings of a UFO. In 1976, I started the Rhode Island Chapter of MUFON (Mutual UFO Network), which is the largest organization in the world with chapters in almost all countries whose mission is the scientific study of unidentified flying objects. We had many people who came to us with their UFO experiences. Some claimed to have memories of being detained by ETs. These experiences caused many of these individuals to have serious problems, such as having to keep their lights on all night because they were too scared to go to sleep. Others could not go to sleep or leave home. Still others became very scared of spiders or other insects after the experience.

Many of these people had heard that under hypnosis more could be learned about their experiences. I decided to take the necessary courses to become a certified hypnotist. During hypnosis sessions, I found that many people were taken from their bed and floated right through the wall to a ship. If it was above the ground, they would be put in a blue beam of light that lifted them up into the ship. Many remembered being put on a table and the procedures that followed. Some described the interior of the ship, and there were many other descriptions of men and women seeing their baby or child. There is so much more, much of which you already found in this book.

Some people believe that hypnosis may bring out things that are untrue. After owning and operating a large and very difficult business for many years, I cannot believe most things unless they can be proven to me. When three or more people who do not know each other describe, awake or under hypnosis, the same ETs or experiences to me, I must consider that they are telling the truth. This is how I learned about many of the ETs, which Jim talks about.

The following are two examples of some other individuals' experiences that, based on my years of research, I am confident are truthful. One individual, with whom I have worked for many years, lives in New Hampshire. One of his many experiences was seeing a reflection of an ET in the glass sliding doors to his porch. The individual was standing inside his house by the stairway. By the description I would say the individual was full grown and what we would call a hybrid.

There have been many healings done by some ETs — one experience comes from a woman whom I have known for many years and admire very much, who had ovarian cancer and was preparing for surgery. She remembered being taken from her bed and awoke on a table that had been indented for her form. She then witnessed the ETs doing corrective surgery on her. She even remembers the instruments that were used.

I have found there are benign ETs and those that are not so benign, just as there are good and bad in all people. It appears to me that there are many more benign ones.

Based on what I have learned over the last 50 years, Jim has experienced exactly what he describes in this book. He consciously remembers more about the ET experiences then any other person I have found. My good friend John Mack said the same.

✛ ✛ ✛

### LYLE J. MICHEL

The government and the press with single-mindedness use one basic approach to confuse people regarding the presence of beings from other planets coming to Earth: They ignore the courtroom evidence.

Evidence, according to a legal dictionary is, … "all the means by which any alleged matter of fact, the truth of which is submitted to investigation at judicial trial, is established or disapproved. Evidence includes the testimony of witnesses, introduction of records, documents, exhibits or any other relevant matter offered for the purpose of inducing the… [fact finder's] belief in the party's contention." In other words eyewitness testimony and physical evidence related to the incident being studied is admissible as proof that the incident did occur in the manner described.

It is important to understand that the position taken by the government and the press has nothing to do with the reality of the ET phenomena. In other words, they know that beings from other planets are routinely visiting Earth and that some species walk among us. Therefore, why does the press and the government work so hard to keep people confused about beings from other planets coming to Earth?

The government keeps people confused because they feel that the people of the world could not or would not be able to deal with the truth, as happened with the 1938 radio broadcast of "The War of the Worlds," when many people panicked and chaos resulted. In this case any risk is an unnecessary risk. It is better to keep people confused.

On the ET issue the position of the press is in part to support the government. The press realizes that if they consistently presented only truths to the people of Earth, the result would be massive demonstrations against the institutions which we require for leadership. Note that I said in part they support the government. They also know that our system of government would not be able to survive without the people knowing the truth on all important issues. Therefore, their method of handling virtually all controversial issues is to tell the people the truth and then to present alternative opinions, regardless of how untruthful or silly these alternative opinions happen to be. This method is used extensively by the press to support the government, as well as to educate the public regarding the truth on all issues of importance to the people of the Earth. There are few exceptions to this practice by the press.

To illustrate this point, let's consider the issue of an ET abductee. A person abducted by the ETs may have near-total recall of their experiences. Jim Sparks can describe in great detail the appearance of the craft and the beings who abducted him. He can also reflect with authority his experiences with them. There is no doubt that Jim Sparks has detailed knowledge of his experiences with beings from other planets. In my opinion he has no motivation to be less than truthful. His first-hand accounts are admissible in a court of law, should our government require his testimony. All you have to do is look at his presentation from the point of view of being in a courtroom with the reader as a member of the jury evaluating his case. By examining the ET phenomena in this manner, you will begin the process of separating fact from fiction as presented by our government and the press.

I've been a student of ET phenomena since 1991. The first seven years of information came completely from television and an occasional newspaper article. Many of the programs on the Discovery, A & E, History and Sci Fi Channels contain significant truths about our alien visitors. These programs also frequently contain disinformation in order to give others a reason to disregard the fact that beings are coming to Earth from other planets. Presenting information in this manner can help those who cannot deal with the truth adjust slowly to the fact that alien visitors are coming to Earth. In other words, those who are afraid of the truth are given an opportunity to stay in denial of this truth until they are ready to adjust to the facts in the case.

There you have it, in an abbreviated form. The cornerstone of the government position is to deny the truth and exercise the strategies of decoy, destruction and trash. Never admit to the truth! Whenever possible, introduce additional information that will confuse anyone interested in the phenomena. Make things up. For example, simply say the event didn't happen. The witness could not have been with the ETs, he was at the movies. The witness was visiting relatives. The witness is delusional. It doesn't matter that none of these statements is true. People who are not experienced with how they are being manipulated will be so confused about the other alternatives to the courtroom evidence supplied by the witness that they will simply go on about their daily activities as if the story they were told were not true. Remember the key to success for the government is to ignore courtroom-type evidence.

Clearly, beings from other planets are coming to Earth. Some are here to visit — in other words they are tourists. Some are here as scientists — to study our civilization. Some are here to help us. They work among us to help us invent things that they know we will find useful. They are helping us to absorb technology at a pace that is comfortable for our civilization. They are helping us to become a sustainable civilization. They want us to one day join their galactic federation.

Several years ago I had the privilege of spending a year taking "A Course In Miracles" from a minister of the Unity Church. I learned a number of important lessons in this course, but one of the most important was that there are universal truths. The mere fact that we do not know or understand something does not change the facts in the case. Beings similar to us are coming to Earth and are among us. Your decision to believe that this statement is not true will not change the fact that they are here and have been for a very long time.

✛ ✛ ✛

## NANCY SMOOT

It is doubtful that anything I could say or write would change someone else's mind about the existence of ET life; it would take a personal experience to do that. Personal experience is a great eradicator of doubt. Jim Sparks and I, along with countless others, have had personal experiences that have banished whatever doubt our belief systems may have held with regard to the possibility of non-human intelligent life. Whether the inhabitants dwell in other realms, dimensions, times, or planets, the home base of these beings is not so much what's in question; it's their very existence that seems to be the topic of debate. When sightings, visions, abductions, inexplicable malfunctions or residual effects, and numerous other paranormal activities have become part of one's personal experience, then one's belief system is changed, whether one desires such change or not. Your inability to accept my statements of what has happened to me will not change my conviction of their authenticity. Subsequent information that crosses my path may color my interpretation of an event's meaning, but it will not cause me to deny that it took place. Personal experience causes one's beliefs to evolve into one's knowledge.

At this time in my life, I personally acknowledge that there is a power greater than human power. How this power is manifested in human experience varies from person to person, and by what name this power is known also may vary from person to person. Events labeled "synchronicities" (chance occurrences that seem to have significant meaning) by one person may be called "miracles" by another. Someone else may think of it as Satanic activity. Much of our belief is based on perspective. And no two people have the exact same perspective of any event, due to the fact that no two people have ever had or will ever have the same set of experiences. Also, experience is colored by an individual's attitude, and attitudes are developed by experience.

When I was nine, I had a prolonged sighting of a silver space-ship-looking craft that rotated in small circles as it rotated in larger circles. This took place at dusk near Scottsdale, Arizona, in February of 1963. With three other teenagers I observed this low-flying craft, about a third of a mile away, for about ten minutes, and then it eventually flew behind a nearby mountain. I cannot state definitively that it was from another planet, but I cannot claim to know who was piloting it or who built it, either. It didn't look like any craft known to me at that time or at any time since then.

My second sighting of a craft of unknown origin occurred in February, 2001, in Las Vegas, Nevada. For about three to five minutes I observed an enormous black triangular-shaped "ship" pass through the dark night sky, drifting silently and slowly only about two hundred feet above me, from the northwest to the southeast. Perhaps this was a new style of blimp. I just don't know what it was, but there were lights all across its leading edge, and it seemed very much controlled by some intelligence. It appeared large enough to carry thousands of people. At the very least, it filled me with wonder.

Jim Sparks has had more odd experiences than anyone I've ever known. Whether these events are in fact "real" or not is debatable; they certainly seem real to him, and I am in no position to argue with him. The fact is that Jim's outlook on life is also very different from anyone else's that I've come across in my lifetime. The events he's described have led him to a most unusual understanding of motivations and intentions of a multitude of people, both human and non-human. They have left him with a philosophy that is so profound, in my opinion, that I am inclined to

225

believe what Jim tells me, even though it sounds impossible. I'll give you an example of what I mean.

One evening Jim and I and two other people had been to a show in Las Vegas. Afterwards, Jim and I took our leave from the other couple and went to a small café where we purchased some shrimp cocktails. There were perhaps fifteen or twenty other people in this café, and Jim and I were deeply engrossed in conversation about his paranormal experiences and their residual effects on him, which is a topic that fascinates me. From what began as typical "white noise," the murmuring of the crowd, there emerged a single raucous voice from a nondescript woman who was approaching the buffet line behind our table. This intrusion escalated into more and more of a "scene" as her voice grew louder. I was not mindful of the content of her utterances, since Jim's comments merited my full attention.

I now became annoyed when this patron's behavior interrupted my concentration. Jim's words captivated me, but at last I felt compelled to turn around and see what the ruckus was all about. The woman appeared to be trembling as if she didn't have full control of her body. At that very moment, she focused her eyes on me and made a disturbingly stunning comment which was directly related to the esoteric statement that Jim had just made privately to me. This woman, a stranger, was about twelve to fifteen feet away from us and could not possibly have overheard our conversation.

What was even more bizarre was the fact that everyone else in the room became motionless, as if they were frozen in time. They weren't staring at us or paying attention to Jim, me or this woman. They just stopped in mid-stream from whatever activity they were doing at the time, as if they were caught in a freeze-frame on a video. A startling silence suddenly overtook this café for several seconds as this woman's eyes met mine. When I turned around to Jim to ask, "What was that?" the room and the woman resumed normal activity with the typical sounds of a café. No one else seemed aware of what had taken place, not even the woman who had made the statement.

Jim's response to my question was, "If you're going to hang around with me, you'd better get used to things like this. They happen to me all the time."

In my mind, if this unbelievable experience truly is typical of what Jim often has to deal with, then I think he's handling his "phenomenon" very well. Jim is a gifted individual whose abilities have raised my consciousness by expanding my concept of reality and by opening my mind to seriously consider the existence of other dimensions and those who inhabit them.

✛ ✛ ✛

### ANITA L. ALBRIGHT

Pandora's Box cracked wide open for me, just like it is has for so many others, one crisp October night in 1994, with my first initial sighting of a UFO.

I watched in awe as a football-field sized black triangular craft, hung eerily directly over me, just about treetop level for several minutes, before it silently and quite slowly, slipped away over the horizon.

Shortly thereafter, my younger sister insisted that I attend a MUFON meeting with her. She nearly had to drag me. Why would anyone (in their right mind) want to get tangled up with the seeming insanity that has always been associated with these phenomena.

I was absolutely convinced it was going to be a certain parade of freaks, geeks and whackos. But I was wrong, very wrong. With that first meeting, I was dumb struck. These were not freaks and geeks, but highly intelligent, often degreed, incredible (credible) people. Many of whom, who with gentle patience, supported me through the pain and agony that one must endure with the realization that you have been an abducted your entire life.

After witnessing that first craft, my world was turned literally upside-down, going from the mundane to the maniacal. Poltergeist and ghost-like activity, black helicopters over my home and work, MIB entering my home on two occasions (doing God only knows what), dozens upon dozens of more sightings, out-of-body experiences, more abductions, virtual reality dreams... all suddenly became common occurrences for me. I was now being led down a road that had always existed somewhere just out of my periphery, that I somehow missed my whole life.

I thought my life could not become anymore bizarre, until I met Jim. It was at the 2000 Ozark UFO Conference in beautiful Eureka Springs, Arkansas where he held a large audience absolutely spell-bound with the most remarkable accounting of alien abduction any of us had ever heard.

That same night, at the Lone Star Bar (a converted hotel room that is opened to the speakers and attendees of the conference) I hobbled along through the crowd on crutches, recovering from a recent knee surgery. Jim seeing me struggle to pour a drink offered his signature gentlemanly assistance. Almost immediately we recognized a mysterious, indefinable connection to one another.

A few days after returning home from the conference, I awoke from another virtual reality dream:

I was standing on a ship, as an adult, watching myself as an infant, maybe three months old, being laid, only inches apart, next to another infant, on a large, flat stainless-steel-like protrusion from the floor. Interestingly, I was experiencing both the adult and infant perspective simultaneously. My infant self turned and locked eyes with the other infant, whom I instantly knew was Jim.

Then there was also another incident, uncovered from hypnosis: I'm six years old, laying in a hospital ward, just having had my tonsils out, when three grays floated through the large windows to take myself and two other boys from the ward, onto a ship.

On board, there was this little, scrawny, sickly looking (very much human) kid in blue jean cut-offs, no shirt, deeply tanned, dark-haired with a crew-cut and barefoot, which was odd considering it was the middle of October.

We were given a red rubber ball and all told to play with it together. Minutes later someone trotted out two little hybrids, a boy and a girl, who appeared to be about our age. They weren't too strange looking, blonde, thin hair, fairly human faces with not too large, almond-shaped eyes, dressed in some sort of plain, long-sleeved smock.

Immediately we all realized that these hybrids appeared to be quite socially inept and really, really needed some playmates. They stood emotionless, stiff necked with their arms held limp at their sides, with their tiny little feet frozen in place.

After the initial shock and introductions, we were given instructions to include them in the game.

We all tried bouncing the ball to them time after time, but with arms still limp, they failed to make any attempt at catching it. Invariably the ball would end up smacking them in the stomach, the face, where ever. Their only reaction would be to turn slightly in unison, as if on cue, stiff-necked, to glance at one another, still blank-faced and clueless. (I am not exaggerating when I tell you it was just exactly like the way the Cone-heads would react and move on Saturday Night Live).

The four of us human kids, finding the whole thing absolutely ridiculous, began to roll with laughter, the laugh till it hurts kind. And to top it all off, our voices echoed and bounced through the ship, inciting further out-of-control hysteria.

This was, after all, something you could never, ever get away with on the school playground, deliberately hitting someone with a ball and then daring to laugh about it!

The thing about this incident was that I knew the two boys from the hospital ward, but who was the other kid dressed in shorts?

Jim, I believe, answered that question one day when he began to recount the details of his childhood to me. He grew up in Florida where the weather in October would still warrant the cut-offs. A childhood illness had left him extraordinarily thin. He and his brother spent every spare minute at the beach or exploring the everglades, barefoot, shirtless and in their old cut-offs, keeping year round, deep tans. Their parents also always insisted in shaving their dark hair.

I was blown away.

Later in my relationship with Jim, he would get sometimes cryptic, sometimes intrusive, messages from his otherworldly friends to give me. These messages contained private and intimate things about me that they shared with him. Things that living hundreds of miles apart he could not have known on his own. And keep in mind, that these messages were coming from the same entities that he claims, who are the walking, talking, seemingly human, flesh and blood type, who just suddenly appear from out of no where, to join him, quite unexpectedly in open public places.

Jim's very entertaining descriptions of how these guys will show up wearing outrageous, mismatched outfits from various different time periods, makes one think about the times we have all seen really odd folk, and have asked ourselves, "Just what planet did they come from?" Think about it, it's kind of weird that these visitors can travel space and time, dimensions or whatever, however it is that they get here, and yet they can't even figure out how to put together a simple ensemble.

These are only a few of the countless, strange and bizarre stories that I have been through with him. Jim is and always will be a sincere mystery to me. He gives me every reason to reconsider any and all of my belief systems (just when I thought there was nothing left to shatter).

"Jim's World" is rich with complexity and intrigue, the veritable rabbit's hole. And I will certainly fall short when trying to describe the depth of honesty I sense and know in him and his absolute humble, rare, self-effacing demeanor.

Jim has brought his story forward at great personal loss and risk. And let me also say, even if he won't, that he continues to be a victim of harassment. Sources, forces, who knows who they are, make his life miserable at every turn. He endures this in relative silence, sharing with only a few intimate friends.

In closing, for those of us who have also endured the physical and emotional pain of abduction, I think Jim, epitomizes something we all hope to find within ourselves. a truly gritty, gutsy determination to overcome and survive through it all.

His story also gives us one other thing... a strange, yet comforting, guilty solace, knowing that someone else has suffered so much more.

✛ ✛ ✛

## DONALD E. WARE

After Jim Sparks drew a record crowd for his lecture, "The Star People," at the Unlimited Horizon's meeting in Navarre, Florida on January 13, 2002, Jim spoke to me personally about one of his most profound alien encounters. He was a bit nervous about talking about it publicly, so he waited until we were on the way home in the car before he related it to me. I feel this encounter is important information for truth-seekers. It is a case of aliens among us.

Jim said that he had found that his many years of alien encounters had enhanced his psychic awareness. Stronger telepathic ability, both in words and visions, seems to be a residual effect of such encounters. He can also feel the energies surrounding the aliens. The energies of the taller supervisor types were sometimes overpowering, much stronger than the energies projected by the "worker beans."

When Sparks was working as a waiter in Florida, he felt a strange compulsion to apply for a similar job at a very ritzy Country Club, and so he did. A year later he was hired and trained. He worked in a tuxedo and served many very wealthy people. Some of the events he worked were in private mansions with hundreds of guests. The profound event occurred at a 1998 fund-raising event at the Country Club for a children's hospital, with 800 attending.

While waiting at the bar counter to have an order filled, Jim got a psychic impression of a VIP arriving with several accompanying security guards. As the group came into the building, Jim could feel the familiar energy of a supervisor-type alien getting stronger. He heard a strong telepathic message to support the children's hospital, and he was certain others received the same message. The man entered the room rapidly, followed by his security team. He looked like a supervisor-type alien; about 5' tall, large cranium, oval black eyes, thin chin and light skin. People turned to watch him. Most people thought it was a human in a mask, but some seemed to recognize his energy and sought his blessing as he

231

passed. His body was lean and graceful, and he walked like the aliens Jim had seen on the ships. He walked straight to Jim and touched him on the shoulder, whereupon Jim was thanked telepathically for being a teacher about humans and their emotions. He told me that he felt that this was a reward for his participating in their encounter programs. He quit his job that night, knowing that setting up this encounter with a powerful alien in our society is why he had felt compelled to work there.

This seems to be one case of an alien choosing the right time and place to mingle with humans in our third-density society. I wonder how often this mingling of species occurs.

# Symbol Analysis

Linda Moulton Howe sent my alien symbol conversions to Mario Pazzaglini, Ph.D., who earned his Master of Science degree in Clinical Psychology from George Washington University in Washington, D.C. Simultaneously, he worked in a double program on his doctoral degree in Sensory Neural Physiology and Abnormal Psychology from the University of Delaware in Newark. Dr. Pazzaglini has studied many symbols provided by people in the human abduction syndrome since the 1980s, including some from Betty Andreasson Luca. He agreed to study my version of the alleged non-human symbols and numbers and to provide his professional assessment, which is reported here in full.

## Assessment of Alleged Non-Human symbols and Numbers Described in Jim Sparks's Story

by Mario Pazzaglini, Ph.D.,
Clinical Psychology and Sensory Neurophysiology

This sample of alien writing is interesting in that it lends itself to layers of analyses. Superficially, it appears to be rudimentary and perhaps purely human-generated. But, the Jim Sparks symbols also present unexpected facets.

In form, this script falls between two general classes of alien writing. The classes referred to are of three types generated by a compilation and study of alien script, which I have collected over fifteen years. These classes are:

1. Geometric forms — circles, squares, angles, triangles.
2. Dot and line forms — where symbols are made of various combinations of dots and lines.
3. Cursive — where the symbols look like Gregg shorthand

Most alien writing from abductees seems to fall in the latter group and now represents the largest of the three groups of writing. The

233

Sparks sample looks like an intermediary between classes 2 and 3 above. Its later iteration as combinations of symbols looks in general like group 3, usually seen in abductee cases. Oddly, it is in this second iteration that dots become combined with cursive forms to produce the final script.

Combining the images from Mr. Sparks's narrative, there are really four levels of variants of this script.

   a) First, there is the script which appears on a flat two-dimensional surface of paper.

   b) Secondly, that two-dimensional form is understood as three-dimensional because Mr. Sparks says that the symbol for A, which looks like a simple horizontal stroke is actually three superimposed strokes of repeated motion on the same line.

   c) Thirdly, the simple alphabetic elements are combined into shorthand condensed forms.

   d) And fourth, the entire text of a script is condensed into one complex symbol with multiple layers of motion and meaning.

This is clearly a very complex system apparently relating somehow to the native alien script as used by the aliens themselves and secondly to a system that would be teachable to humans. Mr. Sparks's symbols may not be the actual and purely alien script. He suggests himself that it is a "common ground for communication between them and us."

Several observations can be made in stages.

## Stage 1 - First Impressions

   a) This is an alphabetic script where one symbol equals one sound, just like our alphabet.

   b) The aliens have presented to Jim Sparks equivalents to human sounds and alphabet which is an odd fact for a supposedly alien source. Even different Earth cultures with the same voice box produce different phonemes. Either this is made up or the aliens are tailoring a system to us humans.

   c) Some alien letters resemble their English alphabetic equivalents. For example:

B is   ʒ   C is   ∪   S is   ∪  one-half of our S.

At this level of analysis, the possibility that this is actually an "alien" script is suspect.

d) There are "follows" which are also found in Earth-based artificially made-up scripts. As the name implies, symbols in these made-up scripts tend to follow one another.

For example:

c ‿ follows d ⌣ while e ⌐ follows f ∟

The fact that there are follows in the Jim Sparks's symbols raises additional questions about its alleged alien source. Is this made-up by a human? Or alien? Or for a human-alien psyche interface of some type? Does the human mind add a note of rigidity to the process of forming an alphabet for communication? Why couldn't the aliens come up with clearer and more distinguishable symbols? Are those particular symbols necessary somehow to provide the aliens with the forms they need to perform subsequent operations with human minds?

Jim Sparks's symbol for the letter R actually does resemble the ancient Greek letter rho; S looks like a type of Greek S or C [sigma]; B is mildly like a Greek beta. Are these accidents? In other alleged alien symbol communications I have studied, there are resemblances to early and classic Greek. So, in this first stage of impressions, one would suspect that this is a humanly produced (consciously or unconsciously) symbol system. It seems to share too many characteristics of pre-existing alphabets and doesn't look well-formed as a coherent system of well-defined alphabetic symbols.

## Stage 2 - Analyses of Symbol Shorthand

In its more complex form, the Sparks's script eliminates many of the above criticisms, and the first impressions become less clear in the third and fourth iterations of the symbols when they are combined into a shorthand script.

Those combined symbols of condensed cursive-style script look very much like examples of script from other abductees. This in and of itself does not make them alien, but it is interesting that widely divergent sources, unaware of what other abductees have described, do write similar looking script, such as Betty Andreasson Luca.

These complex forms are not 1:1 letter-to-sound symbols. Their placement on the page is not linear, but produces a whole gestalt of meaning as described in the text. Perhaps the most provocative and unique aspect of Sparks's description is the requirement for 3-dimensional projection in order for the script to be fully understood. Three-dimensional conceptualizing is rarely mentioned as a characteristic, of other purported alien scripts.

Historically some so-called magical scripts, or sigils, also are said to require a three-dimensional conceptualizing. In a conversation with an assistant to Aleister Crowley, who was a member of the order of the Golden Dawn and leader of the O.T.O. Ordo Temperalis Orientalis (Order of the Eastern Temple) in the early to middle 20th Century, it was mentioned that some portions of the Enochian chessboards used in the Enochian system of magic were to be seen in three dimensions. Aleister Crowley followed directions of Queen Elizabeth I's court astrologer, John Dee, who said he received the Enochian system from a luminous being. Crowley and Dee understood that three dimensions were necessary in order to visualize properly the symbols needed to contact other worldly entities.

There are other cases in which "aliens" have told their abductee-contactee students that the alien script is multileveled. In one of the script samples, it was said that the script was to be "read" by passing a finger over it and that in this way "thought will be produced" equivalent to reading the script. Further, these particular entities said that different levels of meaning could be elicited upon repeated finger passes over the same script.

While we cannot definitely say that the Sparks script is alien, we can say that it does not follow the common characteristics of hoaxed or made-up scripts. It describes a complex system which could form a communication link between totally dissimilar minds — a link between ourselves and the Other, human and alien. But nothing is clear in this elusive phenomenon.

# Stage 3 - Analysis of Numbers

This is an odd number system for an advanced culture. First, there is no zero, which is an essential feature of a computational system. The Romans had a terrible time with their system for this reason. The Arabs and Mayans both had the concept of zero and were able to go quite far with computations. Therefore, six is an odd number to use as a base. It would be better to use 10, or 2 even as in a 0-and-1 binary system; or even 60 as the Babylonians had. Those systems again are more convenient for computations. The Earth-based systems that use 12 or 6 x 2 as in the foot and inch are very complex to work with. Why would aliens use such an odd system? Numbers are numbers. Of course, it's clear we don't understand what the aliens are up to and don't know how they "think." It's possible that their 6-based number system could relate to the six sides of a 3-dimensional cube with zero at the center.[1]

With six "numbers" or "states," there are $6^6$ (6x6x6x6x6x6) or 46,656 possible "states" using the cube mode if each number can be used more than once, or 6! (6x5x4x3x2x1), or 720, states if each number is used only once. 720 is 2 x 360, as in degrees in a circle.

Stan Tenen of the Meru Foundation in Sharon, Massachusetts, has produced a three-dimensional form that rotates in space. Tenen said that its various shadows cast on a two-dimensional surface form the letters of the Hebrew alphabet.

The Meru Project booklet states: "Stan Tenen tracked the spiral of a tube torus out of the middle and took out the shape. He removed the minimum amount of matter to delineate the tube torus and placed it inside a three-dimensional tetrahedron. He found that by shining a light through it so that the shadow of that shape came out onto a two-dimensional surface,

---

1. Editor's Note. A zero is only essential for a two-dimensional number system. Consider a three-dimensional dicelike system where zero is all "snake-eyes" and every number is a unique permutation of dice faces, with one dice per numeric position. Lack of a zero does not constrain computation with an abacus, for example.

he could generate all the letters of the Hebrew alphabet, exactly as they are written and in order.

"He also found that by changing the shape to a different position, he could project all the Greek letters. Then by changing the position again, he could configure all the Arabic letters. He did this simply by moving this particular shape to different positions inside a three-dimensional tetrahedron. There are actually 27 primary symmetrical positions inside a tetrahedron.'

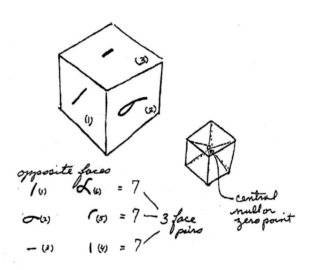

•FIG. 34: A BASE-6 NUMBER SYSTEM WITH CENTRAL ZERO

# Alien Alphabet

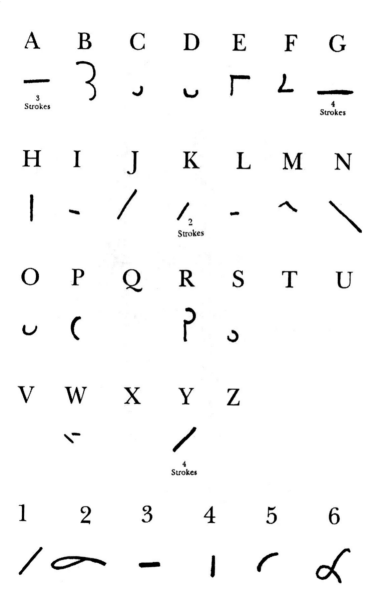

•FIG. 35: THE COMPLETE ALIEN ALPHABET I WAS TAUGHT

# Final and Future Thoughts

by the Publisher

"It appears ever more likely that we exist in a multidimensional cosmos or multiverse.... The Cosmos... far from being an empty place of dead matter and energy, appears to be filled with beings, creatures, spirits, intelligences, gods... that have through the millennia been intimately involved with human existence."

—Dr. John E. Mack

One of the final acts in Dr. John E. Mack's courageous and memorable career was to write a sound endorsement of Jim Sparks's story, as related in this book. Dr. Mack, Professor of Psychology at the Harvard Medical School, was well-known and deeply respected by those who knew him. Dr. Mack saw Jim's story as key to the unfoldment of the true story behind the on-going alien presence on Earth.

Jim Sparks's remarkable conscious-memory recall of his interactions with apparently alien and future-human visitors is sobering. The message is clear: our dear blue-and-white jewel of a planet is dying because of our own mismanagement. While our problems are clear enough, the solutions are not.

Why was Jim taught this odd alien alphabet, with its three-dimensional aspects? Is there more to his story than meets the eye? Stanley Tenen discovered that the Hebrew alphabet can be created by shadows cast from a three-dimensional object rotated in a tetrahedron:

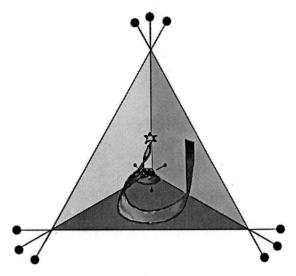

אבגדהוזחטיכלמנסעפצקרשת

•FIG. 36: TETRAHEDRAL PROJECTION OF THE HEBREW ALPHABET

Additional research has shown that the Greek and Arabic alphabets can similarly be generated by shadows. These discoveries might just open the door to a potentially great impact of Jim Sparks's story. Let me explain.

The dramatic emerging view of the truly ancient origins of civilization on Earth, as depicted in Ashayana Deane's Voyagers series, and Zechariah Sitchin's Earth Chronicles series, for example, make it very clear that off-planet visitors have probably been involved with this planet since life began here, and a great many civilizations preceded the earliest ones of which we have surviving records.

The first civilizations seem to have been planted here by alien visitors, and their development seems to have been carefully cultivated by alien overseers. The very alphabets of these civilizations are probably of alien origin.

The Cosmos seems to abound with benevolent galactic federations and great alliances of interstellar civilizations, while we Earthlings fight over dubious religious tenets, limited resources, and invisible political lines drawn across the soils of Earth in this remote backwater of the Milky Way. It seems that Earth will not be invited to participate in these great organizations so long as we remain warlike and disrespectful of the precious natural gifts of Mother Earth.

So how do we get from here to there? Imagine, if you will, finding that the alien alphabet given consciously to Jim Sparks could also be generated by shadows cast by a three-dimensional object rotated in a tetrahedron. This research is underway. If Jim's experiences are real, and there is little doubt that they are real in my mind, and the minds of Linda Moulton Howe, the late Dr. John Mack, and a host of other respected researchers and individuals who know Jim, then what can we conclude?

Firstly, we can conclude that the hidden three-dimensional structure of our two-dimensional languages may be subtle alien metaphors to help us realize that our three-dimensional perception of reality is just a projected shadow from the higher-dimensional reality in which the visitors reside. When our science understands that we live in a reduced-dimensional view of a higher-dimensional universe, many mysteries will resolve, from Bell's Experiment to the Unified Field Theory.

In Bell's Experiment, for example, a subatomic particle is split, and the two halves spin off in mirror-image curving paths. Occasionally, one half-piece will collide with yet another particle and ricochet off at a new angle. At that precise moment, someplace else, the other half-piece also ricochets off at the same new angle, despite having not hit anything discernible. Our science has relegated Bell's Experiment to the "Isn't that interesting?" category, whose implications have been largely ignored. But if every particle has higher-dimensional components, then so does the secondary collision, and the anomalous second ricochet can be understood as evidence that the particle is still unsplit in some unseen dimension. Imagine a flat surface with two worm holes, a worm in each hole. Poke one and the other moves — a mystery in two dimensions, but clear in three dimensions, when one sees the U-shaped tunnel containing just a single worm.

The second conclusion from the reality of Jim's experiences is to observe that we can demonstrate a common source of the major languages of this divided planet — an alien source. Hebrew and Arabic derive from a common alien source, as does Greek, and by implication, English. We can deduce then that we are all alien-derived, all siblings and cousins, and the proof is in the very languages we speak and write.

You may have wondered why an alien alphabet would have characters corresponding to A, B, and C? a, b, and c? Alef, bet, and gimel? Perhaps it is because the underlying multi-dimensional structure of these alphabets was given to various humans at various times, in various ways, by off-planet cultivators, as clues to our origins—clues that would make no sense prior to today's emerging global view of other cultures.

If this conclusion is true, and it may well be, then it inevitably follows that it will soon be time to drop our swords, erase our boundaries, share our Earthly wealth, rejuvenate our beloved water planet, and celebrate the oneness of the human species with those whom the Native Americans have always called the Star Nations — the Keepers of this Garden.

This, then, may indeed be just part of the ultimate significance of this remarkable book.

The Jim Sparks account is one of the richest and most credible documentations in all alien abduction history.

There are small changes that each of us can make in our daily lives to make a difference for the planet.

• Begin replacing regular light bulbs with compact fluorescent ones. You lower the energy used and save money.

• Make sure any new appliances, electronics, printers and FAX machines are designated as ENERGYSTAR.

• Since you can't replace everything, remember turning things off or unplugging what isn't being used saves energy.

• Walk or bike instead of driving a car.

• If you can't walk or bike, combine trips or share rides to reduce your time behind the wheel.

• Reduce your flying time with teleconferences or by combining trips. You can also go on the web to find out how to save your credits.

• Make meat, especially beef, a food for special occasions — save it for the weekend.

• Buy locally!

• Reduce, Reuse, Recycle!

Thanks for joining in this movement to heal our planet and join the galactic community.

—Jim Sparks and his publishers!

# "Talk to Jim"

### Individual Consultations for People with
### ET-Abduction/ Contact Experiences, or just Questions

Based on the overwhelming number of requests for Jim's feedback on people's personal abduction/ ET contact experiences, Jim now offers consultations via telephone, email or Skype chat, in the form of "Question and Answer" sessions.

These consultations are designed to assist individuals who lack a frame of reference in their life due to the bizarre nature of their experiences and have become deeply affected by contact with ETs. They desperately seek some understanding of the implications of this phenomenon to their own life.

Jim's own experiences and his almost total recall, have given him a vast understanding of the phenomena based on years of abductions and "training" sessions with his ET mentors. Therefore, many experiencers who harbor concerns and questions and have read The Keepers become reassured by information he can relay to them.

Some people feel overwhelmed by their own experiences or by memories that have started to emerge after reading about other people's ET contact experiences; others may be more interested in finding out about their own potential role in bringing about the required planetary changes in alignment with The Keepers' recommendations, and there are those who are just curious and seek real in-depth information from a one-on-one conversation.

Reach Jim by email at: TalkToJim@jim-sparks.com

Regular cost per telephone/email/Skype consultation: $100 (US) per hour after confirmation of payment via PayPal.

10% of the proceeds from Jim's consultations go directly towards the operating costs of Your Earth Foundation.

# Emotional Support Coaching

Coaching for Experiencers of ET-Contact and Interdimensional Phenomena with Dr. Gabriele Frohlich

Dr. Frohlich, M.D. is a transpersonal psychotherapist and coach with over 20 years experience. Her psychological work experience extends from mainstream couple- and individual- counseling issues and conflict mediation to ET abduction, interdimensional experiences, and other anomalous phenomena.

Her own experiences from early childhood onward led her on a journey of exploring these phenomena in an in-depth way, including some training in shamanic traditions.

Jim and Gabriele see their understanding of the implications of ET contact and interdimensional phenomena as complementary to each other's positions, in the way that experiences affect human beings on an individual level, but also in the way that their work impacts on planetary developments through human conduct and consciousness.

Gabriele's consultations emotionally integrate any potentially traumatizing aspects, and individual understanding of the meaning of ET contact/ interdimensional phenomena as individuals experience them on a personal level. Her work helps experiencers arrive at a position of self love and acceptance, regardless of the nature of their experiences, and helps them recognize their role in the greater scheme of things concerning their own life and the fate of humankind at this crucial point in human history.

Consultations are conducted internationally via phone or Skype after confirmation of payment via PayPal. Cost per consultation: USD $100 per hour.

The income generated from these consultations enables Gabriele to actively support "Your Earth Foundation."

For bookings please contact Gabriele at: gabyfrohlich@gmail.com

For more information on Gabriele's work please visit: http:// www.global-develop.com

# GRANITE PUBLISHING L.L.C.

HAS THESE IMPRINTS:

WILD FLOWER PRESS
SWAN • RAVEN & CO.
LITTLE GRANITE BOOKS

TO RECEIVE A CATALOG OF MORE OF OUR BOOKS—
EMAIL: INFO@GRANITEPUBLISHING.US
OR
PHONE: 828.894.8444
FAX: 828.894.8454

VISIT OUR WEB SITE AT
HTTP://GRANITEPUBLISHING.US

TRADE ORDERS FULFILLED BY
## BOOKMASTERS
800.537.6727
FAX: 419.281.0200

PERSONAL ORDERS FULFILLED BY
## PATHWAY BOOK SERVICE
800.345.6665
FAX: 603.357.2073

TO JOIN OUR PERIODICAL EMAIL JOURNAL THAT TRACKS
THE EARTH'S TRANSITION TO THE 5TH WORLD,
EMAIL US AT— 5WJ@GRANITEPUBLISHING.US

Made in the USA
Charleston, SC
23 December 2009